'This is an important book because it illuminates a difficult and controversial development. Paola Marion discusses psychoanalytic theory as it relates to the scandal of sexuality in the light of modern conceptions, addressing the problems posed by the present time, including not only the new forms of procreation but also the cruxes faced by current society in terms of the evolution of sexuality such as the queer and the transgender. These new forms of identity constitute a real challenge for psychoanalysts whose clinical practice compels them to question their own theories.'

Anna Maria Nicolò, *Past President of*
the Italian Psychoanalytic Society

'What happens when procreation is no more "only" the combination between a man and a woman, since the "cold third" of technology brings something else and/or someone else into the process which generates a new human being? When other genetic material than the one of the couple (or at least, material treated by a medical figure) enters the Freudian primal scene? And what with the new homosexual or sexually polymorphic parenthoods? Paola Marion masterfully investigates these crucial points from an updated and deeply integrative psychoanalytic perspective.'

Stefano Bolognini, *Past President of*
the International Psychoanalytic Association

I0130449

Sexuality and Procreation in the Age of Biotechnology

Through the lens of psychoanalytic thought about sexuality, the book examines changes in the area of procreation and generation, the disjunction between sexuality and procreation introduced by biotechnology and some new methods of reproduction, and their impact on the essential moments of existence (birth, illness, death) and the most intimate aspects of personal identity (sexuality, procreation, body).

At the centre of this book is the thesis that the disjunction between sexuality and procreation brought about by biotechnology represents a new scenario and introduces elements of discontinuity. What kind of effects on individuals will the modifications introduced by biotechnologies in the field of procreation have? How can these changes affect even the most profound aspects of personal identity, including body and sexuality? How might they interfere with the sphere of desire? The book investigates the new scenarios and the consequences which are emerging, such as an alteration of personal boundaries, both in spatial and temporal terms, which is reflected in our way of thinking about ourselves and our relationships and the assertion of an unconscious fantasy that the limits imposed by sexuality and death can be surpassed.

Offering a psychoanalytic reading of changes introduced in this field, this book will appeal to training and practising psychoanalysts, as well as philosophers, psychologists, and gynaecologists.

Paola Marion is a Training and Supervising Analyst for the Italian Psychoanalytic Society and a Child and Adolescent Psychoanalyst. She is past Chair of the IPA Outreach Committee for Europe (2011–2013) and past Editor (2017–2021) of the *Rivista Italiana di Psicoanalisi*. She has published papers in the *International Journal of Psychoanalysis (IJP)* and other reviews and collections.

THE NEW LIBRARY OF PSYCHOANALYSIS
General Editor: Alessandra Lemma

The New Library of Psychoanalysis was launched in 1987 in association with the Institute of Psychoanalysis, London. It took over from the International Psychoanalytical Library which published many of the early translations of the works of Freud and the writings of most of the leading British and Continental psychoanalysts.

The purpose of the New Library of Psychoanalysis is to facilitate a greater and more widespread appreciation of psychoanalysis and to provide a forum for increasing mutual understanding between psychoanalysts and those working in other disciplines such as the social sciences, medicine, philosophy, history, linguistics, literature and the arts. It aims to represent different trends both in British psychoanalysis and in psychoanalysis generally. The New Library of Psychoanalysis is well placed to make available to the English-speaking world psychoanalytic writings from other European countries and to increase the interchange of ideas between British and American psychoanalysts. Through the *Teaching Series*, the New Library of Psychoanalysis now also publishes books that provide comprehensive, yet accessible, overviews of selected subject areas aimed at those studying psychoanalysis and related fields such as the social sciences, philosophy, literature and the arts.

The Institute, together with the British Psychoanalytical Society, runs a low-fee psychoanalytic clinic, organizes lectures and scientific events concerned with psychoanalysis and publishes the *International Journal of Psychoanalysis*. It runs a training course in psychoanalysis which leads to membership of the International Psychoanalytical Association – the body which preserves internationally agreed standards of training, of professional entry, and of professional ethics and practice for psychoanalysis as initiated and developed by Sigmund Freud. Distinguished members of the Institute have included Michael Balint, Wilfred Bion, Ronald Fairbairn, Anna Freud, Ernest Jones, Melanie Klein, John Rickman and Donald Winnicott.

Sexuality and Procreation in the Age of Biotechnology

Desire and its Discontents

Paola Marion
Translated by Adam Elgar

Routledge
Taylor & Francis Group

LONDON AND NEW YORK

First published 2022
by Routledge
2 Park Square, Milton Park, Abingdon, Oxon OX14 4RN

and by Routledge
605 Third Avenue, New York, NY 10158

Routledge is an imprint of the Taylor & Francis Group, an informa business

British Library Cataloguing-in-Publication Data
A catalogue record for this book is available from the British Library

Library of Congress Cataloging-in-Publication Data
Names: Marion, Paola, 1951- author.
Title: Sexuality and procreation in the age of biotechnology : desire and its
discontents / Paola Marion ; translated by Adam Elgar.
Other titles: Il disagio del desiderio. English
Description: Abingdon, Oxon ; New York, NY : Routledge, 2021. | Series: New
library of psychoanalysis | "Originally published in Italy by Donzelli
Editore"--Title page verso. | Includes bibliographical references and
index. Identifiers: LCCN 2020058089 (print) | LCCN 2020058090 (ebook) |
ISBN 9781032003603 (hbk) | ISBN 9781032003689 (pbk) | ISBN
9781003173830 (ebk)
Subjects: LCSH: Sexual freedom. | Sex (Psychology) | Birth control. |
Reproduction.
Classification: LCC HQ21 .M4555 2021 (print) | LCC HQ21 (ebook) | DDC
306.7--dc23
LC record available at https://lccn.loc.gov/2020058089
LC ebook record available at https://lccn.loc.gov/2020058090

ISBN: 978-1-032-00360-3 (hbk)
ISBN: 978-1-032-00368-9 (pbk)
ISBN: 978-1-003-17383-0 (ebk)

Typeset in Bembo
by MPS Limited, Dehradun

Contents

INTRODUCTION
Lesley Caldwell

Paola Marion's book *Desire and its Discontents: Sexuality and Procreation in the Age of Biotechnology* was first published in Italian in 2017. The English language edition further confirms its importance for contemporary psychoanalysis and the international psychoanalytic community. Marion, a distinguished Roman analyst of adults and children and the current editor of the *Rivista* has long been a leading figure in psychoanalytically informed work in the demanding fields indicated by her title. She has been at the forefront in tackling the theoretical challenges faced by contemporary analysts in the very extended arena of sexuality we now inhabit with our patients and colleagues. Through her clinical interests she has consistently made available the highly nuanced world whose external parameters now present both patient and analyst with continuing challenges and emotional and psychic demands.

Freud's insistence on the centrality of sexuality in the constitution of human subjectivity and its dilemmas had established psychoanalysis as a challenge to ideas of the human and the individual, a challenge whose radicalism, on occasion, has been submerged and evaded in the psychoanalytic world itself. The centrality of sexuality was eclipsed in some post-war national accounts, especially in the British school's concern with the pre-oedipal, the mother–infant bond, and early emotional development. In the European tradition the centrality of sexuality suffered no such eclipse and Dr Marion shows herself to be equally at home in both these sometimes divergent traditions which she brings together in demonstrating their relevance for the adults, children and adolescents she meets in her own practice.

Her initial linking of Fonagy, Stein and Laplanche emphasises the implications of widespread parental failure to mirror the dimension of excitement and infantile sexuality there to be exchanged unconsciously in every infant parent couple. Her investigations explore how the desire for a child operates in relation to the exercise of desiring itself, its distortion into need, and the various ways what seems to be lived as an obligation to the self may lead to the negation of sexual pleasure. Biotechnologies may increase the range of generative and temporal possibilities but they have continuing effects for parents and children, for those who succeed in their wish, and for those who do not.

Marion is interested in the different ways infertility seems to be lived by men and women and how transformations in the sphere of procreation influence the relation with self. Understanding a diagnosis of infertility as frequently experienced as a diagnosis of exclusion in the human project of creating life, she explores how anxiety, loss, depression, failure and guilt can lead to narcissistic wounds for both protagonists.

For those who are successful the psychic arena is equally complicated: fantasies about relationships with the personnel involved, the continuing impact of intrusive techniques, the risk of endless mourning, the range of problems and decisions raised by the psychical implications of technology, for instance the number of embryos to transfer and what to do with those that remain.

She locates the range of new parenting forms, new families, and the range of options that technology offers to those wishing for children but finding themselves without the bodily capacities to have them, in the continuing relevance of what psychoanalysis and its founding texts demand be thought about together. This serves to remind the reader that the challenge of sexuality and the sexual remains precisely that, a challenge, for clinician and patient alike.

Marion is not afraid to question the continuing centrality of the Oedipus complex in the face of the multiple possibilities technology now enables and is open to considering if they could modify its form. This openness leads her to wonder whether structural changes in reproductive options are in the process of modifying our very nature and in approaching these fundamental human questions she brings together Freud, Winnicott, Bion and Bollas to discuss the Oedipus complex as the first interpersonal relation linking bodily relations and fantasy with what she calls "the mind's oedipal function".

Any sense that the urgent issues of the contemporary world and its practitioners will be approached exclusively through the developments that currently shape the intergenerational and reproductive world is put on one side as Marion approaches her themes through a return to Freud and a reading of some of his foundational texts. We are familiar with those who invoke Freud as a way of avoiding the challenges of the contemporary field, but Marion insists that a return to Freud and the radicality of his project is the way to confront how sexuality and its discontents now occupies our consulting rooms, and she demands that we consider its impact for our patients through the struggle to understand the transformations of the present.

While the acute psychological demands and the emotional pain of infertility and difficulties in conceiving, together with the technological solutions that have been forwarded to deal with them, show a world that was literally inconceivable in the early days of psychoanalysis she reminds us of the equally extreme responses Freud's own discoveries posed to the Vienna of his time. Drawing upon her wide cultural knowledge she links what she terms "the end of innocence", ushered in by Freud's account of sexuality, with its anticipation in late nineteenth century European art, citing both the Viennese artist, Klimt and the great paintings of Manet, *Olympia* and *Dejeuner sur l'Herbe,* as part of placing Freud himself in the interrelation of collective life and memory and its impact on the individual.

In bringing together the British and European psychoanalytic traditions she makes detailed use of Donald Winnicott and how his attention to the environment embodies a view of the object as grounded in its own subjectivity so that the qualities of the object itself become an essential contributor to the infant's internal reality.

Winnicott's proposals about an initial state of non–integration and the integration which emerges through a maternal care that gathers in the initial fragmentation of the neonate sees "the subject's unconscious psychic space as in continual and reciprocal relation to that of the object": that is, Marion emphasises, it is not just the infant but the mother who participates in the process of integration that is fundamental for the establishment of the infant's unit self. It is the mother's own integrative journey in terms of her experiences with "that" child that is formative. And she draws a parallel with the work of the psychoanalyst who, in putting together the different temporalities present in every session tries to bring together a patient's diverse experiences. Marion develops the concept of integration and its opposite, disintegration, to address the kind of dissociation present in those cases where the parents keep their child's origins a secret from them. She sees this silence as a "private nucleus which cannot be made accessible to others ... the failure to integrate that particular reproductive process". This silence is quite common with parents who have children born by ART and avoid open discussion of it, and Marion, the analyst, wonders how the apparent feelings of shame and guilt on the part of the parents may contribute to a child's symptoms, how they may stand in for the lack of integration of the child's origins into the family constellation. For these children there are not only the fantasies of exclusion all children have to encounter in the primal scene but the unconscious fantasies of both child and parents around the fact of being/having a parent who has made that child with someone else.

Marion proposes that the real challenges of today lie not so much with the theories of psychoanalysis, though they certainly demand close attention, but more urgently, with the external challenges to our theories, especially for our patients. We are witnessing **openly** multiple expressions of sexuality, and I would stress **openly** since there is nothing new in the forms and practices, the objects of desire and so on, of sexual aim, object and choice. Above and beyond availability, however, Marion sets out to tackle the differences that external changes produce at both psychical and social levels. In doing so she makes the important claim that the body is the place where most of the transformations which have characterised the second half of the twentieth century can be located. It is here that our concerns most coincide with those of our patients since, historically and socially, the terms we now use as a matter of course are all of comparatively recent origin: adolescence itself as an extended period and an object of study, gender and its continuingly sustained challenge to sexual difference, the concept of identity itself, all are recent imports into the theory and practice of psychoanalysis.

Through her scholarly exposition and a deployment of the extra resources offered by literature, the classics, the human sciences, feminist and queer theory alongside the specialist medical technological and biological advances that have so extended the arena of procreation and what it means, Marion uses these specialist accounts with one aim: how, together with her patients, the contemporary analyst approaches the particular difficulties produced by the impact of the possibilities offered by modern science and changing social relations. What, if anything, can be considered invariant, and how do we understand our responsibility as clinicians in the face of our necessarily uncertain answers to such a question.

With considerable empathy she points to a sort of bedrock of human difficulty manifested through those advances that can serve to overcome specific difficulties in having a child, or effecting change in the sexed body to more closely conform to a conflicted gender assignation. Her case studies are expertly woven into a continuing psychoanalytic narrative that prioritises what more the analyst can learn about already familiar psychological organisations from the analysis of patients with the added complexities of assisted reproduction. It is her determination to think as an analyst for instance that produces a hypothesis about one patient that heterologous fertilisation had functioned as a defence sheltering the patient from the invasion of incestuous fantasies reactivated by conception itself; unconsciously she had made sure she was extraneous to the actual act of procreation itself. How can this and other examples be harnessed in the interests of psychoanalytic knowledge more generally. Her cases find resonances with many patients and they invite our responses and whether they would be different when the assisted fertility is taken into account. And they reveal the depths of emotional anguish and the defences deployed to avoid them in pursuing paths that bio technology has made available. Marion acknowledges that psychoanalysis does not offer answers and certainty in its encounter with the contemporary world but what she and it do offer is a practice committed to investigating the repercussions of decisions taken consciously and above all unconsciously, whatever the external circumstances.

Sexuality, grounded in the psyche soma, in body and mind, is shaped by familial personal and social relations, the environment within which we meet ourselves and others, where, if all goes well, we find a place in the world, and an internal place where we are at home with ourselves. But what effects does the separation of sexuality from procreation bring about on the level of identity and the capacity to find such a place?

Marion makes use of Winnicott in another important way in assessing the place of pleasure and unpleasure in the development of psychic life. Winnicott describes the human infant's total dependence on the environment at the beginning when the quality of care, together with the satisfaction of need and the discharge of tension are not only functional but where they introduce elements of pleasure, unpleasure, excitation and desire. In this phase the satisfaction and pleasure in its own body which the infant experiences, are perceived subjectively and it is only gradually that these experiences become part of a shared world, of and with others.

This experience of pleasure requires an encounter, it requires the presence of the other, an adult, as Marion puts it "capable of investing and being invested libidinally, capable of desiring and resonating with what the infantile arouses within him or her: a presence which encounters the infant's 'hallucinatory' fantasy and maintains its illusion". In this emphasis she presents an account of adult pleasure as deriving from presence not absence, of an account of an internal world whose continuing aliveness and creativity derives from finding oneself in the other. For Marion this is reactivated by the waiting for and arrival of a baby, and this is then conveyed to the baby and internalised in that baby's own selfhood and pleasure.

Marion wonders how the expulsion of sexuality from procreation may modify the terms of the relationship with the pleasure-unpleasure principle and its unconscious effect on the child. In developing this important perspective Marion draws on her analytic experiences with patients who seem to lack the experience of being the object of another's pleasure, of a shared pleasure, and bring this wish to their analyst. The desire to share the emotion of pleasure in being together is not something confined to patients conceived and born by one specific means, rather such a capacity contributes to the organisation of the symbolic domain and its dependence on thirdness, regardless of how or who that thirdness is represented by. Marion maintains for instance that "the psychic space created between parent and donor guarantees the entry of 'thirdness'. The unconscious message transmitted by the parental couple – same or other sex – contains the seeds of heterosexuality as much as of homosexuality, and the fantasies around individual truth dispense with historical truth."

For Paola Marion "in order to comprehend 'the new ways of being born', it seems necessary to accept the birth of new ways of thinking about the relationship with ourselves and with the other". Her book offers precisely this commitment to its readers.

Lesley Caldwell
Analyst with the BPA
Visiting Professor at the Psychoanalysis Unit
University College, London
September 2020

PART I

THE SCANDAL OF SEXUALITY

THE RETURN OF THE REPRESSED

1.1 A change of perspective

In 2008, the *Journal of the American Psychoanalytic Association* published an article by Peter Fonagy entitled "A Genuinely Developmental Theory of Sexual Enjoyment and its Implications for Psychoanalytic Technique" in which he proposed a model for understanding sexuality from the psychoanalytic viewpoint, a model centred on an attempt at integration between francophone psychoanalysis and the developmental model that is oriented instead towards exploring the vicissitudes of the mother–child relationship and the domain of needs. Only two years earlier, reviewing the state of sexuality within psychoanalysis, Fonagy (2006) had described how psychoanalytic reflection (at least the Anglo-Saxon variety) had shifted its attention elsewhere: "Psychosexuality is nowadays more frequently considered as disguising other, non-sexual self- and object-related conflicts than the other way around" (p. 1). Moreover, research into the words most frequently used in psychoanalytic theory confirmed this decline in interest. In his 2006 text, Fonagy attributed this shift above all to the decline of Freud's drive theory; to the "desexualisation" performed by object relations theory, which directs its attention predominantly to the mother–child relationship and tends to interpret sexual contents in terms of defence against underlying problems located on primitive levels; and to the presence of pathologies not included in the neurotic spectrum with which the Freud of 1905[1] had been principally concerned.

The subject is taken up again in the 2008 article but with a different slant. Here, in fact, a new model is being proposed, one that integrates research into development and attachment with francophone psychoanalysis, and is able to locate sexuality at the centre of clinical psychoanalytic research. As the author openly admits, his work has been inspired by Laplanche's theory and by another writer, Ruth Stein, who is deeply rooted in the French psychoanalyst's thought.[2] The hypothesis maintained by Fonagy, and supported by the results of an investigation he had himself undertaken, concerns the parent's capacity for attunement with the emotional states of excitation and curiosity which come from the child and have to do with infantile sexuality. Based on the observation that the manner in which the parent mirrors the child's emotions is fundamental to affect regulation, Fonagy demonstrates how this may be deficient or entirely lacking as far as sexuality is concerned. Mothers, parents tend to disavow and hence do not accept emotions relating to this area.[3]

"Incongruent" mirroring generates the experience of having "an alien part of oneself" not recognised by the other, which attacks the coherence of the self while the affective and emotional states connected to sexuality are left as a residue leaving a feeling of "foreignness" and "alienation". This definition of an "alien part" includes a denial of the sexual affects, those of the parents towards the child, but possibly also those of the analyst towards the patient.

What we find ourselves having to face, and which this article rightly puts into focus, is the contrast between the Freudian vision which gave primacy to psychosexuality and subsequent post-Freudian evolution which instead addresses the model of the mother–child relationship and explores the events of the object relationship and the forms of attachment at the origin of psychic life. In other words, since the model of the mother–child relationship prevailed over the oedipal model, erotic impulses, including those in the transference, are no longer located in oedipal sexuality, but are interpreted as secondary to deficiencies in the first object relations, deficiencies which may indeed be traumatic. It is this observation which André Green had brilliantly asserted in his 1995 article "Has sexuality anything to do with psychoanalysis?" where he showed how, in his opinion, contemporary attention to object relations theory, pregenital fixations, borderline pathology, and the observation of infant development has obscured the significance and importance of genital sexuality and the Oedipus complex. The danger is that this denial of sexuality as "otherness" may also extend to the analytic relationship and thereby obscure central aspects of the patient and the use which patient and analyst can make of this negation (Ruth Stein, 1998a; 1998b, 2008).

The conclusion reached by Fonagy, as a psychoanalyst engaged in research and in particular in research into early development, is important because it signals a rethinking about the role of sexuality in the psychoanalytic discipline and within the development of the individual. While we can no longer think about sexuality in the same way as Freud did, we should nevertheless acknowledge its specific nature and centrality in the psyche and also be aware of the risks of "a collusive negation of its significance" (p. 34). He concludes his article with these words: "If I am right about the centrality of psychosexuality to the understanding of conflict, its continued study will pay dividends and renewed clinical interest might reveal new psychological mysteries ... My plea here is for the sensitive clinical and theoretical examination of subjective experiences surrounding the sexual to become once again a key concern of psychoanalysis" (ibid.). The threads of a reawakening of interest in sexuality and its significance in psychoanalytic theory and practice are also being woven by sectors of psychoanalysis which have traditionally been more remote. The 2011 Congress of the International Psychoanalytic Association in Mexico City on the core concepts of psychoanalysis testified to this attention: together with the unconscious and dream, sexuality was one of the three concepts under examination, and the questions to the presenters reflected the demand for exploration of the current state of play and of the analysts' stances on sexuality and its presence in theory and practice.

The shadow cone into which the topic of sexuality seemed to have fallen in psychoanalytic discourse (or at least into a large part of it), the prevalence of other models, and the feeling that something is missing, have prompted me for some years to start reflecting on the topic. Moreover, my work with children and adolescents, both in clinical practice and as a supervisor, brings me continual evidence that the crux of sexuality has a specific salience and that only with difficulty can it be reduced to, or superimposed onto, deficiencies which can be situated in a "before" and "after" of the story. This is not only a question of the "integration of the sexed body" (Laufer, 1984), adolescents' specific challenge and task which compels them to take their own sexuality into account, or the highly conspicuous changes of adolescent sexuality, but also – or perhaps above all – the questions which children bring and address to us in the space of the analytic scenario about the sensations coming from their bodies, their fantasies about "The Power", as Paola Camassa (2014) effectively calls the primal scene, the scene of the parents' sexual coupling. Overall, there are not only traumas which come "before" sexuality; there is also the trauma *of* sexuality.

Lesley Caldwell (2015) emphasises that sexuality has returned to our consulting rooms and that it asks to be considered by acknowledging the radical nature of the Freudian project and overcoming the psychoanalytic community's resistance to it in recent decades. She regards this movement which is winding its way into the psychoanalytic community as "a return of the repressed, which insistently demands to be taken into consideration" (2015, p. 2).[4] The relative return of interest in these topics, including that of infantile sexuality – as Fonagy has shown us – testifies to the sensation that something was at risk of being lost in the psychoanalytic understanding of the human being. The topic of sexuality gathers around itself a range of features which concern us deeply and mark out the steps of our existence. If they are eliminated from the radar of our attention there is the danger of mutilating our image of ourselves and rigidifying the exchange with the other in clinical practice as much as in our relationships. Returning to the radicalness of Freud's project, not so much in the terms in which Freud expressed it, but in the deep meaning that he was able to grasp and define in relation to human and infant sexuality and its unconscious operation, also means acknowledging another of its characteristics. Freud's psychosexuality is a concept which refers to and foregrounds the close relationship between mind and body. The body, the birthplace of the mind, is also its boundary.

1.2 Discontinuity of the present time

Psychoanalysis stamped the last century with its distinctive character. Its categories and codes have influenced the way we conceive not only the field of discontent and treatment but more generally the image of the individual as "no longer master in his own house". In this anthropology of modern times, sexuality has played a key, central role from the start. "The Powerful One" is sexuality itself, which inhabits us and is of fundamental value for every one of us, defining our coming into the world, the hard kernel of our identity, "the truth about ourselves" as Foucault says. Freud's achievement is to have made us aware of the fact that human sexuality is not reducible solely to the biological and instinctual plane, but represents the meeting point *par excellence* between body and mind, between me and the other. He has made us aware how much sexuality determines both the construction of the sense of identity and the identificatory processes, and the capacity for building links, for developing thought and knowledge.

These features still accompany us into the third millennium. The way in which sexuality is experienced and acted does not only reflect each of our intimate stories and our affective experiences, our relational vicissitudes, but also reflects the time in which we find ourselves living. The present is a time of radical changes introduced by the biotechnologies and by advances in medicine which put the most intimate aspects of personal identity into play, specifically the body, illness, and sexuality in its varied expressions. Psychoanalysis is not indifferent to the spirit of the age: "just as the dream occurs in relation to the previous day the unconscious proceeds in relation to its historical and cultural context from which it draws the materials for building its own reality, but this is never the simple picture of what the world offers" (André, 2014). The concept of sexuality also develops and evolves as the culture of which it is a part develops and evolves (Parsons 2014). The evolutions and changes we are witnessing are such that we are compelled to rethink assumptions about human nature and existence that we have taken for granted. As Rifkin (1998) was claiming some years ago in a manner which today looks "prophetic", "Many age-old practices regarding sexuality, reproduction, birth, and parenthood could be partially abandoned ... Our very sense of self and society will likely change."

In recent decades we have witnessed the modification of a bond, that between sexuality and procreation, which had obtained throughout human history and which had not even been altered by the practice of contraception. The disjunction between sexuality and procreation introduced by the new ways of conceiving represents a fracture and a radical leap, and calls back into question the meaning and place of the two terms in the sphere of the individual and the couple. This is the other question which I have been strongly prompted to reflect on, precisely from the viewpoint of its interweaving with the sexuality of individuals. Do the new procreative methods influence it? In what way do the two spheres interact? How is all this being reflected in the fragile

7

and delicate sphere of desire? In addition, the ideological tones in which the public debate is sometimes expressed seem to me to be an effect of the difficulty in focusing on the profound consequences of the break in this ring of the symbolic chain.

There is a profound relationship which each of us entertains with our own sexuality from infancy onwards: our personal psychic elaboration of it invests all forms of sexuality, genital and pregenital, homo- and heterosexual. If sexuality were only a matter of practice or technique, it would be sufficient to learn the Kama Sutra, as J. André (2014) provocatively says; but sexuality, on the contrary, is physical, psychic and relational. The interweaving of these three terms defines the nature and experiences both in individual psychic life and in the couple relationship. It is a link which declares itself between pleasure, stimulation, physical excitation and the fantasies about the object with which we are entering into relation, "an object that is never itself but that one seeks forever and in vain to refind" (Stein, 1998a, p. 598). The desire for the other and for pleasure with and through the other puts bodily, sensual pleasure into play, revealing a tension provoked by the otherness of the other, but also a desire to be one with the other, as the child perhaps sometimes felt in and with the maternal body. This is where the relational game gets complicated and erotic pleasure becomes an attempt to abolish boundaries, to feel more than mirrored, to be entirely wanted and desired by the other, and this brings into play deep portions of our unconscious psychic life, not reducible to a mere interpersonal exchange.

In the sexual context, desire combines curiosity, bodily striving towards the other, and the pleasure which derives from these, with the fantasy of encountering the "absolute" object: "in this, the psychic and the somatic are interwoven, in opposition to the scene of conscious logic in which the body, the living being, is instead absent, and if it makes itself manifest becomes an encumbrance" (Ansermet and Magistretti, 2010, p. 9). But the sought object, the potential source of pleasure, is always other than the original (Laplanche, 1997) and as Stein (1998a) says, its fate is to be "always sought and never found". This insurmountable difference characterises the movement and nature of desire, but also its discontent. The new scenarios which separate sexuality from procreation further complicate the matter. What are the vicissitudes of desire when the plan to have a child is separated from the sexual act which, in the best cases, is so deeply consubstantial with it? What primal scene will lie behind us, and what "Powerful One" must we imagine? What fantasies does it stir up? The primal scene is the point of origin for us all, the founding place and at the same time the starting point of our fantasy and imaginative life. What happens when such a divergence stands so violently at our origin?

The desire for a child may be limitlessly intensified precisely because of its impossibility. Here the gap shifts away from the search for the desired object, which to some extent always fails to live up to expectations, to the search for what one desires and does not attain. The desire may be transformed into a claim for something one cannot have, and of which one feels unjustly deprived. Faced with these new scenarios which concern individuals in the most intimate sphere of their sexuality and fertility, desire seems to lose its link with the shared pleasure of the encounter, of "bodies in relation" (Riolo, 2017), and seems to be dislocated from the striving towards the desired object and linked instead to the very exercise of desiring. In situations of assisted procreation, the gap between sexuality and procreation risks bringing about the absolutising of desire and its distortion into a need, an obligation to oneself, the opposite of sexual pleasure. Desire, which is desire for the other and is directed towards the other, may become distorted and changed into necessity and rigid repetition. The discontent of the desire for the object "always sought and never found" in the way it is desired, is a discontent about the unsaturated, about a void. The discontent of desire in the situations we will encounter later is presented as an excess which can compulsively saturate the mind and emotions of the protagonists.

This step change we find ourselves confronting generates a series of questions which were at the origin of the urge to explore incompletely mapped territories, and to offer a reflection on changes which are sure to "leave [their] mark on the anthropological landscape", as Lingiardi (2006, p. 316n) puts it, thinking about the close interweaving of sexuality and gender. In the experiences which concern us and are the subject of this book – perhaps that return of the repressed mentioned by Caldwell, which insists on being taken into consideration – sexuality stands in the foreground and this is the reason which has prompted me to devote much space in Part I to what sexuality has meant for psychoanalysis and, above all, what psychoanalysis has meant for sexuality. The situations we are called on to think about – let alone decide about – today, radically alter the traditional symbolic schemes of reference concerning the mind–body relationship and bring into play dimensions of subjectivity which may remain in the shadows and be hard to approach without a lens sensitive enough to catch their meaning, their complexity and their dark side. In order to avoid the situation which Seneca described to Lucilius – "When a sailor does not know what harbour he is making for, no wind is the right wind" (Letter 71) – when we address these new scenarios and grasp at least a part of such complex problems, the wind is the tool made available by psychoanalysis for steering us in the right direction.

In the more than one hundred years of this discipline's development, in the multiplicity of languages in which it is expressed, influenced by new cultural and social contexts, our sexuality is no longer Freud's and still less is our world his world. Nevertheless, his contribution represents the key which has opened up the discussion of sexuality in all its infinite variations: the origin of the unconscious, the choice of object, the possible deviations from accepted goals and purposes, the differences between the sexes and the generations, the confrontation with the other and the toleration of otherness, the conflict between desire and identification, the acceptance of excitement and the loss of control over the other in sexual pleasure. Each of us transforms these variations into the dream of our own sexuality. Our task, as Parsons (2014) well defines it, is to see in what way psychoanalysis is capable of taking on and re-elaborating the Freudian legacy concerning sexuality in order to build an understanding of it which fits the times in which we live. We are tiptoeing towards the new scenarios which face us and to which the second part of this book is devoted, fully conscious of how little we still know about them, and knowing even less about their effects on the subjects involved in them, although we take comfort, too, for the slow advances of our scientific knowledge in the words of the poet:

Was man nicht erfliegen kann, muss man erhinken.
Die Schrift sagt, es ist keine Sünde zu hinken.
["What we cannot reach flying we must reach limping ... The Book tells us it is no sin to limp."].

(Freud, 1920, p. 64)

Notes

1 1905 is the date of the first publication of the *Three Essays on the Theory of Sexuality* in which Freud systematised the discussion of sexuality which he had begun in his writings of the 1890s.

2 As we will see in Chapter 4 of Part I, "The time of sexuality", Laplanche's model is based on the asymmetrical adult–child relationship, configured as an unconscious seduction of the infant by the adult, and concerns the communication between the two of them and the unconscious "messages" which the adult sends to the child and which are compromised by his or her sexuality. These messages, which turn out to be enigmatic for the child, infiltrate the process of attachment and nurturing.

3 As Fonagy writes, if the primary role of parental mirroring is "to bind unintegrated aspects of a constitutional self-state into coherent second-order representations of specific affect states" (2008, p. 20), this does not happen with regard to the states and emotions linked to sexual excitement.

4 As we will also see in the following chapters, this defence mechanism which Freud encounters in hysteria has a specific link with the seduction theory and is exercised in an elective manner on sexuality. In *Repression* (1915), Freud describes three phases in its operation: 1) primal repression; 2) repression proper; 3) the return of the repressed.

THE WORLD OF YESTERDAY
The end of innocence

The concept of 'sexuality', and at the same time of the sexual instinct, had ... to be extended so as to cover many things which could not be classed under the reproductive function; and this caused no little hubbub in an austere, respectable or merely hypocritical world.

(Sigmund Freud, *Beyond the Pleasure Principle*, 1920)

2.1 Manet and Freud

At a distance of more than a hundred years, years when the world has witnessed a dizzying acceleration of space and time, it seems really hard to imagine what the birth of psychoanalysis meant and what it meant to listen to a young doctor who, towards the close of the nineteenth century, tells his colleagues what, in his opinion, is the connection between neurosis and sexuality. The setting is the well-known one of *La grande Vienna* – to borrow the Italian title of the fine book by Janik and Toulmin (1973) – the *fin de siècle* Vienna of the declining Austro-Hungarian Empire, but also the Vienna of Schönberg and Musil, Wittgenstein and Mahler, Loos and Kokoschka. It is a contradictory city, lively and active, cradle of new lines of thought and avant-garde movements in the arts, but also the fortress of a traditional bourgeoisie. Above all, it is a city of paradoxes which, while flourishing and astonishing in many respects – from the arts to the sciences – continues to sustain itself with formal values inspired by a devotion to order and the past, to a hierarchical family and social structure, and refuses to see "the bitter pill that lay beneath the sugar-coating of hedonistic aestheticism and *Sachertorte*" (Janik and Toulmin 1975, p. 61). Stefan Zweig's *The World of Yesterday*, what he called "the golden age of security" shattered by the dramatic events of the 'short century', resisted accepting ideas that today "circulate widely in the blood and language of our time" (Zweig, 2011) and failed to acknowledge that subterranean world and those impulsive forces, not amenable to reason, which play such a large part in the subjective journey. Zweig is a direct and refined witness to his era, a valuable guide who describes the "conspiracy of silence" (*Totschweigentaktik*) imposed by bourgeois society and Victorian culture, so deeply anxious about anything to do with sex, which the *bien pensant* middle-European bourgeoisie of the period had considered an anarchic force to be severely regulated and disciplined. Indeed, the very fact that it represented a taboo and was constantly censored was the clearest demonstration of its presence. Like the corrosive satire of Kraus, Freud's ideas on sexuality sounded provocative and offensive for the middle classes of Kakania, as Musil happily and ironically called it.[1] This denial/disavowal of the question was at the origin of a two-track behaviour: on the one hand, manifest irreproachable conduct – especially for women – and on the other, a parallel and secret sexual life – predominantly, if not exclusively, for men – which signalled the centrality of the matter. It could not be explicitly admitted that sexual frustration and inhibition had consequences, just as it could not be admitted that there was a link between sexuality and childhood, at least – as we will see – not in the terms proposed by Freud. He and his hysterics are located, therefore, in the scenario of the declining Austro-Hungarian Empire.

Freud's ideas about how to understand and regard sexuality, and about the role it played in the individual psychic equilibrium, became interwoven with other signs that testified to the fact that the beginning of this change had more distant roots. It is helpful to make a comparison with the visual arts. The language of images puts us in touch with a view of things and of the world that anticipated or ran parallel to the Freudian view of man. As Kandel (2012) writes in his examination of Viennese modernism in Freud's time, it was not only a response to the restrictions and hypocrisies of everyday life, but also a reaction "to the Enlightenment's emphasis on the rationality of human behavior" (p. 11), and succeeded in describing the themes of

sexuality and aggression even in their extreme crudity and contra-
dictoriness. The year 1897 is the date that marks the inauguration of
the Vienna Secession, guided by Klimt who was also its main ex-
ponent. We find ourselves in the presence of a surprising pictorial
turn which seems to reflect onto the screen of art the intuitions of a
psychoanalytic thought still coming into being. With Klimt, and
later with Schiele and Kokoschka, painting overthrows the schemata
for traditional representation of the female body and sexuality bursts
onto the scene. Desire and sexual pleasure are the central theme of
a series of drawings in which Klimt portrays the female body in
the various forms of erotic expression. In the paintings of the gold
phase too, the use of two-dimensionality, the form of the bodies,
and the use of colour communicate the passion and desire that unite
the lovers (*The Kiss*, 1907–1908), but also the force of the drives that
underlie human behaviour. The painting of Klimt and his followers
celebrates the exploration of the subject's inner life, woman's in
particular, and the forces which animate this life: sex, aggression, life,
death. In the radical nature of the turn, "painting proved to be
analogous to creative writing and to psychoanalysis in its ability to
delve beneath Vienna's restrictive attitudes towards sex and aggression and reveal people's true inner state" (Kandel, 2012, p. 90).

Nevertheless, there had been a precursor to this change of direction, one that had signalled a deep fracture in the representation
of sexuality on canvas, not only implicitly recognising its centrality
in human behaviour, but also figuratively describing its scandal.
There was no way back from the linguistic metamorphosis proposed
by Manet in 1863 with his painting *Olympia*. The parallel with
Titian's *Venus of Urbino* (1538) is a subject which art historians have
explored in depth, debated, eviscerated. The links of form and
content between the two pictures have been proved. But Manet's
provocation is still there. Cogeval and Pludermacher (2013) write
that "Titian's Venus is a masterpiece of eroticism … Titian actually
represents a woman touching her sex while she looks at us, a *unicum*
in the history of the female nude" (p. 24). It's true. But – at least to
our eyes – Titian's courtesan maintains a relationship with her
eroticism and seductiveness in which the ideal or idealised aspect of
the female figure is strongly present, as is testified by the reference to
divinity, the softness of the forms and her posture, the warm and
gilded colours of the canvas, the rich and inviting backdrop. In
Olympia, the place of a nymph or goddess is taken by a *mademoiselle*

14

of the *demi-monde* portrayed without embellishments in a crudely realist manner, who looks almost challengingly at the observer: Manet depicts a naked woman, that actual woman, not a female nude. A similar linguistic metamorphosis is proposed by Manet with his famous *Déjeuner sur l'herbe* from the same year as *Olympia*, rejected, as is well known, by the Paris Salon and exhibited in the alternative Salon des Refusés. In this case too, the theme is a revisiting of some classic paintings, principally Titian's *Concerto Campestre* (1510) or Raimondi's engravings (1510–1520), and yet the representation of the scene and the stylistic provocation are so evident that critics unanimously consider the *Déjeuner* "the first truly modern painting" (De Seta, 2013, p. 55). The mythological references and Arcadian themes are dismissed, and the pastoral setting itself, with a woman in the background (the same model as in *Olympia*) bathing in transparent clothing, no longer has any reference to pastoral but projects us directly into a situation which bears witness to the future rather than the past. The sexuality is openly declared, the observer is compelled to look at the scene without idyllic fictions, and is challenged to relocate it in his own space and time. Both paintings deal a blow to the morals and *pruderie* of the time and are the most explicit manifesto of something revolutionary advancing towards a point of no return. Manet's paintings are a constant object of study and critique by art historians and it would be unpardonable to venture into a field that does not concern us. However, the message of his work is also ours and it tells us that something was changing profoundly. We could say that Manet's images "contain more memory and more future than the waking ego can know about" (Chianese and Fontana, 2010, p. 173). Though the theme was as old as mankind, its treatment indicated that a tradition had been overturned, that sexuality, blatantly exposed to the eyes of all and brought back into the everyday life of the earthly sphere, could no longer be considered as it had been before but was becoming something yet more complicated and dangerous.

2.2 The end of innocence

Freud's contribution to the emergence of the scandal of sexuality is part of the history of psychoanalysis and its non-linear journey. The affirmation of his ideas on this point is summed up in a corpus of articles written in the same year, 1896: *Draft K* ("A Christmas Fairy

Tale"), in a letter sent to Wilhelm Fliess on 1 January; *Heredity and the Aetiology of the Neuroses* (in French), *Further Remarks on the Neuro-Psychoses of Defence*, and *The Aetiology of Hysteria*, which represent the manifesto for his thesis about the aetiopathogenesis of hysteria and obsessional neurosis. The theory of heredity was contested in favour of sexual trauma, which Freud considered a determining and specific factor in the origin of the psycho-neuroses. This group of writings had been preceded by the *Project for a Scientific Psychology*, in which this thesis had been anticipated, and by the *Studies on Hysteria*, which – as is well known – mark the high point and simultaneously the definite decline of his collaboration with Joseph Breuer, which had run its course precisely because of their diverging evaluations of the sexual origins of hysterical manifestations.

The Aetiology of Hysteria represents the "gauntlet" thrown down by Freud, at his own risk and peril, to the scientific community. This is the text for the conference held by the Viennese Society of Psychiatry and Neurology in April 1896 where he stated his theory of the aetiology of hysteria as deriving from a childhood sexual trauma. The reception, as Freud wrote in a letter to Fliess (1892–97), was "icy" and the ideas being proposed were branded by Krafft-Ebing, in his own words, as "a scientific fairy tale".[2]

What stopped Freud's ideas being recognised by a scientific milieu in which the studies of sexology and sexual pathology, like the observations about infantile sexuality, represented a broad and thoroughly elaborated scientific field, and even a branch of medical science itself? The answer is contained in the work itself, above all in Freud's contesting of the theory of heredity as being at the origin of neurotic aetiology, a popular theory at the time, and not only among Charcot's students. The idea of the "hereditary taint" also predominated in the Viennese setting, and it is this idea that Freud contests with vigour and a stringent dialectic. Starting from Breuer's claim that "the symptoms of hysteria … are determined by certain experiences of the patient's which have operated in a traumatic fashion and which are being reproduced in his psychical life in the form of mnemic symbols" (Freud, 1896c, pp. 192–3) and describing the operation of the psychoanalytic method which, in this very text, he associates with the work of the archaeologist – *Saxa loquuntur* (ibid.) – he tracks down the "specific" cause of hysteria and obsessional neurosis in a sexual trauma experienced during childhood, in a pre-sexual period, and at the time not recognised as such. "*A passive*

16

sexual experience before puberty: this, then, is the specific aetiology of hysteria" (1985a, p. 152), claims Freud in the article from the same year published in French a few weeks before the conference. On the other hand, the theory of the hysterical "proton pseudos" had earlier been asserted in the *Project* (1895).[3] In this text Freud put forward some concepts that enabled him to resolve the enigma of why, at the origin of the psycho-neuroses, there was a constant link with sexual themes and why those very sexual representations were the only ones subject to the mechanism of repression. The claim "We invariably find that a memory is repressed which has only become a trauma by *deferred action*" (1895, p. 356) introduces two ideas: on the one hand that, precisely because the of the human subject's immaturity at the time when it occurs, the traumatic event is not recognised in its distinctive features; and on the other, the idea of deferred time.[4] This offers an answer to the problems that Freud was setting himself and, above all, defines a temporal form which, based on his reflections about sexuality in human beings, represents – as we shall see – one of the most profound and enduring psychoanalytic intuitions. Clinical practice took shape in harmony with this conceptual stance, using speech to bring back to the light what had been plunged deep into the unconscious and kept there by the action of repression. Such a conception of psychic disturbances, and in particular the new method of treatment which enabled the origin of the disturbance to be brought to light, produced "a sort of therapeutic revolution", as Roudinesco (2014) reminds us.

While Freud – as we shall see – would quickly be compelled to change the initial hypothesis about sexual trauma, the fact that sexuality plays a fundamental role in the genesis of neurosis and repression remains an idea that the founder of psychoanalysis would not abandon, and again in 1922 he would state that "None of the theses of psycho-analysis has met with such tenacious scepticism or such embittered resistance as this assertion of the preponderating aetiological significance of sexual life in the neuroses" (Freud, 1922b, p. 244). The conviction that he had reached the *Caput Nili* of psychopathology would turn out to be false, and yet the arc of the seduction theory, though short, would be intense. Freud's intellectual effort in the late 1890s was directed to the classification of hysteria and obsessional neurosis, to the search for their origin and cause. As we have said, the conviction that sexuality plays a role in neurosis was a widely-held opinion in the medical community of the time, percolated via comments which revealed the protagonists' thinking. Referring to his patients, Breuer spoke of "secrets of the marriage-bed" and Charcot maintained, though in a private remark, that *c'est toujours la chose génitale* going on with hysterics. The conclusions which Freud reached in 1896 are described in Draft K, *The Neuroses of Defence* (1895). In this short text, comparing hysteria, obsessional neurosis, and a specific form of paranoia, Freud considers that, in all three cases, two conditions are indispensable for their formation: a sexual event, and the experience of this event in a period prior to sexual maturity (sexuality and childhood). This is certainly the disruptive element which goes beyond the "*secrets d'alcôve*", the sexual dissatisfactions or distortions of adult life. Freud describes a typical tendency in what he considers "neuroses of defence", where psychic conflict predominates: 1) presence of one or more sexual experiences which will later be subjected to the process of repression; 2) the process of repression is not simultaneous with the experience, but happens at a later time when other circumstances arouse the memory of it, and this moment coincides with the formation of a primary symptom; 3) if the repression is successful, a period of "successful defence" follows – as Freud expresses it – which nevertheless involves the existence of the primary symptom; 4) the phase of the return of the repressed representations follows, and the conflict between these and the Ego is at the origin of the illness and of new symptoms. The claims made in *Draft K* had been anticipated in a letter to Wilhelm Fliess (15 October 1895): "Have I revealed the great clinical secret to you, either orally or in writing? Hysteria is the consequence of a presexual *sexual shock*. Obsessional neurosis is the consequence of a presexual *sexual pleasure*, which is later transformed into [self-]*reproach*. 'Presexual' means actually before puberty ... the relevant events become effective only as *memories*".

Here we are presented with the complete formulation of what is considered the classical seduction theory. It is a theory about the genesis of the neurotic symptom which is characterised by several elements (sexuality, trauma, repression, retrospection) that are so important in Freudian thought, and psychoanalytic thought generally, that they will be maintained – though under different names – even when the theory is revised and reformulated, which Freud will do in 1897. Returning to the letter to Fliess of 15 October, in that year and the following year, Freud is firmly convinced that he has arrived at the solution to the problem, to the source of hysterical psychopathology, which would necessarily open up a new page on this type of disturbance and its causes. The key point in this formulation, which Freud reiterates in *Further Remarks on the Neuro-Psychoses of Defence* (1896b) and then in *The Aetiology of Hysteria* (1896c) cited earlier, as we will see later, does not consist wholly or principally in the reality or otherwise of the traumatic episode – the abuse of the child by the adult, which will in fact be the very reason why the theory is thrown into crisis – but in the idea, which will become central in later psychoanalytic thinking too, of the process of repression and of a temporality that evades the linear dimension. As he had already explained in the *Project* (1895) on the subject of Emma,[5] the trauma is not recorded in the moment when it happens and only becomes manifest in a later period, when another event has the power to stir up the memories of that first episode subjected to repression. We can say that the memory is coloured with meanings only when it is revived in the light of new experiences. Nevertheless, in those years, there was an element of concreteness in the seduction theory Freud was proposing, represented by the idea that the traumatic episode was the result of an incestuous act perpetrated by a perverted adult which made its acceptance intolerable and seemed to justify Krafft-Ebing's comment that "it seems like a scientific fairy-tale". It is curious that this comment reflects the subtitle used by Freud for *Draft K*, "Christmas Fairy Tale", revealing Freud's fear, which also appears in certain passages of his correspondence with Fliess, that his constructions were nothing but a heap of fantasies, a castle in the air. And yet Freud's reaction to the way his work had been received shows how his own doubts did not stop him feeling hurt when the same doubts were advanced by the scientific community around him, which he longed to feel recognised by and to be part of.

A year later, the letter to Fliess of 21 September 1897, which Laplanche calls the "letter of the equinox" because of its date, marks the turn. Once again we are in a hall of mirrors, and the form used by Freud to let his friend know that the day of the seduction theory was over, at least in its so-called "classical" formulation, seems to be the same one that, only two years before, in October 1895, he had used to reveal "the great clinical secret". He writes, "I want to confide in you immediately the great secret that has been slowly dawning on me in the last few months. I no longer believe in my *neurotica* [theory of the neuroses]" (1985, p. 264). A series of factors contribute to this outcome, and Freud lists them in the letter: his failed attempts to bring an analysis to a genuine conclusion, the absence of the hoped-for successes, the awareness that it was hard to imagine every father or adult male relative (uncles, elder brothers) being invariably perverted and guilty, and lastly an exquisitely psychoanalytic reflection: the conviction that no factual realities exist in the unconscious, "so that one cannot distinguish between truth and fiction that has been cathected with affect" (ibid.).

Freud's farewell to the seduction theory cannot be read as a sharp break and a definitive abandonment of the ideas which had sustained it until that moment (Blass and Simon, 1994). Freud was led to this retraction by personal doubts provoked also by his self-analysis and the death of his father, but this did not mean the construction of a completely alternative theory. The conviction that he had found the source of psychopathology revealed itself to be false, and Freud was forced to confront this stumbling-block, having to note that the issue was actually the relationship between reality and fantasy, and to admit that fantasy can be experienced as realistic and can be at the origin of our experience, our behaviour, our sense of identity, as forcefully as real events. What happens on a fantasy level has a reality-value. Blass and Simon describe how this discovery is not so much the result of listening to his patients or the acknowledgement of the oedipal themes in relation to his father which he had explored in his self-analysis, as the fact of having to admit and acknowledge within himself the seductive fantasies he was feeling towards his patients. As these two authors interpret it, "Freud saw that the patients' reports of their fathers' acts were in accord with his own seductive wishes directed towards his patients and he came into touch with his fear that his seductive fantasies were having a real seductive effect on his patients and the kind of material they produced" (Blass and Simon, 1994, p. 690). As he himself admitted many years later, "When, however, I was at last obliged to recognize that these scenes of seduction had never taken place, and that they were only phantasies which my patients had made up or which I myself had perhaps forced on them, I was for some time completely at a loss" (Freud, 1924, p. 34).

The collapse of the convictions he had held until that moment does not seem to have dismayed Freud, who claims, "I was able to draw the right conclusions from my discovery: namely, the neurotic symptoms were not related directly to actual events but to wishful phantasies, and that as far as the neurosis was concerned psychical reality was of more importance than material reality" (ibid). The "crisis", even though he would "not tell it in Dan, nor speak of it in Askelon, in the land of the Philistines" (1985, p. 265),[6] releases an energy which is directed towards new explorations and, above all, signals a sharp turn in the speculative journey being taken by psychoanalysis. Besides acknowledging the primacy of fantasy over reality,[7] it also represents the encounter with the Oedipus complex "which was later to assume such an overwhelming importance" (1924, p. 34). It is not altogether true that Freud stumbled upon the Oedipus complex without recognising it, as Blass and Simon try to maintain (1994), if we think about his self-analysis which had led him to bringing into focus the oedipal scenario in himself, as is testified by the correspondence with Fliess (letter of 15 October 1897) in which he makes an explicit reference to the Greek tragedy. It is true nonetheless that besides the literary reference, specifically to the play by Sophocles rather than to the myth, Freud never made a systematic exposition of the complex; instead, it runs more or less below the surface throughout his work.[8] As is well known, the Oedipus complex is the great theme of psychoanalytic theorising. In the trajectory of post-Freudian psychoanalysis, it has shifted ever further from a specific reference to certain elements of the Sophoclean tragedy (incestuous love for the mother, murderous aggression towards the father figure), to the idea that the oedipal configuration express a function of the mind in pictographic form, a function that accepts the complexity of triangulation, the search for one's identity via the route of identification and, through defining one's boundaries, accepts the differences of gender and of the generations. Ultimately, the Oedipus myth has been interpreted over time more in terms of a myth of seeking and knowing, the solution of which consists in accepting complexity (Bollas, 1993; Britton, 1989; De Simone, 2002).

So, the end of innocence is played out in a dual register. In fact, it first of all compels Freud to set aside an explanation in terms of cause and effect, and to give up his relief at having found justification and comfort in determining external factors (perverted fathers and uncles). That solution showed itself to be unreliable from the moment when Freud, with his work on himself as his starting point, discovers that he has the same impulses and the same fantasies of a sexual nature as those he had previously attributed to his patients. The tragedy of Oedipus represents "a universal event in early childhood" and this is what gives rise to "the gripping power of *Oedipus Rex*, in spite of all the objections that reason raises against the presupposition of fate" (1985, p. 272). To these lines, which are an explicit admission of how strongly present the story of Oedipus was in Freud's mind, he adds some others which indicate a line of thought that is not resolved into a pure analogy but is instead aimed at exploring the psychic mechanism to which the schema of the tragedy gives rise. The operation of repression, a universal mechanism, allows everyone to be Oedipus in fantasy and to recoil from him in horror, to put up a barrier between the world of childhood and the subsequent stages of development and to achieve the founding of the repressed unconscious. Hence, this is a renunciation of factual reality, of the idea that the seduction is a seduction undergone as a real event, a renunciation that will open the way to the full acknowledgement of psychic and affective reality which accompanies the life of the child and intersects with the world of his fantasies.

This is the second significant point about the loss of innocence. The acknowledgement of the existence of infantile sexuality expressed in childhood fantasies ("Everyone in the audience was once a budding Oedipus in fantasy", Freud, 1985, ibid.), of its significance in the development of the individual and in his or her affective and relational dynamics, radically changed the way of looking at childhood, marking a profound caesura with the old image of an innocent child free of instinctual urges and powerful affects. In its Sophoclean version, the myth becomes a structure and model for representing the complex play of psychic forces. While repression, which constituted the prototype of all forms of defence, operates with the purpose of dismissing from consciousness that which is held to be forbidden from the viewpoint of relational reality, but also dangerous for the psychic organisation itself – that which is conflictual, in other words – repressed infantile sexuality becomes constitutive of the unconscious and characterises it. In this sense, the fabric of the unconscious is made of desires, instinctual motions that impel towards pleasure, the satisfaction and premature character of which easily comes into contrast with the demands of reality and the tasks of development.

2.3 *Der kleine Hans*

After the case of Dora in 1901, known as *Fragment of an Analysis of a Case of Hysteria*, that of *Little Hans* (*Analysis of a Phobia in a Five-Year-Old Boy*, 1908) is the second case history presented by Freud. This text is well known to a wider public because of its literary quality and the extraordinary vividness with which the clinical material is presented. It describes the history of the remarkable treatment of a 5-year-old boy affected by phobic symptoms, the genesis of which is reconstructed, going all the way back to the possible source of the neurotic manifestation. It is the only instance of a child analysis in Freud's long career, a case conducted via an intermediary in the person of the boy's father (a follower of Freud's) who presented the Viennese doctor with the material he gathered in domestic situations. The obvious eccentricity of such a setting is only explicable in the context of a profession in its early stages and at that time still living through a pioneering and experimental phase. Freud published this case history three years after sending *Three Essays on the Theory of Sexuality* (1905) to the press and, as he himself wrote, observation has great importance for him in that it permits him "a possibility of observing in children at first hand and in all the freshness of life the sexual impulses and wishes which we dig out so laboriously in adults from among their own débris" (1908a, p. 6). It also provided him with a confirmation of the hypotheses he had put forward about infantile sexuality and expounded in his previous writings, included the move from the "classical" seduction theory to the theme of the oedipal fantasies which inhabit the unconscious and are moved by instinct and desire.

So, for Freud, the case of Little Hans represents an unprecedentedly effective opportunity to demonstrate the veracity of the existence of infantile sexuality in all its multiple manifestations and, above all, in its aetiological valence. As we follow the story, we see the unfolding of the events that concern Hans and the development of his neurosis but, above all, we see the universal characteristics which render sexuality, as it is manifested in childhood, part of "normal" human development and of the relational vicissitudes which accompany growth. We can isolate certain specific themes in particular: the Oedipus complex and the path of the identifications; the topic of masturbation; the difference of the sexes; the sexual theories of children and the epistemophilic instincts.[9]

Hans's story concerns the development of the phobia which starts to show its first signs when the boy is aged about 3, and explodes at the age of 4, about a year after the birth of his little sister Hanna. Hans is afraid of being bitten by a horse when he goes out into the street and this is accompanied by a slight depression in the evenings, anxieties of loss associated with mother and insistent desires to be "cuddled" by her, which he expressed in attempts at seduction and in explicit requests to be taken to bed with her.

"Hans, four and a quarter. This morning Hans was given his usual daily bath by his mother and afterwards dried and powdered. As his mother was powdering round his penis and taking care not to touch it, Hans said: "Why don't you put your finger there?"

> *Mother*: "Because that'd be piggish."
> *Hans*: "What's that? Piggish? Why?"
> *Mother*: "Because it's not proper."
> *Hans* (laughing): "But it's great fun."
>
> (Freud, 1908a, p. 19)

As this exchange shows, in the requests Hans makes to his mother there is not only the fear of losing her, but also (and perhaps especially) the fantasy of attaining a privileged position in relation to her and of gaining exciting and pleasurable sensations. Physical contact can reassure but also excite, and the use of the other's body, her proximity, can have more than one meaning.

Only a year before *Little Hans*, in 1907, one of the twentieth century's key books began to be drafted: Marcel Proust's *A la Recherche du Temps Perdu*, which overturns the realistic and naturalistic conception of time with a new way of narrating. Here too we encounter a famous little boy, none other than the author himself, who tells the story in the first person and becomes its protagonist. In the opening pages of the first volume, *Swann's Way*, we find a description of the protagonist struggling with an emotional problem not very distant from Hans's:

> At Combray, as every afternoon ended, long before the time when I should have to go to bed and lie there, unsleeping, far from my mother and grandmother, my bedroom became the fixed point on which my melancholy and anxious thoughts were centred ... My sole consolation when I went upstairs for the night was that Mamma would come in and kiss me after I was in bed ... Sometimes when, after kissing me, she opened the door to go, I longed to call her back, to say to her, "Kiss me just once more," but I knew that then she would at once look displeased, for the concession which she made to my wretchedness and agitation in

coming up to give me this kiss of peace always annoyed my father, who thought such rituals absurd.

(Proust 1913, pp. 9–14)

We are far from Vienna, in the French countryside, but the boy in the time of the story is only a little older than Hans, and struggling with a very similar problem. As Élisabeth Roudinesco (2014) testifies, it is curious that, even though the two authors had explored the same themes – dream, memory, unconscious – albeit from different vertices, neither of them acknowledged the work of the other: "While Freud and Proust, each in his own way, were modern narrators of the exploration of the self, they also viewed the mother, or her substitute, as the first object of attachment to which human beings turn. And this idea led the writer and the scientist alike to a conception of love according to which each human being desires to be loved by another just as he or she had been loved by a mother – or in the absence of a mother figure, just as he or she would have wanted to be loved."

Hans's anxiety about his mother and Proust's heartbreak at the moment of saying goodnight refer to the child's fondness towards the maternal object, but not only that. As Freud makes clear, Hans's anxiety in the evening before going to bed becomes comprehensible "if we suppose that at bedtime he was overwhelmed by an intensification of his libido—for its object was his mother, and its aim may perhaps have been to sleep with her" (Freud, 1908a, pp. 25–26). The two boys' highly similar manifestations would therefore correspond to a very powerful desire, later subject to repression, and the possible satisfaction of this desire is felt as a source of pleasure but also of conflict and, as Proust teaches us, a transgression of the rules of the household and the expectations of his parents. The dream of the giraffe which Hans has one night, waking him and causing him to take refuge in his parents' bed, translates the boy's incestuous desires, his anxieties, and conflicts onto an oneiric level: "In the night there was a big giraffe in the room and a crumpled one; and the big one called out because I took the crumpled one away from it. Then it stopped calling out; and then I sat down on top of the crumpled one" (ibid., p. 37). It will be father who, in the light of Freud's teachings, solves the riddle of this scene transported into the world of giraffes. Hans has dreamed his own desire for the mother/crumpled giraffe (I want the crumpled giraffe to be mine, so I can sit on top of it and possess it), but also the fear about the challenge to the father/big giraffe (Who does the mother belong to? The big giraffe/father yells, protests).

Hans runs up against his incestuous fantasies and by means of the dream he brings to light the conflict between his desire and the prohibitions which come from the outside world and lead to the idea of a penalty for imagining something forbidden. The castration anxiety gives expression to the fantastical universe linked to the punishments that will follow, including the separation from the love–object possessed by the other and not one's own.

Hans's phobia is expressed in his refusal to leave the house for the usual daily walk. He is afraid of being bitten by a horse or else that a horse may fall over. Taking into account the fact that horses were everywhere in Vienna at that time, Hans's phobia, which is agoraphobic in nature, impels him to stay at home with his mother and not be separated from her. This represents the secondary advantage of the symptom which, by means of the self-imposed restriction, aims at obtaining the desired satisfaction, but also at removing the fear of paternal punishment, displacing it onto horses. The oedipal schema is clearly delineated: on the one hand, the intensity of Hans's desire for his mother, and on the other, the repressed aggression towards his father which enables the boy to maintain a tender and loving relationship with him from the conscious viewpoint. Since, for Freud, the oedipal schema represented a universal invariant, what distinguishes its normal manifestations from the pathological in the development of infantile sexuality? Freud here again resorts to an economic factor: in other words, to the presence of an excess of incestuous libidinal impulses and aggressive urges towards the rival, with a consequent anxiety about emasculation. The difficulties that would bring Hans to the explosion of his neurosis arose when the boy was three years old and had begun to manifest curiosity about his genital organ, his "widdler", and the need to find confirmation that everyone was like him made its appearance in an overpowering manner. Infantile genital sexuality coincides with the child's discovery of his or her own sexual organs, inadequate for procreation but a source of excitation, and pleasurable sensations. The awareness of one's own body and of what the genital organs mean in the relationship with oneself and with others, marks the end of innocence. In this context, we also find infantile masturbation and the fantasies connected to it, which describe the beginning of the whole development of instinctual life: "Masturbation of the ordinary healthy and relatively non-compulsive kind belongs to this keeping alive of the instincts in the absence of full-blown instinctual experience" (Winnicott 1988, p. 54) which will only arrive later. A couple of years before drafting *Little Hans*, Freud himself had written, "I have learned to explain a number of phantasies of seduction as attempts at fending off memories of the subject's *own* sexual activity (infantile masturbation)" (Freud, 1906, p. 274). In the light of these considerations, masturbation began to be seen from a new perspective, no longer as a degenerative symptom, but as part of the individual's normal sexual development, an activity performed by the child on him or herself and which the adolescent will resume in the second phase of growth. The giving up of masturbation signifies the giving up of one's body as a source of excitation and gratification, the distancing of oneself from sexuality and displacing affective investment onto other places and other times. The struggle Hans must make with the desire associated with his phobia is evident in this exchange with his father:

> *Father.* "You know, if you don't put your hand to your widdler any more, this nonsense [*The name given to Hans's phobia in the vocabulary he uses with his father*] of yours'll soon get better."
> *Hans*: "But I don't put my hand to my widdler any more."
> *Father.* "But you still want to."
> *Hans*: "Yes, I do. But wanting's not doing, and doing's not wanting."
>
> (Freud, 1908a, pp. 30–31)

At the moment of "this epiphany at around 3" (Bollas, 2000) the body offers the child autoerotic gratification in which there is a convergence between the discharge of tension and instinctual excitation and the current fantasying that accompanies such activity. The struggle between Hans and his parents reflects the universal process of censorship to which masturbation is subjected. It is perceived as dangerous because it contains a narcissistic element of self-sufficiency which distances the Self from others. But it is also because the fantasies which accompany it put the child in close contact with his or her intertwined feelings of ambivalence. As Hans teaches us, the impulse towards the mother and the fantasies about the paternal figure, recognised as the third who is there before him and exercises rights over the same object of desire and love, unleash a great anxiety

27

in the child. Hans asks his father, "Why did you tell me I'm fond of Mummy and that's why I'm frightened, when I'm fond of you?" (Freud, ibid. p. 44). And Freud comments, "We know that this portion of Hans's anxiety had two constituents: there was fear *of* his father and fear *for* his father. The former was derived from his hostility towards his father, and the latter from the conflict between his affection, which was exaggerated at this point by way of compensation, and his hostility" (ibid., p. 45). The repressed desire to see the father drive off in his carriage and to be left alone with his mother had been transmuted into anxiety about horses. As the clinical material gradually shows, the arrival of the little sister compounds this and brings a complicated problem relating to the question of who to identify with: to be like Mummy who has babies or to be like Daddy who makes babies with Mummy. Hans will give a brilliant solution to this problem, as his father reports:

> Seeing Hans playing with his imaginary children again, "Hullo," I said to him, "are your children still alive? You know quite well a boy can't have any children."
> *Hans*: "I know. I was their Mummy before, *now I'm their Daddy*."
> *Father*: "And who's the children's Mummy?"
> *Hans*: "Why, Mummy, and you're their *Grandaddy*."
> *Father*: "So then you'd like to be as big as me, and be married to Mummy, and then you'd like her to have children."
> *Hans*: "Yes, that's what I'd like, and then my Lainz Grandmummy" (my mother) "will be their Grannie."
>
> (ibid., pp. 96–97)

As Freud comments: "Things were moving towards a satisfactory conclusion. The little Oedipus had found a happier solution than that prescribed by destiny. Instead of putting his father out of the way, he had granted him the same happiness that he desired himself: he made him a grandfather and married *him* to his own mother too" (ibid., p. 97).

The child's departure from Eden means renouncing the Ptolemaic view of existence which had dominated until then, and having to acknowledge that maternal desires exist outside the child's and encompass more than just her or him, that there is a pre-existing couple with their own intimate, independent life. The new intensity achieved by the child in relation to genital sensations, accompanied by the discovery of what we adults call "sexuality", one's own and that of others, represents a taboo the meaning of which eludes him or her, and yet it is capable of changing the child's perception of the relationships between him/herself and other people and between other people. The emerging awareness of this transition represents the "trauma" which the child must face, confronted with sexuality which transforms her/his vision of the world and introduces a fracture between the blessedness of the earthly paradise of time before and the Fall of time after. Censorship and the threat of castration represent what Bollas (2000) calls the parents' "gentle attack" on the child's sexuality, while they link the full realisation and sexual satisfaction to a deferred action which displaces the goal into the future, to a time that is yet to come and will be achieved with adolescence.

Psychoanalysis has recognised how infantile sexuality is an essential element in the child's development. The sexual instinct expressed in terms of bodily excitation and pleasure is directed at an object, the breast, the mother who gives care. The mother is the first and greatest seductress and she reserves for her child "feelings that are derived from her own sexual life" (Freud, 1905, p. 223). It is precisely through being cared for that the child perceives the sexuality and seduction coming from the adult. And it is also in this way that the adult's sexuality "infiltrates" the relationship with the child and is perceived by him or her as something far from clear, "enigmatic" (Laplanche, 1997, 2007), which prompts the elaboration of fantasies and the construction of the child's own theories in search of an explanation. When the mystery of sexuality makes itself present in the child's mind, the whole infantile universe is given a twist. The parents are now regarded with different eyes, and meanings are attributed to their relationship that it did not previously have. The child's encounter with sexuality is at the origin of what Klein calls the "epistemophilic instinct" (1923). The urge to know and to research is undoubtedly related to sexual life, as Little Hans has shown us. Curiosity, the desire to know, is attracted by sexual matters which contain the enigma of enigmas: where do babies come from? Where do I come from? It is the same riddle that prompted Oedipus in his journey to Delphi. For some time, what the parents do together in their room remains a mystery to which the child tries to give solutions in her/his own way. The answers that the child devises in relation to these basic questions lead to the construction of infantile sexual theories or theories about birth which can take on the most varied permutations in the mind and fantasy of children.

The vicissitudes of Little Hans struggling with his own sexuality and the birth of his sister, which introduces a problematic variable into his infantile universe and dramatically confronts him with anatomical difference, stimulate the child's thinking and his attempts to give an answer to the first great problem of life, the problem of origins. The instinctual impulse, albeit via metamorphoses and dissimulations, is revealed in infantile fantasies and sexual theories, and the working out on an imaginative level of the body's functioning, of instinctuality and excitation, is expressed in fantasy and in the form of play (Klein, 1950; Isaacs, 1948). The universe of infantile sexuality is located half way between the "enigmatic message" coming from the adult and the child's endogenous impulse, which in its own way seeks an answer and a means of dealing with something that is unknown but is also a source of pleasure and excitation. All of this sets up an intense "creative" activity in the child, expressed in the need to "translate" what seems obscure, to imagine it, to fantasise it. The curiosity about sexuality, which animates the child and is transformed into an urge towards research and knowledge, persists in the adult as a permanent source of desire and creative activity.

The discovery of sexuality "destroys the innocence of a self and mother" (Bollas, 2000, p. 14) and introduces a profound divergence between need and desire, between a maternal object predominantly perceived in the light of one's own satisfaction and an object with her own independent desires. Thus, the seduction scene does not originate in only one of the two sides but in a space of intersection between infantile sexuality and the message from the parents who offer themselves as exclusive objects of the child's love and who desire and wish for that love. Now seduction is no longer the prerogative asserted by a perverse adult over a child but rather a complex network of fantasies where the infantile desires are interwoven with the adult's sexuality which infiltrates their responses to the infantile demands. Recent readings of *Little Hans* (Blum, 2007; Chused, 2007; Stuart, 2007)[10] highlight how Freud was motivated above all by the search for proofs to confirm his idea of the oedipal schema, and of infantile sexual fantasies and desires. Based on the movements and transformations which the psychoanalytic theoretical and clinical corpus has achieved over the years, the common emphasis is on how much Freud's attention and interest in this text remain focused on the child's intrapsychic and fantasy world, without considering the way the environment contributes to Hans's neurotic solution, still less asking how far the boy's case was the history of his attempt to master events coming from outside, which were traumatic for him. It was an environment whose quirks and intricacies must have been well known to Freud, not only because Hans's father (a musicologist) was one of his followers, but more particularly because Hans's mother had been one of his patients and he was well acquainted with her turbulent and dramatic family circumstances. The "accusation" levelled against him is that he elided over the contribution of the object's – the mother's – response to the boy's phobia, neglecting the way her previously verified depression and problems could represent a possible and potent cause of the boy's symptomatic crisis.

Of course, to go back to Little Hans is also to go back to the infancy of psychoanalysis. Our modern awareness of the importance of the object's response to the child's emotional and affective demands necessarily changes our point of view. How much of Hans's distorted response to the vicissitudes he had to deal with is in fact attributable, not just to his intrapsychic dynamics, but also to the relational aspect that proves unable to acknowledge the boy's narcissistic vulnerability and the difficulty of the task he found himself presented with? Today we have a better and deeper knowledge of the other side of the story, the side where the parent is not only the object of the child's desire, but the child is also the object of affective investment for the parents and can conversely be more or less inadvertently used for dealing with their anxieties or avoiding painful separations. And seeing it from the children's side, we could ask ourselves what bodily sensations and also what fantasies may result from an excessive closeness, from a physical proximity that does not respect boundaries. Freud does not take the nuances of the mother–child relationship into account, or the role of trauma related to the mother's post-partum depression. This "absent-mindedness" may find an explanation in the abandonment of the seduction theory and actual trauma. The renunciation of what he had so long believed had been a clean break, but was also traumatic for Freud himself: "My confidence alike in my technique and in its results suffered a severe blow" (1924, p. 34). The full acknowledgement of how much psychic reality counts in the neurotic solution, the awareness he had reached in his self-analysis of the fact that we have all been Oedipus, cleared the way, on the one hand, for the study of infantile sexuality and the world of fantasy, but on the other hand it blinded him to the converse side of the story: that is, to the influence which the environment exercises over the child, both consciously and unconsciously. Freud's theoretical aims, the desire to find confirmation of his hypotheses obscured a more subtle boundary, a more arduous one to confront, "the sorting out of what is called reality and fantasy" (Winnicott, 1988, p. 59). It is a decisive matter for the subsequent development of these topics and we will return to it later on.

Notes

1 "This name was invented by Robert Musil, and combines two senses on different levels ... It is a coinage from the initials K.K. or K. u. K., standing for 'Imperial-Royal' or 'Imperial and Royal,' (königlich und kaiserlich) which distinguished all the major institutions of the Habsburg Empire ... But to anyone familiar with German nursery language, it carries also the secondary sense of 'Excrementia' or 'Shitland'" (Janik and Toulmin, 1975, p. 13n).

2 Richard von Krafft-Ebing (1840–1902) was a leading figure in the Viennese medical and psychiatric circles of the period. He owes his fame to the publication of *Psychopathia sexualis*, an encyclopaedic treatise on deviant sexual behaviours.

3 This is a concept derived from Aristotelian logic which indicates a false premise in an argument, from which false assertions follow, even if the deductions are correct from the formal viewpoint. Freud applies this mechanism to his reading of the hysterical symptom and, in particular, to the case of Emma. As we will see in due course, the sexual event when it first occurs is not recognised as such, and this gives rise, on the basis of an initial mistaken assessment, to the mechanism of the "proton pseudos".

4 Strachey's version is well known to be somewhat misleading since the German of the 1895 text reads "*nur nachträglich*", "only at a later time". The concept of *Nachträglichkeit* will be examined in detail in Chapter 4, Section 2.

5 Emma is a patient whose symptom is to do with not being able to enter a shop on her own. The patient connects her inhibition to the memory of an episode which occurred when she was 12 years old (after puberty, Freud specifies) when, having gone into a shop, she sees two shop assistants laughing and, "in some kind of *affect of fright*" (1895, p. 353), she runs away. While the girl consciously associates her fright with the idea that the shop assistants were laughing at her and that one of the two attracted her, another memory later came to light

that was not present at the moment of the scene in the shop. This was the memory of an episode of seduction experienced at the age of about 8 when, having gone into a shop to buy sweets, she had been molested. Freud concludes by saying, "Here we have the case of a memory arousing an affect which it did not arouse as an experience, because in the meantime the change [brought about] in puberty had made possible a different understanding of what was remembered" (ibid., p. 356).

6 Reference to the biblical combat between David and Goliath.

7 To explain this transition, Freud (1924) uses Livy's narrative about the kings of Rome as a metaphor. He writes that his mistake was like that made by someone who believes that Livy's history is "historical truth" instead of taking the account as the result, in the form of writing, of a reaction to times that were wretched and "perhaps inglorious". In other words, the attempt to use narrative to construct a reality very different from what it was in fact.

8 *The Ego and the Id* (1922) is the work where Freud perhaps gives the most extended treatment of the Oedipus complex and its evolution. The triangular nature of the oedipal situation, coupled with constitutional bisexuality (see Part II, Chapter 7, below, pp. 125–50), become central in determining object choices and the identificatory path on which the definition of the character is based.

9 As is well known, Freud has been accused of being "phallocentric", of considering the Oedipus complex solely from the male viewpoint and not taking adequate account of the girl's development, attributing its specific nature to anatomical difference (1925), from which so-called "penis envy" would derive. This hypothesis would be completely revolutionised by Melanie Klein, for whom there exists a "feminine phase" of attachment to the mother which involves both males and females. The specific nature of female sexuality does not consist in "envy of the penis" but in the early knowledge of the existence of the female genital organ, the vagina. Above all, Klein introduces the element of curiosity, exploration, and knowledge (the epistemophilic instinct) directed to the contents of the mother's body. The urge to know (epistemophilia), like the urge to look (voyeurism, scopophilia) plays an important part in libidinal development. Questions about sexuality, also given the child's immaturity, are the basis of the urge towards exploration and knowledge (Klein, 1932). However, these themes are also clearly detectable in *Little Hans*. First with Klein, and then with Wilfred Bion, attention has more and more shifted towards a model of relations between objects and a myth, that of Oedipus, which becomes less about sexuality and more about knowledge.

10 To mark the centenary of the publication of *Analysis of a Phobia in a Five-Year-Old Boy*, the JAPA (*Journal of the American Psychoanalytic Association*) devoted a special section to the rereading of Freud's text based on documentation which had become available over time. In his essay, Blum (2007) indicates some newly acquired sources: the publication of Hans (Graf's) autobiography in 1972 and the documents contained in the Sigmund Freud Archives which can be consulted for information about the interviews conducted by Kurt Eissler with Hans and his father (Graf, 1959, 1952).

3

PSYCHOSEXUALITY
A new form of thought

3.1 On this side and the other side of the *Three Essays*

The recognition of the existence of infantile sexuality and the significance of its fantasies in the development of the individual – as Little Hans has shown us – is a decisive step, heavy with consequences for the conception of sexuality as a whole. Indeed, it means admitting the presence of a sexuality that is neither genital nor procreative, with all that this entails, as we shall see. It is a scandalous claim that deepens Freud's distance from the scientific community around him and which he addresses and clarifies in *Three Essays on the Theory of Sexuality* (1905). The work is the product of a long transition which began with the composition of the group of papers from 1895 to 1898, some of which we have referred to in the previous chapter, and entails a leap forward in the theory, given that it fully acknowledges the influence of sexuality on the structure of human nature (Green, 1995).

The text[1] consists of three essays: *The Sexual Aberrations*; *Infantile Sexuality*; *The Transformations of puberty*. This raises a question about the sequence chosen by Freud, which does not correspond so much to a logical order as to internal demands of the reflection that the author was undertaking. In fact, Freud starts out with adult sexuality in order to arrive at the infantile, and not the other way around. Adult sexuality is considered in the light of all the possible deviations or variations from what was starting to be considered a normal type of sexual evolution, one that is genital and procreative. For this

35

reason too, the publication of the text represented a radical over-throwing of traditional viewpoints that sounded like a challenge to common sense, to a world of shared and familiar opinions and be-liefs. It is not by chance that the *Three Essays*, together with *The Interpretation of Dreams* (1900), are considered (in Strachey's words) to be Freud's "most momentous and original contributions to human knowledge", but this is also what makes it "universally unpopular" (Jones, 1953). Indeed, the sexual instinct was regarded by the sex-ology and psychiatry of the period as a reproductive instinct in the service of the perpetuating the species, and the sexual goal was circumscribed by the genitals, not involving the surface or other parts of the body as sources of pleasure and excitement, except in pursuit of the final goal. As a consequence, this led to the exclusion of sexuality from infancy and the belief that it would only become manifest at the moment of puberty.

One question which the historians of psychoanalysis have often asked is whether Freud's position can be described as a radical break with that of his contemporaries (Sulloway, 1979; Roudinesco, 2014; Van Haute and Westerink, 2016). Freud's opinion was that his col-leagues – psychiatrists, neurologists, sexologists – shared a Darwinian approach to the question, focusing on the sexual instinct as an instinct with a reproductive purpose. While his speculations distanced him from the mainstream of contemporary thinking, there were never-theless already present in this medical corpus some ideas which Freud himself would later develop. Let's think, for example, of Krafft-Ebing's (1886) position, recognising the force and importance of the sexual instinct on the human organisation as a whole, anticipating "Freud's insight that any theory of sexuality would have a general anthropological dimension and that the sexual drive was a culturally productive drive through sublimation" (Van Haute and Westerink, 2016, p. 566). However, two points distinguish Freud's speculation in quite a radical manner. The first concerns the invention of psycho-sexuality. The term defines the constant psyche-soma link and in-dicates the work that the psyche is compelled to do in virtue of its links with the body, and inaugurates a new perspective from which to view already widely known phenomena. In the second place, he calls into question the approach to the difference between normal and abnormal sexuality. His starting point is the consideration of the multiple varieties in which human sexuality expresses itself, thus challenging both the idea of a sexuality that only begins with puberty and the idea that there may be a clear distinction between a sexuality that is normal and one that is not.

3.2 The perverse scenario

Freud works at extending both *spatially* and *temporally* the traditional boundaries within which sexuality was enclosed. By describing the perversions[2] (First Essay), Freud extends and simultaneously "fragments it", establishing the existence of a sexuality that does not coincide with the sphere of genital and procreative sexuality, and is "beyond the limits of the difference of the sexes, of the sexed" (Laplanche, 2007). In *Fragment of an Analysis of a Case of Hysteria* (1901) Freud concluded his account of the treatment of young Dora (whose story we will return to) with these words: "sexuality is the key to the problem of the psycho-neuroses and of the neuroses in general" (p. 115) and adds that neurotic symptoms "are nothing else than *the patient's sexual activity*" (ibid.). Claiming that the disposition to perversion is part of normal psycho-sexual development, he overturns the widely held opinion which in-terpreted perversion (and masturbation, for that matter) in terms of degeneracy or constitutional predisposition. He brought to light, on the contrary, a pervasive sexuality which declines definite and accepted goals and purposes (genitality and procreation), affectively investing the entire surface of the body. The sexual drive[3] is also considered in its pregenital journey, marked by the erotogenic zones, by partial and/or provisional sources and goals, and is recognised within an infantile sexual universe, which still awaits unification with the primacy of genitality. Apart from some extreme activities that exceed the bounds of modesty, disgust and tolerance, says Freud, as far as the rest are concerned,

> Everyday experience has shown that most of these extensions … are constituents which are rarely absent from the sexual life of healthy people … No healthy person, it appears, can fail to make some addition that might be called perverse to the normal sexual aim; and the universality of this finding is in itself enough to show how inappropriate it is to use the word perversion as a term of reproach.
> (Freud, 1901, p. 160)[4]

Hence the conclusion which leads him to call the child, in virtue of a sexuality played out in the sphere of the pregenital, "polymorphously perverse".

It is this "polymorphous perverse" sexuality which Meltzer (1973) regards as part of adult sexuality and Kernberg (1992) considers to be indispensable in normal erotic activity. Indeed, it expresses the unconscious fantasies of the two partners about their relationship with their own oedipal and pre-oedipal objects coming together in sexual play. According to Kernberg, "an essential factor in maintaining the intensity of a passionate love relationship is the inclusion of polymorphous perverse sexuality" (1992, p. 270), just as it is essential to understand "the playful use of 'exploitation' of each other as part of sexual play" (ibid.). Integrated polymorphous perverse sexuality therefore has the aim of containing and "linking" the unconscious fantasies, and also conflicts, in the couple's play at that particular moment in their evolution. However, perversion maintains a certain specific character which Laplanche and Pontalis (1967) define as "deviation from the 'normal' sexual act when this is defined as coitus with another person of the opposite sex directed towards the achievement of orgasm by means of genital penetration" (Laplanche and Pontalis 1967, p. 306). Orgasm is obtained with other sexual objects, involving other bodily areas, or by modes of behaviour to which one is subjected, as in fetishism, transvestism, or in sadomasochistic behaviours. Thus, perversion is characterised by an atypical mode of obtaining pleasure. All of this is accompanied by two central features which, according to Freud (1905), define its character as "sick" and consist in *exclusiveness* and *fixation* (p. 161), indicating the compulsiveness of a ritualised and circumscribed erotic activity.

However, the consideration of homosexuality is different. Insofar as it is discussed in the first essay on *The Sexual Aberrations*, homosexuality belongs for Freud in the wide variety of sexual activities and orientations that may characterise the human individual. After critically discussing the two options then current as explanations of homosexual phenomena – degeneracy and innate character – he concludes that both are "crude" and unsustainable, and shifts his reflections onto the link that is set up between sex drive and sex object, claiming that it is we who wish to maintain a predetermined and too intimate link between the two. In a note added in 1914 he was to be still more explicit about this: "psycho-analysis considers that a choice of an object independently of its sex – freedom to range equally over male and female objects – as it is found in childhood, in primitive states of society and early periods of history, is the original basis from which, as a result of restriction in one direction or the other, both the normal and the inverted types develop" (ibid., p. 144). He goes on to claim that, for psychoanalysis, even heterosexual choice cannot be seen as something obvious, to be taken for granted. What must be emphasised in this approach is the relationship between drive and object because – as it is already possible to see in Freud's work and that of his epigones – this is the focus of the transformation towards which the subject of perversion and its interpretation is moving.

According to some (Blass, 2016a), in Freud's text there remain two lines of thought that are apparently hard or even impossible to reconcile: one that accentuates the instinctual character of the drive, which in the beginning lacks an object; and a second line according to which the relationship with the object is inherent in the drive from the outset. Without going into a historical examination, the contradiction helps us to shed more light on some trends which mark the way the concept of perversion has evolved. The way that perversion has been seen is accompanied by the revisiting of the very concepts of sexuality (Parsons, 2014) and of object.[5] We are witnessing a progressive shift from the viewpoint that sees neurosis as the negative of perversion to the idea that perversion is a complex psychic operation which, like neurosis, is generated by means of compromises between impulses and defences. Whereas, in the 1905 text, Freud still considered perversion as an un-sublimated pregenital residue transformed into a symptom, in *A Child is Being Beaten* (1919) the idea that comes to the fore is one of perversion as a defence, essentially a failed attempt to "circumvent" the Oedipus complex and castration anxiety. Other hypotheses will later be advanced: in the object relations school, the role of pre-oedipal aggression is emphasised to the point that, based on the aggression towards the parental couple, all subsequent sexual relationships will be perceived and experienced in the light of this experience. This is a "perverse" interplay between idealisation of the love object and the paranoid transformation of the oedipal rival, generating a difficulty in identifying with the parent of one's own sex and the inhibition of a sexual relationship with the other sex. Janine Chasseguet-Smirgel, and the French school in general, introduce a different point of view. In one respect, this author shares the Freudian approach according to which perversion confronts us with a regression or fixation to a pregenital partial drive, but in another she underlines the pervasiveness of the anal-sadistic phase in perversion – what she calls "the anal-sadistic universe" – which contains the cancellation of sexual and generational differences.

There is another type of cancellation which characterises certain perverse scenarios: that of the difference between pleasure and pain described in some passages of that twentieth-century literary text which runs through certain stages of our journey like a watermark. In the pages of *À la recherche* devoted to one of his characters, Baron de Charlus, revealing first his homosexual tendencies (*Sodom and Gomorrah*, pp. 3–19) and then his sadomasochistic ravings (*Time Regained*, pp. 159–185), Marcel Proust captures and describes something profound that may accompany the perverse scenario. On discovering that suffering and pleasure can be confused with each other ("I concluded from this later on that there is one thing as noisy as pain, namely pleasure," p. 10), he adds that "if there is something of aberration or perversion in all our loves, perversions in the narrower sense of the word are like loves in which the germ of disease has spread victoriously to every part" (*Time Regained*, p. 184) in the illusion of achieving a dream by means of a deformed reality. In the transformation of suffering by sadomasochistic practice – the baron is chained to a bed in a seedy hotel and simultaneously suffers and enjoys the pain of blows from a whip – in this desperate search for "his own dream of virility", we find the origin of that particular type of negation, *Verleugnung* (disavowal), which Freud attributes specifically to perversion and which consists in making two mutually irreconcilable positions coexist.[6] This seems to be the specific mechanism of the perverse solution, at least of a certain type of practice in which difference seems to be cancelled, both between pleasure and pain and between genders and generations, and the acknowledgement of castration coincides with its disavowal. Sexual action aims to master the castration anxiety (anxiety about separation and about difference) and to circumvent the acknowledgement of parental sexuality as it is enacted in the primal scene.

Subsequent psychoanalytic reworkings have given ever more substance to the idea that perverse behaviours represent a defence against object relations. In this sense, the perverse character of a behaviour would not depend so much on the object choice (homosexual, heterosexual), nor on the use of "polymorphous sexuality", as Meltzer (1977) and Kernberg (1992) maintain, as on the quality of the relationship that is set up: that is, how far the relationship includes the acknowledgement of the otherness and subjectivity of the other. This view has received support from a new way of considering the external "object", the other, as related to internal aspects of the subject, and thus – to be clear – as an object of projections or identifications, thereby overcoming the idea that the object can be reduced to a simple "medium" for the satisfaction of the drives. The quality of the perverse relationship, in which the relation between aggression and eroticism remains a central element, is also closely correlated to the level of personality we find ourselves being faced with: neurotic, borderline, narcissistic (Kernberg, 1992).

The majority of authors, albeit with different emphases and nuances, seem to concur in believing that the question hinges on the subject's capacity to tolerate reciprocity in relating, the privacy and identity of the other person. In 2000 the *International Journal of Psychoanalysis* published an article by Michael Parsons entitled "Sexuality and Perversion a Hundred Years On" (later included in his book *Living Psychoanalysis* 2014) in which the author sets out to show how the conception of sexuality and its interpretation depend not only on the transformations of psychoanalytic theory, but also on specific historic and societal conditions.[7] In this respect, the concept of perversion has also undergone a transformation of Freud's original idea which interpreted it as an un-sublimated pregenital residue. What Parsons emphasises is the change of perspective that has been introduced. The psychoanalyst's attention is directed less to the object choice and more to the evaluation of the qualities of the object relationship that is set up: "The shift, where perversion is concerned, lies in defining it not by the nature of the external object or of the behaviour aimed at, but in terms of the quality of object-relatedness, and whether sexual excitation is used in the service of, or to obstruct, object-relatedness. This offers a broader and more nuanced view of perversion" (Parsons, 2014, p. 80).

This all takes us back to the vicissitudes of sexuality from the earliest phases of development onwards. Those that McDougall (1982) calls "neosexuality" represent the ways in which – from the first phases of development – the subject invents a personal "erotic theatre" (p. 273) which responds to contradictions and conflicts encountered in infancy around the fabric of sexuality, both that within the parental couple and that of the parental couple towards him or her. In the perverse scenario, the subject creates a game of illusion which controls and defines. The partner, submitting to the subject's requests, has the role on the external plane of dismissing a conflict which is, in fact, all internal, intrapsychic. The original situation that may have represented a traumatic experience in infancy is converted into adult triumph where the dehumanisation of the other protects the subject from the risks that a close relationship holds for him/her. "Technique of intimacy" is a term used by Masud Kahn (1979) to express the aim of perverse action which is the greatest striving for a distorted intimacy and, at the same time, the greatest defence against a mutual and shared intimacy.[8] Though with varying emphases and nuances, the descriptions of perversion (in the specific sense, not that of polymorphous perverse sexuality) concur in defining it as a defensive operation which robs the other of his/her subjectivity, denies otherness and the mutuality of the relationship in an attitude of possession, domination, submission. Such an arrangement places the relationship with the other at the centre of the question.

3.3 Some controversies about infantile sexuality

In the second essay, devoted to infantile sexuality, Freud makes the temporal extension of sexuality that I referred to earlier, recognising its existence and origin in a period before puberty, indeed in infancy, and introducing the concept of "infantile amnesia" in order to explain its apparent absence. It is expressed in phases characterised by the prevalence of different "erotogenic zones" ("oral phase", "anal phase", "phallic phase") awaiting their unification under the supremacy of the "genital phase". On this point, we find ourselves faced with a new contradiction in Freud's text because, though he seems to be using the idea of phases to propose a linear, developmental process, this impression is more apparent than real. In fact, Freud had already clarified the concept of *Nachträglichkeit*[9] (posteriority, *après-coup*), which here finds a complex formulation via the question of the two times of sexuality, the "vicissitudes" of libido and the recognition of the "transformations of puberty", to which he will devote the third essay. It will be precisely this conception of temporality, as we will see later, that guarantees infantile sexuality its specific status in psychoanalysis.

Freud had addressed the concept of drive in one of the last sections of the first essay, "Component Instincts and Erotogenic Zones". The middle part of this section was added in 1914, thus reflecting the influence of the *Papers on Metapsychology*, which he was busy drafting in those years: "By an 'instinct' [*Trieb*] is provisionally to be understood the psychical representative of an endosomatic, continuously flowing source of stimulation, as contrasted with a 'stimulus', which is set up by single excitations coming from without. *The concept of instinct is thus one of those lying on the frontier between the mental and the physical*" (Freud, 1905, p. 168; my italics). Freud is very explicit here. Addressing the concept of drive and inserting it into the revised text, he makes clear his intention to distinguish it from the model of the instinct understood as a response to a natural need. Instead, sexuality is understood in terms of a deep link that is established between the "endosomatic, continuously flowing source of stimulation" and its psychic representation, thereby signalling both the superseding of the reduction of sexuality to "biological" terms, as Laplanche observed (1970), and the full introduction of the concept of psychosexuality. As I was saying earlier, this term serves specifically to indicate the work required of the psyche by virtue of its links with the body. It is not by chance that Freud posits a nexus between infantile sexuality and the drive to know, which Klein will later call "epistemophilic". He claims that sexual problems reawaken the impulse to research, to knowledge. The question, "Where do babies come from?" is the mother of all the enigmas that concern the infant mind, together with the riddle of the Sphinx. The search in this direction is also pursued in the third essay, devoted to puberty, and allows us to explore the nature of the sex drive more deeply in the light of the evolution of psychoanalytic theory.[10]

There are some concepts in Freud's text which have given rise to an intense debate about their meaning and resulted in divergent strands of interpretation about the topic of infantile sexuality and its role in psychoanalytic practice and theory. These are the notions of object, attachment (*Anlehnung*) and autoerotism. They are cruxes which do not only concern Freud's contribution to the interpretation of sexuality, of its genesis and role within individual development, but are also at the centre of a long subsequent debate (Widlöcher, 2000). The debate can be broadly summed up around the question of attachment and the primary love object aimed at the satisfaction of the needs of self-preservation on the one hand, and the origin of infantile sexuality and the infantile sexual fantasies linked to autoerotic activity and the drive on the other. The crossroads at which psychoanalysis has found itself after Freud has required a choice between adopting the vertex of child development or that of libidinal development.

(Conrotto, 2002)

As we have seen before, in the definition of the object as it is formulated in relation to the goal of the drive, we can trace the aporias in Freud's thought and hence also the matrix giving rise to the different lines of thought which have branched off from it. If we ask ourselves what Freud meant by object of the drive in the sense of "instrument" by means of which the drive attains its goal, the answer is not unanimous. The definition he offers in the first essay, "the person from whom sexual attraction proceeds", is overturned by the analysis of sexual deviations which introduces the order of "partial objects" as Freud puts it in his 1915 work, "*Instincts and their Vicissitudes*", speaking about the variability of the object of the drive, which may take the form of a part of the subject's body and not of a whole person. Therefore, some say it is improper to force interpretation towards an outright interpersonal perspective from the outset or, as Blass (2016a) maintains, we must highlight a sharp contradiction between belief in primary auto-erotism and narcissism and the simultaneous recognition of a link between instinct and object.

The notion of "attachment" (*anaclisis, Anlehnung*) introduced from the first edition of the *Three Essays*, represents the element which enables us to overcome the contradiction. It is not only a funda-mental idea in Freudian theory of sexuality, but a conception which helps us to comprehend the genesis of infantile sexuality and the problems posed by the relationship with the object, leading us out of the shoals of the dilemma, primary object love versus narcissistic or autoerotic state.[11] What do we mean by "attachment"? This term defines the process through which the subject initially "attaches him/herself" to the object which satisfies his or her needs (the breast, for example, in relation to hunger) and through the exercise of the somatic function and the satisfaction of the need discovers an additional pleasure, not reducible to the allaying of the current physical demand. In this way, Freud sets up a relation between the sexual drives and those of self-preservation while at the same time distinguishing them from each other. Indeed, the problem of the

44

relationship between them concerns the object-perspective, the fact – in other words – that the further pleasure which accompanies the satisfaction of the need and of the drives to self-preservation is necessarily in a rapport with an object and only later on will the affective investment be withdrawn and expressed in the form of autoerotism. This notion therefore appears decisive for clarifying the possible relationship between "attachment" and "sexuality" (Widlöcher, 2000; Laplanche, 2007): decisive in that it requires a differentiation, without one ruling out the other, between the notion of instinct for self-preservation, which corresponds to adaptive aims, and the conception of drive.

"Instinct", writes Laplanche, "is relatively fixed in the species, is for the most part innate … [whereas] drive (the model for which is the sexual drive) varies from one individual to another, is 'contingent' with regard to its aims and objects, and tends to be 'polymorphously perverse', at least close to its point of origin" (Laplanche, 2018, p. 40).

The impulses to self-preservation – and the self-preserving function of sexuality is included among these – oriented towards the object and to the search for satisfaction of the need in order to re-establish the internal equilibrium, function as a support for the drive which is nevertheless restless, in search of excitation and, above all, not genetic. In this phase, the sexual element is intertwined with the satisfaction of the need, and only later will it be split off from the need and give rise to autoerotic gratification. As the consequence of a taking-away, of an absence, the subject will re-live on itself (autoerotically) the satisfaction it has known with the object. For this reason, and to achieve greater clarity, French authors tend to distinguish "sexuality", whether infantile or adult, from "the sexual", by which they mean "that instinctual component which cannot evolve in a maturational sense, nor be integrated into the domain of self-preservation, but will always remain 'excessive' and 'deviant'" (Conrotto, 2002, p. 9). And that is not all: this difference between need and drive enables us to go back to the question we left unresolved at the end of the first chapter, the "sorting out of what is called reality and fantasy" (Winnicott, 1988, p. 59). In fact, the object which satisfies the need, whether it is the mother or another adult, is not an unsexed object, but is also an object with its own reality, bearer of desire and of its own sexuality which enters the primary relationship and influences the additional pleasure, not reducible to the satisfaction of need, that I was speaking about earlier. It is this which the child may or may not experience in the attachment process and which will later be transformed in the world of fantasy, as is well shown by an episode from therapy with Giovanni.

Giovanni is a boy aged about 11 with a diagnosis of high-functioning autism (Asperger's syndrome). In one therapy session, as soon as he has entered the room he hides under the table, saying it's his "shelter". He picks up the mother and father dolls, undresses them, and moves them around, saying they are wandering about. The therapist observes that they are naked. Giovanni says, "She always goes around naked." After a while he adds, "And the daddy is naked too … and then the mummy gets married to superG." At this point the therapist intervenes, "And what will her husband say? … She's his wife." Giovanni: "Nothing, he gets chased away. SuperG marries his wife and chases him away." In this brief exchange, the boy's fantasies about his parents' bodies are evident, but also the couple relationship and the primary scene expressed in transferential play.[12] Shortly after this session, Giovanni introduces a new character into the therapy, the "fire-raiser", interpreted in his play sometimes by the girl-doll and sometimes by the therapist. Giovanni will tell the "fire-raiser's" story: she was born to a king and queen who abandoned her because she had a "willy" and didn't acknowledge her. So the "fire-raiser" wandered around, setting everything on fire, and feeling like "a poor, desperate wretch". The "fire-raiser" is a complex character and personifies more than one aspect, also linked to Giovanni's history. His mother had reacted to her son's birth with a violently depressive withdrawal. The "fire-raiser" seems to be associated with the question of the boy's sexual identity rejected by the mother's mind (the king-queen couple) in her postnatal depression, an identity which, in the pre-pubertal phase, Giovanni is starting to perceive through states of excitation that are burning like a house on fire inside him. On the other hand, the "fire-raiser" also represents the analyst (who is often called on to play her in the game) who is a live object, who excites him and whom he would like to appropriate. The game and its characters express the conditions in Giovanni's internal world, the emotions passing through him, and above all his encounter with the transformations induced by his incipient puberty. The games with the wife and husband and the "fire-raiser" permit the opening out of themes and emotions linked to infantile sexuality which have been "rekindled" by his bodily development and are now perceived as a conflagration. They are themes and emotions which had not found

46

space in the parental mind when they needed it, had not found containment and been worked through, and so the child had not felt himself to be the object of an affective investment in terms of shared pleasure. Giovanni's therapeutic journey well shows the work of *engagement* that the psyche must do in order to accept the transformations it encounters because of its relationship with the body, and which explode at the onset of adolescence, and also shows the patient's need to encounter a "sane" enough object who may help him to deal with such incandescent material.

The central characteristic of human sexuality which differentiates it from that of other living species, and which psychoanalysis has focused on in order to draw out its consequences, is its being in two times separated from each other by a so-called latency period.[13] In the radical changes it imposes, adolescence represents a quite distinctive and also traumatic moment, as much on the psychic front as in terms of bodily development. Indeed, the subject encounters a body which has become a stranger to itself and is now inhabited by the sexual instinct. The attainment of genital supremacy through the "surplus" of sensations arriving from the body, does not ratify the encounter with sexuality, which has happened well before, but allows it to be identified as such. But the second time of sexuality, which specifically defines adolescence cannot be reduced to a simple retroactive attribution of sense and meaning to something that did not have it, or only partly had it, up until that moment. "The finding of an object", writes Freud in the third essay, devoted to the transformations of puberty, "is in fact a refinding of it" (Freud 1905, p. 222), thus affirming that the subject re-establishes the original relationship with the lost infantile object which was replaced by autoerotic activity. And yet this rediscovery also includes a transformation. Indeed, how far is the rediscovered object really the original one? Is it instead the one that replaced it with autoerotic displacement through the transformation of experience into fantasy and illusion?

3.4 Freud's legacy

As we have already seen, sexuality has not only been at the centre of psychoanalytic interest, but marked its very origin. The consideration of sexuality – based on the hysterical symptom – and the unconscious are the two pillars on which Freud built his doctrine.

47

Perhaps it is not by chance that both *The Interpretation of Dreams* (1900) and the *Three Essays* (1905) were subjected to constant revision by their author over the years (Haynal, 2006). The life of the drives was recognised for its value and significance, its language was described and the ways it is expressed in play, fantasy and dreams were identified. We may wonder what is left of this system. Is it still with us today? To take up Green's (1995) question-provocation once again, "has sexuality anything to do with psychoanalysis?" What remains of the Freudian scheme with regard to this point and what is its legacy? Briefly, what meaning do we attribute to sexuality and infantile sexuality today in our theoretical-clinical apparatus?

If we compare two very similar passages from Freud and Winnicott, we can grasp the shift which psychoanalytic theory has undergone. In *Fragment of an Analysis of a Case of Hysteria* (1901) Freud reflects on the treatment of a young patient, Dora, who later became very famous because further horizons of psychoanalytic practice opened up for Freud as a result of his work with her.[14] The patient's symptomatology confirms his ideas about hysterical phenomenology and hysterical conversion, but the ongoing analysis faces Freud with the question of the transference which is revealed for the first time on this occasion, compelling him to recognise its strength and value. It is a discovery that will signal a radical change of direction, making possible "the invention of the analytic situation" (Kohon, 2018, p. 196). The patient's difficulties reveal her internal conflict about the choice of love object and sexuality, a conflict which will become clear in her own relationship with Freud. He often shows himself to be troubled by the patient's resistance to his interventions and this could perhaps explain the form of his interpretations – "dry and direct", as he says himself – which sound hard, sometimes even intolerant. In one particular passage, Freud refers to his hypothesis, which he shares with the patient, that the symptoms are connected to masturbatory activity in childhood. The patient denies it, claiming to remember nothing of the kind. But, some days later, Freud's catches a symptomatic act by the patient as it happens and interprets it as a confirmation of his idea:

> But a few days later she did something which I could not help regarding as a further step towards the confession. For on that day she wore at her waist ... a small reticule ... and, as she lay on the sofa and talked, she kept playing with it—opening it, putting a

finger into it, shutting it again, and so on. I looked on for some time, and then explained to her the nature of a 'symptomatic act' ... Dora's reticule, which came apart at the top in the usual way, was nothing but a representation of the genitals, and her playing with it, her opening it and putting her finger in it, was an entirely unembarrassed yet unmistakable pantomimic announcement of what she would like to do with them – namely, to masturbate

(Freud, 1901, pp. 76–77).[15]

About seventy years later, another patient, this time of Winnicott's, is struggling with a symptomatic act. In this case, the patient is sucked back into a fantasying activity which excludes her from the achievement of her desire and blocks it in a cycle with no way out.

The patient started with: 'You were talking about the way in which fantasying interferes with dreaming. That night I woke at midnight and there I was hectically cutting out, planning, working on the pattern for a dress. I was all but doing it and was het-up. Is that dreaming or fantasying? ...' We talked around the subject, how the fantasying is unconstructive and damaging to the patient and makes her feel ill ... I pointed this out to her and she gave me an example at the moment while I was talking. She said that while I was talking she was fiddling with the zip of her bag ... She could feel that this dissociated activity was more important to her sitting there than listening to what I was saying.

(Winnicott, 1971, p. 32)

Winnicott's attention, unlike Freud's, is captured not so much by the meaning of the symptomatic act and its relation to sexuality, as the by differences between dream, fantasying (daydreaming), and real life. I have recalled these two clinical fragments not only for the striking similarity of the symptomatic act which they describe and the mirroring of the two patients: Dora who plays with her reticule "which came apart at the top" and Winnicott's patient who fiddles with the zip, pulling it to and fro. I have recalled them because they seem to draw the arc that divides the original Freudian model of psychosexuality, with its repercussions in clinical practice, from the permutations it has undergone over the history of psychoanalysis.[16] Winnicott directs his attention to the difference between fantasying and dreaming.[17] In the session before the passage I quoted, there had been a dream in which the patient "knew that she was engaged to be married to a slob ... a man of a kind that she would not in fact like. She turned to her neighbour and said: 'That man is the father of my child'" (ibid., p. 30). Winnicott concentrates on the capacity for dreaming, which represents an advance on fantasying and, therefore, an advance in the patient's personal working-through, and yet he overlooks the dream's oedipal significance. Commenting on the passage, Lesley Caldwell (2005) emphasises that reading it gives the impression that "something seems to be left out" (p. 6). I also wondered what unintegrated aspects might be referred to by the patient's resorting to dissociated activity and why Winnicott does not address its oedipal meanings (at least as far as we can deduce from the text), even in their transferential valency. And I wondered if, and in what form, the patient's dissociated activity may be picking up on a dimension linked to sexuality and to inhibited excitations, to unexpressed fantasies relating to this psychic sphere that are not being detected and accepted in their communicative and transferential valency. The interpretative line followed by Winnicott confirms not only a divergence between sexuality and the sphere of needs, but also the idea that the sexual material which may appear in the transference, in dreams, and in free associations should be seen as a defence against an underlying pathology located on a more primitive level of development, as we have been shown, after all, by his clinical example (Marion, 2011, 2013).

There is no doubt that an examination of the post-war situation in psychoanalysis prompts us to say that sexuality no longer carries the weight it did in the Freudian *corpus*. The main currents of present-day psychoanalytic thought, such as the Kleinian-Bionian model, object relations theory, the theory of the Self, etc., have shifted the centre of their interest towards other parts of the mind and other problematic areas.[18] For a good part of these theories, sexuality seems to have become less relevant as far as the development of the individual is concerned, and the focus of clinical interest has shifted towards the primitive levels of the mind: narcissistic, borderline and character disturbances. These types of pathology do indeed seem to be better discussed in the light of other categories such as object relations theory, the mother-baby relationship, the question of whether or not the primary needs have been satisfied, and the possible traumas that can come into play at this level. In the light of developments after Freud, sexuality and the pleasure/unpleasure principle are no longer thought of as the central organiser of the individual's elaborative and fantasying activity, and attention has been turned more and more towards the early psychic levels, to the archaic phantasies of undifferentiation and possession. The very centrality given by Winnicott to the environment and to what is at stake in the early exchanges in the mother-baby relationship goes in this direction.

The Kleinian revision translates the language of the instincts into that of emotion and unconscious phantasy. The primal scene and the child's phantasies about it (the "oedipal situation"), besides sustaining the impulse to know (epistemophilic instinct) represent the pivot around which the events of the depressive position are structured.[19] Kleinian theory emphasises the feelings of dependency, loss, and exclusion connected to the renunciation of the maternal object and the full recognition of the parents' relationship as a couple as distinct from the parents' relationship to the child. The former is bearer of sexuality, desire and creativity, the second of the needs for care and nurturing, of the feelings of excitation and aggressiveness translated into phantasies and deriving from the position of exclusion: "This recognition produces a sense of loss and envy, which, if not tolerated, may become a sense of grievance or self-denigration" (Britton, 1989, p. 85).

In this position, which signalled a radical new direction in the subsequent development of psychoanalysis, there is profound divergence from the Freudian model. The recognition of the centrality of the relationship with the maternal object from the start of life has given priority to the breast and to orality at the expense of the genital phase, just as the pleasure/unpleasure pairing has been replaced by feelings of aggression and love (Green, 1995). Dana Birksted-Breen (1993) maintains that the interest of British psychoanalysis has gradually shifted from sexuality to concentrate on separation anxiety and the emotional and defensive levels connected to it. In a recent review of the Kleinian-Bionian model, Grotstein (2009) dwells at length on this point, above all on how the concept of sexuality may be used as a defence against the recognition and awareness of need and dependency, which are instead considered primary: "sexuality screens and defends against the awareness of infantile states of dependency and neediness" (p. 240). The "need" prevails over the "wish", just as the self-preservative life drive does over the sexual. In the subsequent evolution of the model in Bionian terms, interest has instead been directed towards the maternal capacity (reverie) for elaborating the "raw" emotional states and the child's capacity for tolerating frustration, which will later make possible the function of thinking and the apparatus for thinking thoughts. "While attention has shifted to mental functioning, to dream-thought, and to what forms dream-thought," as Ferro (2007, p. 64) claims in accordance with his Bionian model, it is evident that the topic of sexuality becomes just one of the possible languages in which the patient and the analytic couple may narrate each other, losing its specific character. To use another of Ferro's (1999) vivid expressions, it represents a "narrative genre or dialect in the consulting room" derived from the quality of the encounter between the minds of the analyst and analysand.

The same relational theory (Greenberg and Mitchell) privileges relational exchanges, overshadowing the Freudian concept of psycho-sexuality which instead entails a close link between the mental and the corporeal. It seems to me that the comparison between the case studies of Freud and Winnicott testifies to this evolution of psychoanalysis and to a different way of looking at psychic problems. The importance of the object has put the drive into the shade, even though it is hard to consider a drive without an object. The object of the drive becomes central in defining the drive itself, as we have seen in reference to the debate about the question of the object originating with the *Three Essays*. As Green (2008) puts it, "the correct method should be a drive-object model, not the one without the other" (p. 1039).

Set against this trend is the panorama of French psychoanalysis, in which sexuality has never left the scene. Sexuality is not understood in terms of sexual behaviours but as the "sexual", a ubiquitous ingredient which accompanies the journey of subjectivation and the symbolic processes. In the article cited earlier, Green (1995) maintains that his own analytic experience has induced him to think of the relationship between narcissistic pathologies and sexuality in an opposite way to the Kleinian scheme. The symptomatology of those patients in whom the role of sexuality seems to be entirely contingent or irrelevant shows instead how far its apparent deletion may function to protect and obscure the deep meaning of the pathology: "the sexual and genital fixations were like the heart of an onion covered by many layers" (p. 874). In fact, the awareness of the importance of sexuality and genitality exposes these patients to a severe danger, that of having to recognise otherness, the difference of the other, and with this the frustration and the connected feelings of rivalry and jealousy, a danger to be avoided at all costs.

Narcissistic problems, and the borderline and character disturbances which characterise the non-neurotic structures of many of the patients we are faced with today, have therefore induced psychoanalysts to turn their attention elsewhere and radically modify their approach along lines quite different from the early Freudian scheme. The focus has shifted to the search for a "before" and a "beyond", to the care of psychic functioning and the widening of the range of mental instruments for thinking and dreaming one's own psychic world. The subject of the "sexual" has lost centrality and specificity in psychoanalytic theory in favour of other models, and attention to the domain of need has obscured whatever pertains to desire. But the question to be asked at this point is whether there really is a category of needs and a human environment in the early phases of development that is not interfered with by desire and sexuality, a "naturalness" of need, a pure expression of necessity (André, 2011). Or, adopting another conceptualisation, we can ask ourselves if a "'sacred' innocence of primary narcissistic unity" really exists (Ogden, 2009, p. 128). If we think about the strength of the maternal desire invested in the baby's body as she cares for it (Freud, 1905; Bollas, 2000; Lemma, 2005), or its absence and the consequences of that, as the brief clinical vignettes have shown, we may doubt that there is a clear separation. And we may doubt it still more if we think about the "powerful transgenerational continuity of oedipal experience" (Ogden, 2009, p. 128) which involves the transmission of unconscious parental phantasies, including those concerned with desire and from the earliest phases of the relationship.

Notes

1 Freud would return continually to this text over the years, testifying to the central place occupied by the *Sexualtheorie* in his speculations. The successive editions (including the final one of 1924) and the additions which each new edition entailed (Lucchetti, 2010; Ferruta, 2012) mirror the changes addressed by Freud's thought over the arc of his life.

2 It is not my intention, nor is it within the scope of this book, to address the topic of the perversions, which is a specific and very complex chapter in psychoanalytic theory. The reference to Freud's essay only lies within the discussion of the wide-reaching changes we find ourselves facing in the theme of sexuality.

3 The drive is a concept which Freud sharply distinguishes from that of instinct, giving rise to various well-known controversies about translating it, especially into the English language which lacks a precise

equivalent to the German, *Trieb*. The drive is defined (Laplanche and Pontalis, 1967) as a *pressure* which impels the organism towards a goal and this goal may be reached in an object or by means of it. The object of the drive is not biologically determined and is interchangeable, just as the modes of satisfaction are variable and linked to the functioning of determined somatic zones (erotogenic zones). The sex drive is initially fragmented into partial drives which achieve a local pleasure (organ pleasure) and genital primacy follows a complex evolution. From the economic viewpoint, the libido constitutes the only measure of the sex drive. The sex drive is linked to a play of representations and fantasies which characterise it.

4 So we must think that as far as Freud is concerned, what defines a "normal" sexual activity is a question of the general consent or degree of moderation maintained in the manifestation of the so-called "perverted" activity.

5 A decisive element causing a break with previous tradition will be introduced by Melanie Klein and her conception of object. Whereas for Freud the object is mostly conceived as the object of an instinctual impulse and at the service of the satisfaction of desire, object relations theory introduces a new perspective in which the object is endowed with characteristics and qualities (good/bad) in relation to the impulses of the subject. According to Klein, the infant is in relation to objects from birth and this arouses feelings of love, hate, gratitude, envy. On the one hand, the object is a mental representation which mirrors reality, but on the other the subject's projective processes contribute to how the external object is perceived. The object thus becomes a goal and part of the subject's fantasy and emotional world.

6 From the 1923 paper *The Infantile Genital Organization* onwards, the term *Verleugnung* (from the verb *verleugnen*), translated as "disavowal" or "repudiation", acquires an ever more marked prominence. It is a specific defence closely connected to the perversions and concerns the disavowal of a reality that turns out to be traumatic for the subject. It is interesting to note the etymology of the German word *leugnen* (contained within *verleugnen*), "to deny", which derives from *lügen*, "to tell lies". This is a particular negation, a "disavowal" or "repudiation" based on a lie, which has to do with Freud's original idea of female castration. The refusal to accept the lack of the penis, despite the perception which confirms this absence, maintains the false conception that there is a penis. In this sense, two irreconcilable positions coexist in the mind, giving rise to a deceptive solution.

7 In demonstrating his thesis about the evolution of the concept of sexuality in time, and hence also in relation to the concept of perversion, Parsons also draws on the evolution that has occurred in the field

of painting and the arts, recalling, like me, the reaction received by Manet's picture *Le Déjeuner sur l'herbe* and likening it to the reactions following the publication of Freud's *Three Essays*. He suggests a parallel with Anthony Caro's sculpture, *Table Piece Y-98. Déjeuner sur l'Herbe II* (1989), which in a similar way to Manet and Freud, challenges the viewer in 2000: "What does the Caro sculpture stand for? How has psychoanalysis reworked Freud's conceptualisation of sexuality, to give us our own contemporary understanding of it?" (Parsons, 2014, p. 68).

8 In the preface to his book *Alienation in Perversions* (1979) Masud Kahn states that "the pervert puts an impersonal object between his desire and his accomplice: this object can be a stereotype fantasy, a gadget or a pornographic image. All three alienate the pervert from himself, as, alas, from the object of his desire."

9 We use the German term here to indicate a conception of temporality specific to psychoanalysis. The term often used in Italian is *"posteriorità"*, which does not fully render the sense of the German term. In German the adjective *nachträglich* means not only 'posterior' (*später*) and 'subsequent' (*folgend*), but also "supplementary" (*ergänzend*). The irregular, transitive verb *nachtragen*, from which the adjective and noun derive, also has this dual meaning of "bring after" and "add". A third meaning is "to bear a grudge". The term has stirred up many controversies about its translation, especially about the English one, "deferred action", adopted in the Standard Edition, which does not catch the complexity of the German term where the sense of retroactivity is central. The French translation, *après-coup*, is clearly more successful, and is very often used in place of the German term.

10 In the third essay, the section which deals with libido theory was added in 1914 and expresses some conclusions that Freud was reaching and which we have already mentioned: libidinal energy is distinguished from other forms of psychic energy and the sexual processes must be kept distinct from other processes, such as nutrition. The libido is directed towards sexual objects that may satisfy it and, when this process is interrupted, it returns to the Ego, generating that special state that is narcissism, including its most severe derivatives in terms of pathology.

11 According to Laplanche and Pontalis (1967), the state of autoerotism, which concerns the way the infant may give itself pleasure through an autoerotic activity such as suckling, cannot be considered a state without an object since it is preceded by a stage in which satisfaction has been achieved by means of an object and by means of the allaying of vital demands, such as hunger.

12 In psychoanalysis, "primal" or "original scene" (*Urszene* in German) means the "scene of sexual intercourse between the parents which the

child observes, or infers on the basis of certain indications, and phantasises" (Laplanche and Pontalis, 1967, p. 335). It is to Freud that we owe the discovery of the "primal scene" via the famous dream of The Wolf Man (1914), but it would be Klein who gave us its fertile elaboration. Klein "will identify in the 'primal scene' the prototype of unconscious phantasy, with its various permutations according to the level of libidinal development, whether oral, anal, or phallic. Assigning to each phase of psychosexual development a specific unconscious phantasy about the representation of the primal scene ... Melanie Klein found an effective, and fully psychic, way of getting round the problem of integrating the precipitates of bodily sensations" (Norsa, 2006, p. 4).

13 By latency period, Freud and psychoanalysis after him mean the years running from the resolution of the Oedipus complex (4–5 years) to puberty and which register an "obscuring" of the sexual drive, which will powerfully re-emerge during adolescence. The concept of latency underwent an evolution within the *corpus* of Freud's own work from the idea of a period of organically conditioned development fixed by heredity to a more properly psychological idea in which latency is understood as a manifestation of the Ego's functions. With the move to the structural model, substantial modifications are made to the location, role, and phenomena of this phase of psychosexual development. The Superego, arising as a consequence of the renunciation of the oedipal sexual objects, becomes the explicative element and dominant feature of latency. On the one hand, as a psychic agency, the Superego is configured as the heir of the Oedipus complex and the establishment of human sexual life in two stages; on the other, as the outcome of the long duration of infantile dependency which typifies the human species compared to that of animals (Marion and Bonaminio, 1986). Besides the evolution this concept has undergone in psychoanalysis, we may wonder what its present-day meaning might be in the light of the changes that have happened to childhood. As we will see later, latency seems to have become a questionable concept (Guignard, 2010). We need only think about the quantity of stimuli, including the sexual, to which children are subjected in the modern world to wonder what type of latency we can be referring to.

14 Dora was a young woman of 18 from an upper middle-class family. The first time Freud saw Dora, she was suffering from a nervous cough and aphonia, symptoms which ceased spontaneously some time later. Dora was later brought back to Freud with psychological symptoms: the girl was particularly dissatisfied with life, behaved rudely to her father and rebelled against her mother who wanted to make her do her share of the domestic tasks, tried to avoid every kind

of social relationship, and wanted to leave her family. All this was diagnosed at the time as "*petite hystérie*". The Ks were friends of Dora's family. Frau K had a relationship with Dora's father and Herr K seemed to turn a blind eye to this relationship, trying to gain Dora's attention in exchange. The girl, disgusted by the situation, had accused Herr K of molesting her, but nobody had believed her. In fact, when Dora was fourteen, Herr K had invited her to a church festival, arranging things so that she was left alone with him at his business premises where he suddenly clasped her to him and kissed her. That event had remained secret during the following months and emerged only during the course of the analysis. Freud believed that the seduction by Herr K had produced erotic excitation in Dora, later transformed into a more acceptable sense of nausea. Freud saw her somatic symptoms (fainting fits) and her threats to her father as her revenge against the father she was oedipally in love with. In the same way, she was by no means indifferent to Frau K, with whom she had once shared a room and could admire her "adorable white body". Moreover, Frau K would introduce Dora to the secrets of sexuality by lending her a book, then considered pornographic, by Mantegazza. The situation with Frau K puts Freud in contact with a deeper level of Dora's problems: that is to say, her homosexual love for the maternal figure, re-experienced through the relationship with her friend. And yet Freud's "imperative" attitude during the treatment, aimed at imposing his view of things, seems to be part of the reason why it was prematurely broken off. In the Postscript to the case, Freud ponders the reasons for its lack of success, criticises himself, and attributes the unfavourable outcome of the therapy to an error on his part. He states that he did not master the transference in good time. The Postscript is a document of great historical significance because, with Dora, Freud really constructed his theory of the transference (unconscious reliving of passed episodes in which the therapist is seen as if he had been one of the participants), which then became the pillar of every psycho-analytic treatment. Besides being the only one about a woman (the other so-called "case histories", five in all, are about males), the essay has assumed importance precisely because "what could have been 'a classic Victorian domestic drama' is now a family novel of mysterious complexity" (Kohon, 2018, p. 197).

15 In this passage we find ourselves faced with an interpretation by Freud that is so direct and expository that it leaves us puzzled, especially about the impression it gives us that he is imposing his own convictions on the patient.

16 Naturally, it is simply a question of examples chosen for their vividness, and this is their sole purpose, with no suggestion that they reflect

the overall articulation of the arguments developed by Freud and Winnicott in their writings.

17 In this book, Winnicott pursues the development of one of the most important and significant points in the formulation of his theories, that of the mechanism of dissociation as distinct from repression. In what Winnicott calls "an organized sequence of fantasying" the patient lives a parallel life "dissociated from the main part of her" (Winnicott, 1971, p. 29), so that she can never make herself feel present to herself and complete. This is the central theoretical-clinical point of interest in Winnicott's formulation. In the debate between infantile sexuality and attachment, Winnicott expresses a dual position. He acknowledges the influence of sexuality in neurotic pathology, whereas – on the strength of his experience with regression – he attributes the genesis of severe pathologies to alterations in maternal and environmental holding. These forms of holding would be predominantly a matter of need.

18 The following passage is intended to give the reader a brief sketch of how psychoanalytic theory and practice have moved along different lines, in some cases diverging radically from the original scheme. It is not part of this book's aim to enter into a detailed review of the various positions and the debate they have occasioned.

19 For Klein, the depressive position represents that stage during which the infant becomes able to integrate his or her fragmented perceptions and to accept the other, the mother, as a whole object. Persecutory feelings and anxieties are balanced by feelings of love, and the infant can begin to be concerned for the object. For the "oedipal situation" and its influence in analytic work, cf. Lupinacci, 1994; Britton, 1989.

TIME IN SEXUALITY

ahimè, non mai due volte configura
il tempo in egual modo i grani! e scampo
n'è: ché, se accada, insieme alla natura
la nostra fiaba brucerà in un lampo.

(Eugenio Montale, *Vento e bandiere*)

4.1 The status of infantile sexuality

"Without the drive concept and without any other similar alternative motivational framework, the motivational and structural centrality of sexuality seems to float in metapsychological space. If sexuality is not mandated by a pressured expression of inner necessity, *why* does it become so essential in personality development and psychopathology?" (Mitchell, 1988, p. 94). The question asked by Mitchell, reviewing the metapsychological model in the light of relational theories, gives a clear sense of the post-Freudian psychoanalytic debate about the subject of sexuality. In particular, it captures a central theoretical crux which signals the "slippage" of the vertex from the classical Freudian scheme centred on the drive concept – to which some sectors of psychoanalysis, especially in francophone culture, remain faithful – towards the idea of sexuality as an expression of a relational matrix and schemata.

Mitchell's query, like those with which we closed the previous chapter, brings into play the question of "sexuality without drive theory" (ibid.), the question of its genesis and nature. Where does it originate from? How can we imagine the *incipit* of a pregenital infantile sexuality in the absence of a "physiological" underpinning that ensures its presence? How is it perceived by the subject? In following the evolution of the discussion and the different answers that have been given to these enquiries, we get the impression that we are indeed being presented with sharply distinct positions but, seen from another vantage point, they may contribute to a more integrated view of the problem of sexuality, in some ways also answering the question posed by Winnicott which I recalled at the end of the first chapter, about the "sorting out of what is called reality and fantasy" (Winnicott, 1988, p. 59). We can picture this view as the meeting between two different theoretical positions and say that, following the attention paid by psychoanalysis to object relations and the mother–baby relationship, the work which the psyche must address by virtue of its links with the body is now extended and inserted into a complex relational and experiential fabric. The stimuli coming from the body are inscribed in a network of responses from the environment, and the mind works to organise, represent and give meaning to this reality.

Returning to the questions about the genesis of sexuality, two hypotheses above all have dominated the scientific scene. The first and more traditional concerns the connection between sexuality's emergence and the absence of the object that satisfies need. For Freud (1905), orality represents the archetype of infantile sexual functioning, which "attaches itself" to one of the non–sexual functions "serving the purpose of self-preservation" (feeding, for example) and "does not become independent of them until later" (Freud, 1905, p. 182). This independence is the effect of the diminution of the object which satisfies the need. In the void that is created in that moment and at the origin of the feeling of frustration, the infant will find itself wanting to repeat that pleasure[1] and will try to recreate it "in hallucination" using its mnestic trace in a self-sufficient way, independently of the outside world. In a *second phase* the initial experience of attachment comes over the infant again so that he reproduces it as he sucks his thumb, but also transforms it, thereby giving life to the fantasied scene. It is the divergence between need and desire,[2] and the birth of autoerotism.[3] According to this hypothesis, the nascent sexuality finds its point of origin and its support in a behaviour linked to the preservation of life; and, in

60

the human species, the setting-up of the pleasure-unpleasure principle, from which the "sexual" derives, travels in parallel to that of self-preservation. Infantile sexuality, which is the object of repression, is thus constituted as a permanent dimension of unconscious psychic life, the engine of desire and curiosity, and represents a central characteristic of the process of subjectivation.[4]

A second hypothesis about the genesis of infantile sexuality, maintained especially by Laplanche, concerns its "exogenic" nature. This author claims there is a sharp distinction between instinct and drive. The former concerns genetic programming and the adaptive and self-preserving features, which also involve sexuality (the instinct to procreate and perpetuate the species, for example) and are only manifested at the time of pubertal development; whereas drive refers specifically to infantile sexuality, *"la sexualité humaine pulsionnelle"*, which is an *expanded* sexuality not linked to sexual difference and not timetabled in accordance with a genetic programme. This hypothesis is specifically characterised by a focus on the centrality of the adult–infant relationship and the attention it pays to the human being's "fundamental anthropological situation" (Laplanche, 2007), which is founded on an asymmetrical starting point. By virtue of this constitutional asymmetry, the adult–infant relationship is characterised by a generalised condition of "seduction" (this is Laplanche's theory of "generalised seduction") of the latter by the former. In Laplanche's perspective, the "seduction" concerns adult–infant communication: the "messages" sent by the adult and inadvertently compromised by her/his *"sexuel"*. They are messages that turn out to be "enigmatic" to the infant mind which is not yet in a position to comprehend them since "the adult has an unconscious ... a sexual unconscious essentially made of infantile residues" (ibid.), whereas the child still lacks one.

Years before, in his paper *Confusion of the Tongues Between the Adults and the Child: the Language of Tenderness and of Passion* (1932) Ferenczi recognised the importance of the sexual trauma which derives from this disparity and tried to describe its outcomes: "If *more love* or *love of a different kind from that which they need*, is forced upon the children in the stage of tenderness, it may lead to pathological consequences in the same way as the *frustration or withdrawal of love* quoted elsewhere in this connection" (p. 228).[5]

Laplanche's theory and, for that matter, Ferenczi's position both invert the terms of the object's presence/absence. In fact, in this case, instead of it being the loss of the object which sets in motion the

61

fantasying displacement and the autoerotic substitute satisfaction, it is its very presence that starts the process. The thesis hinges on the theory of "attachment" (*anaclisis* or *Anlehnung*). In this view, the two types of functioning that I referred to earlier come into effect within the "attachment" (*anaclisis* o *Anlehnung*) itself: one adaptive, genetically programmed, instinctual by nature, the other a drive linked to libidinal development and corresponding to other principles of functioning. The unconscious contents of the adult caregiver infiltrate the processes of attachment and nurture of the infant, who perceives them as something extraneous and incomprehensible, but also as a source of excitation. The infant's symbolising function and his impulses to fantasy have their origin in these very messages which come from the adult, and they prompt him to an intense elaborative activity, a work of "translation" as Laplanche claims, in order to release their "enigmatic" meaning: "the adult-*infans* dialogue, as reciprocal as it may be, is nevertheless parasited by something else, from the beginning. The adult message is scrambled. On the side of the adult and in a unilateral direction, there is the intervention of the unconscious. Indeed, I would say of the adult's infantile unconscious, insofar as the adult-*infans* situation is a situation that reactivates those unconscious infantile drives" (Laplanche, 2007, p. 103).

However, the exchange cannot be thought of as happening in only one direction. Rather, it is an exchange in two directions. The flow of meanings follows the adult–infant line by virtue of the "fundamental anthropological situation," and yet the child, his presence and reactions, challenge the adults and interrogate them in more or less conscious ways about their own bodies and their sexuality (Marion, 2016c). Bollas (2000) vividly describes this encounter: "the mother and father seduce the infantile instinct. They want themselves to be taken as its object. The instinct – if we allow its theoretical existence as a primal fantasy – drives toward the breast like a lover saturated with pre-existent erotic knowledge" (p. 33). The bidirectionality of this process appears to us with surprising clarity at the onset of adolescence when the events of sexual maturation (puberty) provoke a serious conflict with the previous representations, which are both the representations that the teenager had of her/himself, and the representations that the parents had of the teenager.

The difficulty of this phase and its bidirectional character are well illustrated by this clinical example which helps us to clarify the point.

Ludovico is 13 years old and was identified some years earlier because of repetitive behaviours and problems with self-esteem. Ludovico's history is characterised by bereavements and a climate of depression which has marked the family atmosphere. The patient seems to have managed all this by means of a rigid and obsessive structure which has helped him to hide violent drive-impulses connected to self-denigration, anger and aggressiveness. The arrival of puberty bursts into the cage which the patient had built for himself and explodes it. The fear of losing control, of "letting loose the crazy hormones", as Ludovico puts it, is accompanied by a sexual identity that is being put continually in doubt. In one analytic session Ludovico starts talking about problems connected with masturbation; he masturbates in the shower. The therapist observes that maybe he thinks this is a way of wiping out not only the traces of the act but also the fantasies that are occupying his mind. The boy is terrified that other people (his parents) can see his fantasies, which he is ashamed of and feels guilty about. Ludovico claims he is not like other teenage boys, that he doesn't get anywhere with girls. The therapist tells him that perhaps masturbating really is an adolescent thing and what it offers is a way to know yourself, to know your own body. Even so, Ludovico goes on to say that he only masturbates in the shower and that way it leaves no traces. The therapist comments that, just as nobody must know his fantasies, so nobody must see the products of his excitation, of a body that is changing and not the way it was before. Ludovico says he still feels a bit small. He's no longer tied to his mother's apron strings, or maybe a bit, yes. But if his mother found out he'd had a puff of a cigarette "she'd hit the roof". At this point, the therapist comments that maybe he is so tied to an image which he thinks his mother has of him, and he so doesn't want to disappoint her, that he struggles to recognise that there is also a different mother who is happy to see him growing up to be strong, with a manly body. Ludovico thinks for a bit and then comments, "But you aren't an ordinary mother."

As this clinical vignette illustrates, and as we will see later on, an intense psychic work accompanies the subject's break with his own childhood and the consequent transformations of puberty. For Ludovico, the regressive impulse towards childhood, represented by his fears, is always lurking and it threatens his striving towards change. The conflict faced by the adolescent – to grow up or remain a child – is the same conflict that the parents are going through: whether to continue to see him/her as a child or to recognise that s/he now has sexuality. The "deferred action" of sexuality comes to be realised and at the same time challenges and interrogates the environment on this specific point. The integration of the "sexual body" which, as Laufer (1984) says, is the adolescent's specific task, has previously been the task of every adult who is no longer an adolescent. And how the adults have arrived at and lived through their own adolescence will influence the way they see their children's adolescence and adolescence in general, as Ludovico's story shows us.

I was saying earlier that the combination of the drive model and the relational model may contribute to a more integrated view of the problem of sexuality. The impulse coming from our bodies is necessarily articulated in a world of relationships, and the environment's response is not a matter of indifference for the outcome of the experience of sexuality in ourselves.[6] "The mother's desire of the self's infantile body is crucial to one's sexual well-being," writes Bollas (2000). "If the mother has underestimated the infant then auto-erotism will stand in for the lack of maternal sensorial care" (p. 31). The need to keep the two viewpoints together also enables us to answer the delicate question about the hallucinatory satisfaction of desire. That is, in what way would the infant translate the satisfaction of nutritional need or the pleasure obtained from physical care into pleasure of a sensual/sexual nature? According to Laplanche (2007), "if the sexual has not been part of real original experience, it will never be reproduced in fantasy or in its symbolic elaboration". Maternal care, which in a first phase occurs above all through contact – Winnicott's "handling" and "holding" – and testifies to the recognition of the other's (the child's) body, is a potent vehicle for transmitting pleasure and establishes itself as an important foundation for subsequent experiences. With the arrival of genitality, what Bollas (2000) calls "this epiphany at around 3" which we have seen in the case of Little Hans, many other things will happen, but how they develop and what their outcome will be depends greatly on the quality of the response to initial needs that the child feels he or she has received from the environment.

4.2 *Nachträglichkeit*: A particular form of temporality

There is another viewpoint from which sexuality plays a central role in the process of subjectivation. I am referring to the question of time. Sexuality's biphasic character is regarded as one of the two features which define the human species, the other being the human infant's long period of dependency. We can picture the structural function of sexuality specifically in relation to the constituting of temporal processes. The body imposes a demarcation of time closely connected to the stages of sexuality, in this respect reaffirming the close psyche-soma link: and not only in relation to the young child's encounter with his or her own genitality and the entry into adolescence through the transition of puberty, but also through the subsequent steps which mark the cycle of life, such as pregnancy, the menopause, the andropause, etc. They are turning points around which a temporality is woven that is not only marked by the linear direction of time, but also by a folding in on itself, as if the new step were recapitulating and simultaneously rereading those that preceded it.

Psychoanalysis makes use of a complex temporal model which breaks up a unitary view of time and highlights the plurality of dimensions by which the human being is inhabited (Green, 2000). These dimensions are expressed in dream-space, within which past and future converge in the present of the dream (Freud, 1899a), in the atemporality of the unconscious, and in the concept of the compulsion to repeat which introduces a complex anti-time movement, as much a repetitive insistence as a return to a state of quietude. To these dimensions is added *Nachträglichkeit*, that particular form of non-linear temporality which characterises psychoanalytic thought in a specific way that is closely linked to the question of sexuality and trauma. As we have seen (cf. *supra*, Chapter 3, p. 61, note 9), the translation of the term *Nachträglichkeit* has provoked much controversy, especially because of the difficulty in maintaining the two meanings included in the German, both "posterior-subsequent" and "additional". To the temporal recalling of two events in succession, between which an associative link is established, is added the reference to a further meaning, initially absent, which the first event acquires by virtue of the second.

This is a conception of time's passing which comes to light very early in Freud's thinking (1895) and is at the origin of the theory of psychic functioning and pathology. Describing the dynamic of the hysterical symptom, he claims "We invariably find that a memory is repressed which has only become a trauma by *deferred action*" (p. 356) and in a letter to Fliess from 14 November 1897, referring to precisely these effects of "deferred action", he speaks of having given "birth to a new piece of knowledge". It becomes clear in the group of writings from 1896 (*Heredity and the Aetiology of the Neuroses*; *Further Remarks on the Neuro-Psychoses of Defence*; *The Aetiology of Hysteria*) that this concept is situated in the theory of seduction and infantile trauma which, in those very years becomes replaced by elaboration in fantasy, which influences the memory itself. The fact that "a memory only later becomes a trauma" and that it "arouses an affect which it did not give rise to as an experience" (1895, ibid.) is closely linked to the Freudian theory of trauma at two different times. But what exactly does he mean? The memory of the past scene is newly stirred up and received by a subject whose psychic and organic life has changed from the one who lived through the first scene at the time. This is the general characteristic of the human organisation caused by the delay of puberty which "makes possible posthumous primary processes" (ibid., p. 359) and leads to the "understanding" of what had previously only been lived through. The arrival of puberty stamps the succession of events which distance the first occurrence from the second with that particular turn that makes possible a different interpretation of the memory and a re-reading of it in the light of what the encounter with a sexed body enables the subject to grasp. In order to describe the functioning of *Nachträglichkeit,* Freud, who introduces this theory in the *Project for a Scientific Psychology* (1895), uses the famous clinical example of Emma (as we have seen earlier, speaking about the *"proton pseudos",* cf. *supra*, Chapter 2, p. 38, note 3). As a child, around the age of eight, Emma would have had an experience of sexual caresses from a shopkeeper when she had gone to buy sweets. At the time when it occurred, the experience had not had a specific traumatic sexual significance for the girl, and had been repressed. Only later, *a posteriori, nachträglich*, at the moment of pubertal development and in the presence of a similar episode, that first event is restored to memory and reread as a sexual seduction. The traumatic aspect linked to a sexual scene may thus come to light.

In the journey which sees Freud engaged in replacing the traumatic fact, understood as a particular situation, with the elaboration which the subject makes of the event in fantasy and which therefore goes on to influence the actual memory, the 1899 work *Screen Memories* marks an important step. An infantile memory does not draw its specific screen significance only from the relationship that exists through association between it and another forgotten content, but also because of the fact that it is used in the context of a present situation, in this case having more to do with a fantasy being expressed in the form of a memory. The infantile memories "were *formed* ... and a number of motives, with no concern for historical accuracy, had a part in forming them, as well as in the selection of the memories themselves" (1899b, p. 322). This refers to a fantasy which is constructed and takes the form of a memory. The past may be reconstructed *a posteriori* (*nachträglich*), even on the basis of who we are in the present, of our current desires and aspirations.

This particular temporal movement finds a striking representation in a painting by Giovanni Bellini (1433–1516), the *Holy Allegory*. The picture is well known for its mysterious and arcane character, and the difficulty in deciphering it is testified by the multiplicity of interpretations which have been made over time without arriving at a single definitive version. The panel makes one think of a dream-scene and the potency of the artistic creation seems to have succeeded in using space to give a visual representation to the multidimensionality of time and, in particular, to that special form of temporality that is *Nachträglichkeit*. The painting is divided into two parts. In the foreground a marble terrace with a diamond-patterned floor surrounded by a balustrade encloses one space, separating it from another, external one. Various figures are situated within this space. In the background and separated from the enclosure, a watery landscape opens out, as magical and tender as only Bellini's landscapes can be, surrounded by a backdrop of rocks and a group of houses. The middle of the terrace is occupied by a group of little children, one of whom is wearing a white shirt and sitting on a red cushion, at the foot of a fruit tree which one of them is shaking. The child on the cushion has a fruit in his hands and looks at it intently. To the right and left of the little boys there are two groups of adults: to the left the Madonna and two female figures, to the right St Sebastian and Job with their eyes on the little boys. Following certain lines of interpretation, the terrace with the balustrade represents the sacred space. The woman seated on the throne to the left of the children would be Mary in an attitude of devotion, together with the two other women, probably saints or representations of the theological virtues. Their gaze is directed at the child on the cushion who would represent Jesus with the apple, symbol of original sin, in his hand, while the blood-red cushion would be a clear allusion to his sacrifice. The male figures to the right,

Job and St Sebastian, represent humanity before and after Christ, but also martyrdom and forbearance, and they are looking back in time at the "traumatic" point of origin (Jesus, the apple, the red cushion). The figures outside the enclosure also refer to other temporal dimensions: St Peter and the foundation of the Church, and St Paul who pursues the infidel with his drawn sword. What I mean to emphasise in this brief description is how Bellini's *Holy Allegory* seems, in a surprising manner and in a single space, to give form and visibility to the co-presence of the multiple temporal lines which pass through this very space. While Jesus at the centre of the scene seems to gaze intently at the point of origin (the apple) of the task of redemption which awaits him in the future dimension (the cushion he sits on), like a second time enclosed in the first, the other figures, located in other temporal dimensions, seem to look at this original scene with the *nachträglich* gaze of a second time which addresses the first and, while giving it a meaning that is inevitably transformed and charged by the weight of the events that have occurred, finds its own meaning in it.

But, Laplanche (2007) wonders, and we do with him, is this resurfacing of memory, this "construction" of the recollection, enough to reverse the arrow of time? The concept of *Nachträglichkeit* in fact expresses something more. It does not only contain within it a double direction of time, from the present to the past and from the past to the present, but performs a transformation on the trauma itself. Indeed, the first scene experienced by the subject (the scene of seduction, for example) is now invested from within, and it is this inner investment through which "a memory *only later* becomes a trauma". As an example of this, Freud takes the dream of the *Wolf Man* (1914b) which functions simultaneously as "traumatic seduction" and as "transformation of the first trauma" (André, 2009).[7] I would not dwell on such a complex case if it were not for its close association to the dual problem that we are addressing, of temporality and sexuality, and the way Freud addresses it. In fact, I will confine myself to seeing it exclusively from this viewpoint, leaving aside all the other, multiple implications for psychoanalytic theory and practice.

Over the course of his treatment, the patient, whom Freud describes as "entirely incapacitated and completely dependent upon other people" (1914b, p. 7), recovers a dream that he would have had around the age of 4 and which had been very distressing at the time. This is the famous childhood dream of the wolves in which the patient, while he is in bed, sees the window opening in front of him. Outside the window there is a large walnut tree on which some white wolves are sitting. There could be six or seven, and they have features which suggest both foxes (their long tails) and dogs (their pricked-up ears). In the grip of terror that the wolves will devour him, the patient wakes up. The analyst's work concentrates on the interpretation of the dream and, starting with the associative work done around it, comes to identify a traumatic event from some years earlier when the patient was very young, consisting in his having witnessed a sexual act between his parents, an episode which would not have had any pathogenic effect at the time when it took place. Only at a later time, when the boy's development had reached a certain point and attained genital organisation, did the scene he had observed come to be "latched onto again" and understood by means of an effect *a posteriori*.[8] The period of the dream corresponds with the one in which the oedipal dynamic is at its peak and, among the principal desires which constitute the engine of the dream, Freud identifies those for a satisfaction of a sexual nature set in motion by the oedipal processes and the identifications. "The strength of this wish made it possible to revive a long-forgotten trace in his memory of a scene" (ibid., pp. 35–36). The trace left by having witnessed the primal scene is reactivated at a later time.

The interpretation of the dream, so strongly tilted towards re-construction and moved by the search for a cause at the origin of the infantile neurosis, also gives us a measure of the distance between us and Freud in terms of the theory of technique. What seems inter-esting to me, however, is another claim that Freud makes in this text, which is how the very recovering of this scene should not be un-derstood as a recollection re-emerging from the abysses of memory, but rather as *eine nachträgliche zum Verständnis vordringende Bearbeitung* (ibid., p. 64 in the *Gesammelte Werke*), which we can translate as "a revision *a posteriori* which pushes ahead towards understanding". Also in the final note to section 8, speaking about the objections which might be raised to the validity of his reconstructions, Freud gives an explicit definition of the mechanism of *Nachträglichkeit*, recognising "the part played by phantasies in symptom-formation" and "the 'retrospective phantasying' of late impressions into childhood and their sexualization after the event" (Freud, 1914b, p. 103, note 1).

These brief notes suggest that we have moved some way from the idea of a causality to be retraced in primary elements, whether in the form of a single traumatic recollection or in the form of a pathogenic representation. Instead, through the idea of a non-linear temporality, attention is recalled to a complex psychic movement which continually winds and unwinds like a spool of thread rather than in a single direction.[9] Psychoanalytic treatment progresses in spirals rather than cumulatively and, in the light of new acquisitions, what has gone before is constantly reviewed and acquires new meanings. The *nachträglich* reworking is consubstantial with the progress of the analytic journey in accordance with which the events of the past take on life and existence as a result of the transferential vicissitudes and the experience of the analyst-patient couple, and is also consubstantial with the psychic economy which separates the time of the meaning from the time of the experience.

After 1920, with the structural theory, the idea of *Nachträglichkeit* seems to be relegated by Freud to the background, as if it were encountering that period of latency which characterises its own process, in favour of the concept of the compulsion to repeat which gains the upper hand. A repetition which tends towards transformation is replaced (or dominated) by a repetition which identically repeats the repetition itself: the stalling of the treatment.[10] That the concept of *Nachträglichkeit* in Freud and after Freud has fallen into a sort of oblivion or latency, to come to light again only many years later thanks to Lacan, is indeed an interesting aspect of the question, precisely because *Nachträglichkeit* seems to have suffered the very fate it expresses. And the reasons in play in that *a posteriori* have included the contrast and divergence attested by the different interpretations of the concept in the various psychoanalytic communities (Marion, 2010, 2012).

4.3 The trauma of sexuality

The fate of *Nachträglichkeit* is closely linked to the vicissitudes encountered by the question of "trauma" in psychoanalytic theory and hence to all the evolutions and involutions undergone by the interweaving of trauma and sexual theory. Beginning with Freud, the original formulation has undergone significant paradigmatic shifts, and these vicissitudes represent one of the thematic cruxes around which post-Freudian psychoanalytic debated has revolved. The terms of this debate, partly because of the way they have influenced the consideration and use of the category of *après-coup*, have their roots in the terrain ploughed by Freud, but which Freud then sowed with different crops.

Except in francophone psychoanalysis, there is no doubt that the translation brought into being by the Standard Edition has influenced and even altered the original Freudian conception of time.[11] Rosine Perelberg (2006) recently proposed a fertile clarification of the way that *Nachträglichkeit* should be understood which seems to bring order to the concept's controversial interpretations. Perelberg describes two ways of understanding it, the one "dynamic", the other "descriptive".[12] While the "dynamic" conception recognises the centrality of the infantile state of neoteny, the compulsion to repeat, trauma, and infantile sexuality, in the second definition the concept acquires value and importance at the expense of the trauma-sexuality coupling, that very intertwining from which the concept had its origin, and it attains a broader but also less defined meaning. The "descriptive" conception can be considered closer to the adjective *nachträglich* rather than to the noun and should be understood as a "retranscription of memory" by virtue of the circular dimension of time and based on a subsequent experience (Modell, 1990). By contrast, in the "dynamic" interpretation, *après-coup* seems to regain its original and specific meaning, giving centrality to the possibility of establishing a link between trauma, castration and the Oedipus complex, as we will see shortly. It is therefore not simply a matter of retrospectively assigning significance but rather of considering the discontinuity between infantile and adult sexuality via the re-structuring which takes places when the Oedipus complex is reached, along with the incest taboo and the setting-up of the difference between genders and generations.

Bollas's "epiphany at around 3" refers to the attainment of the genital phase, to the transition which the child faces in his or her development at around the age of 3 and is known as the Oedipus complex.[13] As *Little Hans* has shown us, this is a developmental phase in which the bodily sensations deriving from the genital area become acute and are invested by the child with new interest. Curiosity is accompanied by the impulse to explore one's own body. It is certainly not only a need for knowledge that maintains these urges. Rather, the discovery of pleasant sensations deriving from the genital organ at that moment of development and the capacity to procure it actively maintain the curiosity and the desire to know. This overall picture includes infantile masturbation which in *après-coup*, *nachträglich*, enacts what the child has experienced through maternal care and the fantasies connected to it. Winnicott (1988) writes that "infant sexuality could have remained a term describing the compulsive genital exercises of certain infants who are deprived ... It has more value however as a description of the beginning of the whole development of instinct life" (p. 58). In the light, first, of Freud's reflections, and then those of his epigones, infantile sexuality is seen, like masturbation, in a new light, no longer as a degenerative symptom, but as part of the individual's normal sexual development, an activity which the infant performs on him or herself is resumed by the adolescent in the second phase of growth in order to explore a body that has finally become sexually mature.

The new picture that is established produces a change in the mental representations and in the perceptions that the infant has of her or himself, and of their relationships with their mother and father, and of the parents' relationship with each other. The psyche is engaged in a new work of elaboration imposed by the sensations which this new phase of development sets in motion. The infant faces the divergence between pregenital and genital, between a before in which there is a mother dispensing care and nurture, and an after in which clearer prominence is gained by the awareness of his/her sexuality and parental sexuality. The "transformation of the mother-as-comforter into the mother-as-sex-object" (Bollas, 2000, p. 14) is caused by this change in the infant's state, and it is growth which makes awareness of it possible and produces the transformation of the image that the infant has of the mother and of her/his relationship with her, as well as of the image s/he has of the relationship between the parents. The mother comes and goes, as Lacan says, indicating a mother who is not always there, present, available to the child: not only a mother but also a woman. The transition from a relationship of maternal dependency made of exclusive care and attention to the gradual discovery that the mother is something more, beyond the child him/herself, is a sexual object, an object of desire for someone else, irrupts forcefully and leaves its mark on the previous equilibrium. This new consciousness "destroys the innocence of a self and mother" (ibid.). The utopia of innocence precedes the Fall, which instead signals the sun setting definitively on the image of a mother with no desires for anyone other than the infant, the pregenital mother. The previous experiences of castration (weaning, sphincter training, etc.) are joined by this castration which has sexuality at its epicentre. The attaining of this new awareness marks the resolution of the oedipal dilemma in favour of a complexity that makes it possible to think about links, differences, the passing of time, and one's own position in time.

The difficulty of abandoning a position of exclusive centrality and accepting that one is the product of a desire that preceded us is well represented in the problems faced by Vera, a girl who had recently turned 7. Her parents seek help because their daughter has had a lot of trouble sleeping for a couple of years, difficulties which are becoming ever more intrusive and imposing strain and tension on the members of her family. During the analysis it clearly emerges that Vera's problem is situated in her inability to manage the conflict between the ambivalent feelings she feels towards the figure of her father and her attachment to the mother she would like to keep wholly for herself. She would like to be a good, generous, cheerful girl like the stereotyped little images of perfection that she draws. Instead, Vera is engaged in a hard struggle with contrasting, conflicted feelings which do not leave her in peace, and which particularly explode at the moment when she goes to sleep and when her parents should also be going to sleep. The father is in charge of desire for the mother. He represents the third who takes the mother away from Vera, produces other pregnancies not wanted by the girl, destroys the peace of the dyadic relationship and the innocent world of before. He is the object of conflicting and ambivalent feelings on the part of the girl who simultaneously loves him and suffers the contradictions that live inside her. And so Vera tries to recover the lost dimension of the mother–infant relationship in the transference, playing at cooking and making her therapist cook lovely things for them to savour and enjoy in a banquet *à deux*, to which no one else is admitted.

The infant's physical and psychic immaturity puts the awareness of sexuality on hold. It will be resumed on the arrival of pubertal development when the subject is struck by a new and even more profound bodily transformation. It is the moment of the first real manifestation of the instinctual sexuality written into mankind's biological and hormonal structure. Orgasmic excitation, which offers a new form of pleasure and discharge, confronts the subject with a sort of "subjective revolution", to use Rousillon's (2010) happy expression. The second time of sexuality, which defines adolescence, is also the second time of trauma, a trauma that has to

73

do with encountering a body that is a stranger to itself and with the work that the psyche must carry out in order to cope with these transformations. What happens during adolescence cannot be reduced to a simple retroactive attribution of sense and meaning to something that did not have it until that moment, or only had it partially. Through the radical changes it imposes, adolescence represents a traumatic moment in itself, both on the psychic front and in terms of bodily development. The subject encounters a body that is a stranger to itself, a body inhabited by the sexual instinct which reattaches itself to infantile sexuality, but there is a distance and a difference between the two. Infantile drive sexuality, as Laplanche defines it, and instinctual sexuality come together at the point of adolescence, and the second reawakens the first. The "pubertal" (Gutton, 2000) describes the psychic work that accompanies the transformations of puberty and designates the subject's break with her/his own infancy (as Ludovico has shown us). The infantile sexuality is now invested from within and this very investment, in the second time that is puberty, performs a transformation on the past sexuality, making "a memory become a trauma only later on" (Freud, 1985: a translation of the wording in the Italian edition, *OSF*, ii, Boringhieri, Turin 1967, p. 256. Vol. II of the S.E., p. 356).

The oedipal reworking comes onto the scene, and the forms in which it presents itself tell us about the solutions which the individual has found for her/his previous dilemmas and about his/her ability to negotiate with the incestuous fantasies reactivated by puberty, to accept and define her/his position in space and time. By means of a *nachträglich* movement, infantile sexuality is brought back into play, reinterpreted in the light of the present and invested with new awareness and a new temporal perspective. What had been deferred, delayed into the future, becomes the present in a brief span of time, a present whose fabric is also interwoven with the vicissitudes of our infantile sexuality. Indeed, adolescence introduces a "new temporality" (Baranes, 1991) which includes a new feeling of the future. That future gathers together the legacy of everyone's past, which is revisited in the light of the powerful transformations in progress.

In the transition to puberty and adolescence we see the mechanism of *Nachträglichkeit* at work. The interpretation of the phenomenon solely in terms of retrospective resignification turns out to be not only reductive but misleading, and does not take account of the fact that the "blow", "that which unhinges" (rendered literally by the French translation *après-coup*), which has now acquired a use all over the world, is by its nature traumatic and psychic (André, 2009). The traumatic aspect is due to the fact that an event lived *then* (for example, an "enigmatic message") has had no way to be fully *integrated* into a meaningful context (Laplanche, 2007; Marion, 2009). Thus, the attribution of meaning to the event consists in complex work of association, working through and integrating the experience which had been left mute, "asleep", when it occurred, a work set in motion by a later incident or by organic maturation.[14] As we have also been able to see, thanks to the dream of the *Wolf Man*, the model of sexuality, understood as infantile sexuality in its traumatic power and as a residue that has not been worked through, remains the pillar on which *Nachträglichkeit* stands. But this is not the case if we consider it from the developmental viewpoint, in which case sexuality makes itself manifest according to a model of development in phases and in one direction.[15] The traumatic wounding consists in the gap between what happens and what can be understood and integrated, in what takes the form of background noise, and can only *a posteriori*, after passing through its latency period, attain a condition in which it can be transformed into sound.

How do we identify the work of *Nachträglichkeit* in its "dynamic" sense, as Perelberg (2006) defines it, in the analytic session and in work with patients? A young man brings his analyst a dream in which he is a child aged around 6 or 7. He finds himself with others of the same age in a cellar where there is a gas heater. In the dream, he and his little friends throw a can of petrol onto the heater, giving themselves a bad fright because, as soon as they have done it, they realise that the heater could explode. This does not in fact happen. Through the dream and the associative work that follows, we see how the patient is able to represent something which, until that moment, had remained in the background and not been articulated.[16] Indeed, by means of a highly vivid dream–image, something comes onto the scene which has to do with his infantile fantasies about the maternal object, relived in the analytic situation. The mother/analyst loses her connotations as an idealised figure, which she had been up to that moment, and takes on the likeness of a heater ready to explode if he arouses it with his petrol. The dream well describes the patient's revisiting of his infantile sexuality in the light of events within the analytic couple, and especially describes the fantasies which (together with his infantile aspects/the children with him in the dream) he was cultivating in relation to the incestuous object and the feelings of guilt linked to transgressiveness.

In a later phase of his analytic journey, the patient brings three dreams in a row. In the first he is setting out on a voyage and knows that he must investigate something involving petrol and coal. There is a woman beside him, with petrol dripping from her clothes. He is worried, she might catch fire. In the second dream he is shut away in a fortress and fearing an attack by a group of black men. In the third dream he is with his son and his father. They have to take shelter in a hotel, but his father says he can stay outside, perhaps there isn't enough room. The patient insists that his father should go in; there really is room for him. In this sequence of dreams we see the transformations being effected on the themes introduced by the dream of the heater and the working-through of the oedipal question.

The dream-images testify to the evolution that the theme of infantile sexuality has undergone over time and the multitude of temporal lines which have intersected with each other. The heater on the brink of exploding has been transformed into a woman, the analyst, walking beside him, and her excitation (the can of petrol in the first dream) into a problem he must investigate. The awareness of a journey that he needs to make – while acknowledging the dangers it nevertheless entails: for example, setting the woman on fire – has replaced the first dream's feeling of anxiety and fright. They are dangers that are also represented in the second dream with the black men's attack on the fortress, an expression of the oedipal question that is being raised again in his fear/desire to besiege the "maternal fortress" with a destructive assault. The acknowledgement of the third, the father, occurs in the third dream. The patient seems to come to terms with the paternal sexuality which interposes itself into the mother's relationship with the child. The paternal figure may be welcomed into his psychic space, and with it the chain of generations which links the father, himself, and his son and represents the renunciation of incest, "a victory of the generation over the individual" (Freud, 1925, p. 216). The "dynamic" interpretation of *Nachträglichkeit* recognises the centrality of the oedipal scenario and the interweaving of infantile sexuality with trauma, as the patient's dreams show us. The oedipal scenario describes the confrontation/clash with thirdness, and what Freud called "castration anxiety" should be thought of not as an act of retaliation and a threat but in terms of anxieties about the acceptance of separation and boundaries which sink their roots into the playing out of the sexual triangle of which the infant is one vertex.

4.4 Conclusions

In this *excursus* I have tried to revisit certain phases which have characterised psychoanalytic reflection on the topic of sexuality. Psychoanalysis opened the way for sexual discourse, recognising both the centrality for the human being of the mind–body link (psychosexuality) and the discontinuity between infantile and adult sexuality through the complex challenge of the oedipal transition and that of puberty, which rewrites sexuality, recognising above all how it represents a decisive ingredient in mental development, in the impulse to create links and knowledge. The main currents of present-day psychoanalysis have shifted the focus of their interest and attention towards the domain of relationships and needs. There are theoretical reasons underpinning this revision, such as calling the drive theory into question, and the advent of other models of psychic functioning, and also clinical reasons, such as attention to narcissistic and borderline pathologies for which, at least according to some psychoanalysts, the problems are situated at primitive levels and are recognisable in the sphere of needs and the mother–infant relationship. On the other hand, the return of the repressed seems to be imposing itself and asking to be taken into consideration, both in order to recover the meaning of the subjective experiences related to the sexual (Fonagy, 2006,) and to rework Freud's legacy and build a suitable comprehension of sexuality for our time.

The scandal of Freudian sexuality has been tamed (Green, 1995), resolving itself into what Corbett (2009) provocatively describes as a transition in which "the burlap of desire too quickly becomes the pashmina of mutual recognition" (p. 216). And yet there needs to be an integration between a drive model which asserts the role of the body in its rapport with the psyche and a relational model within which the mind–body link undergoes various permutations (Lemma and Lynch, 2015). Thus, we can imagine the sphere of sexuality as a two-headed Janus which preserves a close link with the economic dimension of trauma[17] by virtue of its link with the body and with the psychic work this requires, and simultaneously locates and crystalises this dimension within a relationship, straddling the subtle boundary between "what is called reality and fantasy" (Winnicott, 1988, p. 59). The various "formations" through which infantile sexuality is expressed (in the primary process and in defensive distortions, in the experience of pleasure and unpleasure, in the creation of conscious and unconscious fantasies, in the play of identifications) are not set up definitively once and for all, but are continually reprised and in some ways rewritten in the light of subsequent experiences, but also transformed. At the culmination of the Oedipus complex the child lives and recalls but also, via the new and unprecedented phenomena introduced by the genital phase, reorganises the previous modalities in which his/her desire and the pleasures received have been expressed. "The finding of an object" during puberty "is in fact a refinding of it" (Freud, 1905, p. 222), but a refinding that alters the original by means of autoerotic displacement and its reworking in fantasy. Puberty and genital maturity present the subject with an organisational crisis and impose a profound restructuring which affects the subject in both the vertical dimension relating to the inner world and psychic structures, and in the horizontal dimension which plays out on the relational plane. Adolescents find themselves dealing with everything that has its roots in their past development and primary relationships, a set of experiences which may or may not have gone well, but must above all confront something new and unprecedented which once again calls into question the coincidence between the anatomical body and the body as a reference point for one's identity. In adolescence, infantile sexuality must be "disassembled" and "reassembled", making room for new modes of psychic work and new solutions.

The oedipal configuration may be thought of as a *deposit of time*, prompted and set in motion by the changes that each of us must face at any time over the course of our lives. Ogden (2009) speaks of "reworking and reorganization" which goes on throughout an individual's life. The narcissistic and object-related conflicts which accompany the processes of existence require a continual work of newly questioning and transforming links and of forming new connections in order to "contain, organize, and give meaning to the incessant internal and external changes which happen to us and make us other, insofar as we remain ourselves" (Cahn, 1998, p. 54).

At the end of this journey in which I have tried to show the psychoanalytic view on the topic of sexuality, especially the contribution that psychoanalysis has made to changing the meaning and interpretation of sexuality by revealing its complexity, it is now time to direct our attention to the present: a time – the present – shot through with such radical changes that it seems hard to think about it with the tools we have available to us. The new technologies in the area of reproduction – this will be the subject of the book's second part – have brought about transformations that were unthinkable only a few decades ago. The sexuality-procreation binomial which has accompanied the history of humankind for millennia, has undergone a profound split. In what way is sexuality, core of personal identity and profound impulse towards the construction of links, "the truth about ourselves" as Foucault calls it, affected by these new changes? What effects does the separation of sexuality from procreation bring about on the level of identity and relations? How do these new scenarios question psychoanalysis? How does its theoretical and clinical heritage built up over more than a hundred years address the new dimensions of subjectivity?

As we have seen, there are two respects in which trauma is at the origin of psychoanalysis. Psychoanalysis was born with hysterics and with thinking about the trauma of sexuality resulting from the immaturity of the psychic apparatus and its inability to address and manage the desire and message coming from the adult, which is the starting point of that internal fracture which causes repression. In relation to the historical and social context of the period, it has been the fate of psychoanalysis to be constituted as traumatic, both for the medical and scientific community and in relation to public sentiment and morality. Something is happening today which can likewise be read in terms of trauma. The caesura presented by the biotechnologies, the separation of sexuality from procreation, is the new scandal and throws a system of values, codes, and shared identities into crisis, interrupting the linearity of the generational chain as we knew it until a few decades ago. The questions all this poses for psychoanalysis, but also the contribution it will make to a complex reading of the events in progress, is what we will try to address in the pages that follow.

Notes

1 It should be noted that the German term *Lust* (pleasure) expresses both the meanings Freud is thinking of when he speaks about pleasure: as much the pleasure linked to the appeasement which derives

from the satisfied need as the pleasure linked to the increase of tension and excitation provoked by the desire.

2 Lacan gives this need-desire binomial a different interpretation from that of the Freudian tradition. Whereas for Freud the motivation for the desire is based on the pleasure/unpleasure principle, for Lacan it is connected to an essential lack experienced at the moment of the infant's original separation from the mother's body at the time of birth. The infant's desire is that of being the mother's phallus, hence its desire is the desire for the other which can never actually be fulfilled. Here, we will not be following Lacan's thinking, neither on this specific point nor on other matters. Its complex theoretical elaboration and its "eccentricity" in relation to so-called "classical" psychoanalysis would require their own specific commentary.

3 According to this hypothesis, which Freud will reiterate in *Formulations on the Two Principles of Mental Functioning* (1911), the pleasure principle is connected to primary processes which aim to obtain pleasure and obtain it in a hallucinatory form. Freud here refers to dream-work, still being convinced in this period that the oneiric function is directed towards the allaying of desire "in a hallucinatory manner" (p. 219). It will be the subsequent disillusion that prompts the psychic apparatus "to form a conception of the real circumstances in the external world and to endeavour to make a real alteration in them" (ibid.). With this, the setting-up of the *reality principle* is achieved.

4 The term subjectivation is used to mean the personal journey of evolution and maturation which accompanies the individual from the cradle to the grave. It is a term introduced by French authors (Cahn, 1998), and besides its geographical connotations, it is a helpful term in that it insists on the process by which the individual takes on her own subjectivity and which involves external and internal factors and their systemisation in mental functioning. According to Cahn, the process of subjectivation tries to hold together the contrasting and simultaneously interdependent aspects that link the various registers of development in their diachronic and synchronic dimension. Unlike the term "development", it excludes the idea of a linear and progressive temporality.

5 Ferenczi presented this paper at the Twelfth International Congress of Psychoanalysis held at Wiesbaden in 1932 and it represents a contribution to the deeper investigation of the dynamics and effects of trauma on the infant mind, the distorted solutions to which it can give rise, and how this is reflected in the analytic situation. For a detailed examination of Ferenczi's contribution to the psychoanalysis of children and the question of trauma, cf. Borgogno (1999). Ruth Stein (1998a,b) notes the difference between Laplanche's conception of

seduction and Ferenczi's. Indeed, whereas for Ferenczi parental sexuality is directed at the child in substantially traumatic and confusing terms, Laplanche identifies in the "enigmatic message" of adult sexuality a stimulus and encouragement to deviate from the line of the needs for self-preservation.

6 It is interesting to note how in Freud, the recognition of the relationship with the mother emerges unequivocally here and there, and with conviction, not only in the *Three Essays* (1905) when he speaks of the mother as the greatest seductress, but also in *Formulations on the Two Principles of Mental Functioning* (1911), note 4, for example, where he responds to the objections of those who might say that an organisation founded solely on the pleasure principle and forgetful of the reality principle cannot keep itself alive: "The employment of a fiction like this is, however, justified when one considers that the infant – *provided one includes with it the care it receives from its mother* – does almost realise a psychical system of this kind" (p. 219, my italics). This aside seems fundamental to me, and illuminating about how we can understand the way Freud's idea of a primary relationship and the presence of the object may nevertheless be present in the background.

7 This is the account of the analysis of a young Russian, aged 23, who had come to Freud because of problems that were obsessional in nature. The therapy concentrated on the patient's infantile neurosis via the recounting of various scenes of seduction which the patient would have undergone during childhood, leading to the recovery of the famous dream of the wolves. In particular, the patient's infantile neurosis would have developed during a first change undergone at the age of 3½, coinciding with the arrival of an English governess. His character changed, showing signs of irritability, violence, and sadistic behaviours. A second change was produced at around the age of 5 with the emergence of anxieties and phobias. The phobic symptoms were later replaced by obsessional features which broke out into a thoroughgoing neurosis with religious content. This symptomatological picture seemed to have been spontaneously resolved towards the age of 8.

8 The work of interpreting the dream unfolds over many pages and it would lead us off our subject to follow it in detail. In his interpretative work, Freud utilises and brings to fruition the rules that govern unconscious functioning and the primary processes, to which the dream belongs and which he had described in chapters VI and VII of *The Interpretation of Dreams* (Freud, 1899a). The work of condensation, displacement, transformation, and distortion into its opposite, etc., provides the key for Freud to penetrate the mystery of the dream.

81

9 This particular mode of functioning does not only apply to the psychic economy, but also describes the functioning of the analytic situation. Many observations about *nachträglich* functioning are put forward, supported by clinical illustrations, as in *A Child is Being Beaten* (1919) and *The Psychogenesis of a Case of Homosexuality in a Woman* (1920). Freud seems to be aware of having identified a mechanism which not only oversees the psychic's way of proceeding but also regulates the functioning of analysis.

10 The notion of the compulsion to repeat is at the heart of the 1920 essay, which marks the turn to the structural theory, although the concept of repetition had been addressed since 1914 (*Remembering, Repeating, and Working-Through*). With the concept of the compulsion to repeat, Freud expresses the failure of the process of working-through which occurs in certain clinical situations and risks compromising the treatment. One of the central points of the text concerns the relationship between the pleasure principle and the compulsion to repeat, which seems to signal the existence of a "secondary benefit". Freud claims that "it is incorrect to talk of the dominance of the pleasure principle over the course of mental processes" (1920b, p. 9). The need for repetition, as it is also expressed in play (the famous example of the cotton-reel game appears in this text), indicates that besides the repetition of needs, there also exists a need for repetition. There is not only the denial of time, which functions as a defence against change, bereavement, and death, avoiding the recognition of the oedipal transition and its role in the sequence of generations and their history (Bollas, 1992; Rose, 2007), but it is also the case that "the impulse to work over in the mind some overpowering experience so as to make oneself master of it can find expression as a primary event" (Freud, 1920b, p. 16).

11 Critically discussing the expression "deferred action" adopted in the Standard Edition of Freud's works, Thomä and Cheshire (1991) maintain that the doubts concern the dynamic by which the concept operates rather than the choice of translation. The authors challenge the possibility that a second time acts on a first time with the effect of retroactive causation producing a determining impact on the traumatic characteristics of the first time; instead they aim to distinguish between the process of causation and the attribution of meaning. A significant example of this type of "contentiousness" in post-Freudian psychoanalysis, which brings the question of *Nachträglichkeit* and its destinies back into play, can be found in the debate which has occurred from to time around hysteria and its diagnoses. Without going into the merits of such a highly elaborated confrontation, the discussion may be succinctly summed up as hinging on the question of

whether hysteria should be considered a clinical entity with, at its centre, the dimension of sexuality, the traumatic dynamics relating to oedipal conflict and the processes of identification reprised at a second time, or whether it should be interpreted as a defence, psychotic in nature, against archaic anxieties (cf. for example, the panel discussion on hysteria chaired by Laplanche at the 1973 IPA Congress in Paris, in Scalzone and Zontini, 1999).

12 It should be observed that consideration of *Nachträglichkeit* in the psychoanalytic context is based on the analyst-patient relationship based on the transference-countertransference dynamic.

13 We are referring to the classical dating by Freud and maintained by various post-Freudian authors, as opposed to the change made by Klein in her revision of the theory which puts the oedipal phase back to the first year of life.

14 Winnicott's short paper, *Fear of Breakdown* (1963), stands as a brilliant intuition and description of this temporal movement within treatment. Although the word *Nachträglichkeit* is not explicitly mentioned, this text vividly portrays the working of *après-coup* in analysis. The primitive breakdown which happened but was never experienced re-emerges and gives rises to situations of impasse and being traumatically held in check. Haydée Faimberg (2005, 2006, 2007) was the first to call attention to the value of Winnicott's intuition and to highlight it. In a recent paper she writes, "In other words, as I understand the *fear of breakdown*, the broader concept of *Nachträglichkeit* is needed *in order to understand Winnicott's construction and his implicit conception of psychic temporality*" (2007, p. 1229, italics in original). Using a "broader" concept of *après-coup*, Faimberg proposes a *nachträglich* operation on Freud's own text. Freud's discovery of infantile sexuality creates a new connection between the two temporal phases included in *Nachträglichkeit*. Faimberg calls the first scene "a moment of *anticipation* (an *already there*)." It is followed by second moment or "phase of *assignment of retroactive meaning*" (ibid., p. 1226). Throughout her clinical work, which is centred on listening and interpretation, Faimberg reveals the moment when the meaning of something that was "already there" is discovered for the first time. The movement she describes cannot by any means be reduced to a "retranscription", but is connected instead to what Freud in 1937 called work on "constructions".

15 For Laplanche (2007) it is necessary to distinguish between drive and instinct. Whereas he considers instinct to be genetically programmed and adaptive, the drive is not genetic and owes its appearance to the adult–infant relationship. Infantile sexuality is a drive-sexuality by nature, linked to unconscious fantasies. Whereas the object of instinctual sexuality is always an object located in external reality, the

object of infantile sexuality is an object of fantasy; that is, an object linked to excitation and tension, which will never be fully attained in the real scenario. According to Laplanche, "it is between birth and puberty that *la sexualité humaine pulsionelle* and the infantile sexuality discovered by Freud is situated" (2007, p. 43).

16 In my account of this dream and the later ones, I have omitted the various interpretations they could be given in terms of the transference and the field, and of "syncretic and pictographically narrable expression of the emotional facts occurring in the consulting room, in the mutual fantasy formations activated in the bipersonal field" (Ferro, 1996, p. 59).

17 By "economic" dimension in psychoanalysis we mean an event characterised by a greater intensity than the subject is in a position to deal with, one which is therefore configured as more invasive than the subject can bear: "In economic terms, the trauma is characterised by an influx of excitations that is excessive by the standard of the subject's tolerance and capacity to master such excitations and work them out psychically" (Laplanche and Pontalis, 1967, p. 465).

PART II

BEING BORN IN THE AGE OF BIOTECHNOLOGY

THE NEW FORMS OF PROCREATION

When we cannot understand something,
we always fall back on abuse.
An excellent way of making a task lighter.
(Sigmund Freud, *Little Hans*, 1908)

5.1 The narcissistic wound

The Bible tells that Rachel, the much-loved, favourite wife of Jacob, being unable to have children, decided to make use of her servant Bilhah, who gave birth to Dan and Naphtali. This is how Thomas Mann describes the episode in *The Stories of Jacob*:

Poor Rachel! Was she happy? By means of a recognized resource in such cases, she had to a certain extent weakened the force of the divine decree. But her yearning heart was confused by the fact that her merit was waxing in a stranger's body. It was a half-merit, a half-joy, a half-self-deception, sanctioned by tradition since needs must, but without flesh and blood confirmation in Rachel herself, the very children would be only half-real, the sons whom Bilhah would raise up to her and to the husband whom she so fruitlessly loved.
(Mann, 1927–42, p. 213)

And the same applied to Abraham's wife, Sarah who, faced with such a prolonged infertility, decided to make use of her slave Hagar. However, we know from history that things were not always so simple, and the choice, unwillingly made in the hope of overcoming a stalemate as painful as it was humiliating, entailed high costs on the emotional level. Thus, while on the one hand the relief seemed great at the time, on the other hand it was not easy to deal with the subsequent feels of rivalry, envy, jealousy and the complicated affective dynamics which this situation created and would continue to create. I have recalled these stories from so far back in time not only because they seem to be a sort of ancient precursor to one of the many modes – that of surrogate motherhood – which are associated with the new maternities, evidence of illustrious precedents, at least as regards the dichotomy between the social and the biological mother. I have also recalled them because, in their literary guise, they catch that affective register which recurs in our present reflections on the new ways of being born. Indeed, my focus is on exploring the meaning and impact which the transformations in the sphere of procreation that we are facing today may have in terms of our relationship with ourselves and with the other.

The theme of motherhood has always, and for every one of us, been the place of our origin, "where we start from" as Winnicott (1986) puts it. Psychoanalysis can be credited with having shifted the discourse about the maternal from the biological to the psychic, illuminating the unconscious nature of this desire and its enigmatic features, as well as the contradictions connected to it: indeed, in the gap between unconscious and conscious desire are located those slippages of thought and affects which stop us continuing to think about the experience of motherhood and the project of motherhood as a linear event to be taken for granted, fixed in the biological. Chiara Saraceno (1997) talks about a "post-Freudian" mother to indicate how psychoanalytic reflection has modified the frame of reference, introducing elements of complexity that can no longer be easily dismissed without gross oversimplification. The shift from the biological to the psychic has opened the way to the world of fantasy and affect which accompanies the experience of motherhood: a crucial experience in the identificatory journey of the subject and profoundly linked to the fantasies about oneself, one's own body, one's parental ties, one's origin. The experience of motherhood is configured in its essence as a "crossroads of relationships", real and fantasied, which move in two directions along the space–time coordinates: from outside to inside, from before to after, and vice versa. Indeed, motherhood is in relation to the external (social, political, judicial) and at the same time is deeply rooted in the woman's subjectivity; in the context of her body, her desire, her affective dynamics and choices, her oedipal experience and her identifications with her own mother. And it is in relation to an "original" that is only individual in an illusory sense, which is rooted in previous relationships before projecting itself towards the future through the chain of intergenerational transmission.

It is not my intention to pursue the history of motherhood, whether in terms of continuities or ruptures (D'Amelia 1997), nor would I be qualified to do so. Nevertheless, we can acknowledge that, over a couple of generations, motherhood has recorded two fundamental caesuras (first, the pill, then assisted fertilisation), which have split what has been a unity for millennia: procreation and sexuality. While contraceptives have freed sexuality from the blackmail of generativity, they have not altered the sexuality-generation bond, whereas the disjunction between sexuality and procreation introduced by the new modes of generation represents a rupture and a radical leap when compared with previous contraceptive solutions, introduces a change of scenario, and calls into question the meaning and place of the two terms in the spheres of the individual and of the couple. The very fact of conception via techniques of Medically Assisted Procreation (PMA),[1] far from referring to a one-off event, evokes a set of experiences that are not easily reducible to unity. The transmission of meanings and shared codes which has, up to a certain point, guaranteed the sense of continuity, seems to suffered a breach in the linearity that has accompanied it until now, and we seem to have passed through the Pillars of Hercules where the desire for a child had stopped, as at an inviolable boundary, until only a short while ago (Marion, 2003). The non-coincidence between biological and social motherhood, and the widening out of new possibilities thanks to the techniques of assisted fertilisation are having an impact on the symbolic dimension of generation; so much so that we have to wonder if what Green claimed in 1995 still holds true: "If any one of us breathes the air and is alive, it is as a consequence, happily or unhappily, of a primal scene, in other words, to be fully explicit, of a sexual relationship, happy or unhappy, between two sexually different parents, whether we like it or not" (p. 880). This very image of the primal scene seems to have been drastically questioned by the new ways of coming into being.

Returning to the theme of infertility, where everything starts from, we recognise that we are dealing with an experience with a profound impact on both the body and the psyche, which affects both halves of the couple and challenges the integrity of their relationship. This is where we begin our journey to try and follow the stages of a process that aims to counter such a negative impasse, but has at the same time disrupted the traditional procreative methodology that is as old as humankind, passing from the original therapeutic objective to modalities which redesign and redefine the expression of human nature in its foundational links. The sexual relationship, which signifies the physical, affective and ethical encounter between two people, is now interfered with or replaced by ever more sophisticated but also alienating technological procedures.

The diagnosis of infertility is the first traumatic passage that the couple must go through, the first failure in a plan, in a deeply rooted desire for realisation that is not fulfilled: "It is important to remember that infertility is both a disease and a life crisis affecting one's life dreams, sense of meaning, sexual functioning and spontaneity. Infertility may interfere with love, self-esteem, sense of control, and security in one's body and in the world" (Rosen – Rosen 2005, p. xvi). As the biblical stories describe, this provokes strife in oneself and in the couple, with substantial consequences. In fact, the diagnosis of infertility produces a far from negligible effect on one's feeling of self-esteem and one's self-image, which undergoes alterations, though with different permutations in the two sexes. In the woman, what seems to be most in play are reactions of anxiety, feelings of loss and depression, whereas men feel a blow to their sense of potency and masculinity. This has consequences which reflect on the sexuality within the couple, and indeed sexuality is generally the first area to suffer the cost. In men, the experience of fertility and sexual sufficiency are intimately correlated, and the emotional reactions to infertility alter and/or undermine the sense of self as potent and sexually adequate (Keylor and Apfel, 2002). In their article, Keylor and Apfel quote a study by Conrad et al. (2001) which highlights and describes the difficulties of emotional self-regulation in infertile male subjects. According to this study,

the stigma of infertility leads men to defend against shame and exposure through the continuous suppression of negative feelings and to avoid sharing them within a containing relationship. In turn, unrelieved stress from the lack of 'authentic emotional communication' compromises the bioregulation of the immune system and leaves these patients vulnerable to somatic illness.
(Keylor and Apfel, 2002, p. 71)

In women, the experience of infertility is perceived as a failure, letting themselves and their partners down and failing to fulfil the woman's familial and social mandate to ensure the continuance of the generation. The failure is coloured by more or less conscious feelings of guilt which have an impact on not only at a woman's representation of herself but also at her image of her own body. Sexuality is compromised by it in the sense that, instead of being an expression of desire, pleasure, the libidinal link, it is emptied of spontaneity and subjected to the dictates of medical procedures.

The narcissistic wound resulting from impeded generativity is important and the trauma risks being resolved into endless mourning. Set against the constellation of distressing emotions and painful states of the self are defensive psychological processes activated in order to address and counter them. "The belief that one is making use of an omnipotent, or nearly omnipotent, means of overcoming every difficulty in procreation", in the words of a pioneer in the field of ART, the reproductive gynaecologist Isabella Coghi (2005),[2] reverses the feeling of total impotence and defeat which the trauma of infertility produces. And that is not all: for centuries infertility has been viewed as the result of a divine curse, a source of shame to be hidden and covered with secrecy.[3] We can see this set of factors as having two consequences: on the one hand, the secrecy which couples tend to maintain about resorting to assisted fertilisation; on the other, the great insistence of their demands and how hard they find it to stop the procedures in spite of failures, thereby colluding with what happens from the perspective of the physician, who may feel committed to a mission that is not exactly life-saving or curative but concerned with something more powerful, the generation of life.

In interpreting the problem of infertility, the psychoanalytic viewpoint has changed substantially. Studies of psychogenic infertility begun in the 1940s and pursued over the following decades (Benedeck, 1952; Deutsch, 1945; Jacobson, 1946; Langer, 1958; Allison, 1997) tended to explain the impossibility for the woman to procreate in terms of an unconscious rejection of her own femininity and sexuality, and in terms of ambivalent feelings towards her mother and motherhood. Langer (1958), for example, interpreted infertility in Kleinian terms as the consequence of the daughter's envy of her mother's creative power. The envious attack on maternal fecundity and the aggressive fantasies in play are resolved into the failure of identification with a fertile mother.

91

Pines (1990) arrived at the same conclusion, identifying the reasons for female infertility in the conflicted and frustrating relationship with one's own mother. The general orientation, at least with regard to the female perspective, was towards finding explanations for the condition of infertility in psychic causes. This orientation was strongly questioned the more it was realised that the relation between psychological states and physiological functioning cannot be conceived in terms of linear causality and is, on the contrary, much more complex: the psyche influences the soma, but also vice versa. Various studies, conducted over long periods of time (Eisner, 1963; Seward et al., 1965; Denber, 1978), have been unable to demonstrate the existence of specific psychological characteristics that might describe infertile women and differentiate them from the control group and from fertile women. Moreover, the same instances of conflict and ambivalence towards femininity and motherhood that are revealed in infertile women can be identified in women with children. More recent studies (Facchinetti et al., 1992; Greil, 1997) agree in putting forward an integrated model in which the stress from infertility or infertility is taken into consideration as a greater component in activating and determining the endocrinological and immunological responses. The intensity of the stress depends on many factors, from the length of the infertile period, to the personal, relational and family context of each specific couple, to the way individuals and the couple react to stress, and the interaction of these factors also determines the degree of depression that affects the individual.

This approach completely changes the focus we adopt, no longer looking at the causes of the trauma, but instead taking its consequences into account and assessing them. If, as Sharon Zalusky (2003) claims, rather than moving on the plane of causes which, as things stand, cannot be demonstrated and are in fact the outcome of a complex multifactorial interweaving, we take our cue from the consequences, this offers us a more solid basis to start from. The search for a cause or causes undoubtedly makes the frustration more tolerable and can make one think, however illusorily, that once the reason has been identified a remedy can also be found. By contrast, for both the patient and the analyst, turning one's attention to the consequences means maintaining uncertainty and doubt, but also being able to identify the emotional reactions of anxiety, distress, depression and rage provoked by such a situation. Compelling the patient to seek and define the causes in psychological terms (it is envy of the mother, it is the conflict with femininity, etc.) exposes the patient to a task which, instead of helping her, risks making her feel doubly guilty, and may lapse into the need on the part of the analyst to demonstrate the validity of his theories. On the contrary, acceptance of not-knowing implies a sharing of the limit on the part of the analyst and his theories which mirrors the limit that the patient is having to deal with.

Indeed, the trend in current psychosomatic medicine is to consider body and mind as two categories of the same organism and to pay attention to the two systems, psychic and physical, which may express the same problem from different vertices (Solano, 2013, 2016). The organism's response to a given existential or relational condition may be expressed on a mental or a corporeal level. The recognition that pathology is expressed through the body at a non-symbolic level, but in a specific and organised way, means accepting that the somatic disturbance expresses a malaise that is the fruit of a complex fabric of experiences and concerns the individual in his or her relation to the internal and the external.[4] This may also hold for infertility or infertility. Nevertheless, we must also bear in mind their impact on both physical and mental levels, to the point that the effect of infertility is considered in the same way as an important physical illness or the mourning of the loss of a partner (Hynes et al., 1992). As we have seen, the area of sexuality, Freud's psychosexuality, conjoins psyche and soma in a close bond and becomes the privileged site for expression of a malaise on two levels, the corporeal and the psychic. If we adopt this type of unitary perspective, the outlook is one of re-establishing a dialectical circularity between the different levels of functioning by which the organism expresses itself and of recognising the language in which the subject speaks.

In concluding these reflections, we can endorse the claim of Apfel and Keylor (2002) who, while reminding us that every case is unique and cannot be superimposed onto others, maintain that patients involved in this type of situation share the same feelings of bereavement, anxiety, desperation, depression, and envy of others who have children: "The loss of parenthood is multifaceted and involves more than the loss of fertility; there is loss of spontaneous sexuality, of the pregnancy experience itself, of children and genetic continuity. There is stigma and isolation" (p. 93). To this is added the stress of submitting to complex medical procedures which often turn out to be painful and humiliating for the couple. And it is on this last point that I will now be concentrating my observations because, from both the patient's and physician's or analyst's viewpoint, the subjects involved in these processes are confronted with dilemmas and decisions about genera- tion which are still new, compared to the convictions and – I would say – habits that have accompanied the evolution of humanity in the millennia before us. This provokes an "adaptation syndrome" (Coghi, 2005, p. 73) in relation to a new scenario which, although it has been around for almost forty years, is moving more quickly than our ability to comprehend its deep and disturbing meanings and has not yet been fully integrated into a new conception of generation.

5.2 Overcoming nature's limits

"Is it better or worse to be born in the age of biotechnology?" With this question Isabella Coghi (2005) began her contribution on the problems connected to Assisted Reproductive Technology (ART) highlighting that "adaptation syndrome" which, at the time when she was writing, still characterised the universe of assisted fertilisation and, in her view, was still far from being fully worked through. And today? More than ten years have passed since she made these observations and the technology has evolved further and become more sophisticated.[5] The compilers of the Istisan Report (*Investigation into the workings of medically assisted procreation in Italy*, published by the Istituto Superiore di Sanità) confirm that the percentage of pregnancies achieved (in 2009) seemed to be constantly growing compared to the years 2007–2008, and this growth is assessed as "the logical evolution of a phenomenon in which technical innovation and improved procedures play a constant role that is reflected in the results obtained and the safety of patients" (p. 53). These conclusions seem to be confirmed in the 2014 Report (updated to 2016) which shows a steady, though slight, growth with a perceptible increase in FIVET (Fertilisation in vitro and embryo transfer), ICSI (Intracytoplasmic sperm injection), and FER (Frozen embryo replacement). The authors of both these reports reveal a constant increase in the age of the patients being treated, which – as we know – is the element most likely to obstruct an attempted pregnancy: "the patients' age is a decisive feature in determining the results that it is possible to obtain with the application of assisted fertilisation treatments" (p. 53).

This last fact heralds the "technological vertigo" (Ansermet, 2015) which shifts the intervention of biotechnology from in its initial therapeutic objective (problems of infertility) towards demands that "impact" on the familiar anthropological schema and prompt us to imagine an extreme extension of the capacities of medicine and science, and hence the absence of any barrier to our plans. In reality, the difficulties connected to initiating a pregnancy because of increasing age sound like a strong reminder of a limit imposed by our bodies and by nature.

The "National Register of Medically Assisted Procreation" offers a detailed, helpful and exhaustive map of PMA within Italy. Lurking behind the data are the stories of patients in the throes of procedures with acronyms that do not reveal the degree of commitment required by the process. A first point refers to the various steps on the path that participating individuals have to follow. Though they vary according to the technique being used, they consist of: ovarian stimulation which subjects the patient to a hormonal bombardment; an intervention made under light sedation to aspirate ovules; transfer of oocytes into a test tube in contact with spermatozoa (FIVET) – or alternatively, injection of the spermatozoon into the cytoplasm of the oocyte (ICSI) – waiting for fertilisation to occur (36–48 hours) and the subsequent transfer into the uterus. All these processes are accompanied not only by constant ultrasound monitoring, medication, doses of hormones, the collecting of seminal fluid on demand, etc., but also by a profound emotional tension which embraces both partners in the couple. The physical effort, with the woman in the front line, compounds the emotional and psychological effort because the couple is involved in a sequence of waiting, hoping, and possible disappointments that run from a low ovulatory response to failed fertilisation to non–implantation. As many gynaecologists now know, the worst enemy of this procedure is disappointment (Flamigni, 2002), and the protocols for trying to avoid this are ever more detailed and precise, with a consequent increase in the burden on the individuals involved and the creation of a vicious circle.

The choice of ART is a way of reacting and taking a stand against a destiny that is felt to have been unjustly imposed. Scientific and technological progress offers opportunities, unthinkable only a short time ago, to counter and help resolve painful and incapacitating impasses. And yet it must be acknowledged that procedures as complex and sophisticated as these catapult the couple into a medicalised scenario where action predominates and both physician and patients are concentrating all their energies on obtaining a result. There is no space for doubt or self-questioning, and no time for the couple to think through the adventure they are embarking on. If and when it comes, the disappointment represents the moment when the patients emerge from their biotechnological "vertigo" and deal in real time with the trauma of failure which manifests itself as the iteration in a second time of a trauma already experienced in the first time of their infertility but then short-circuited by the hope of a technological solution. The Promethean fantasy which has accompanied their journey, and may at some more or less conscious level have been shared with the medical team, reveals its limits.

Another very delicate problem is the number of embryos to transfer and what to do with the ones left unused. In this case too we find ourselves in a dramatic face-off with reality. The decision to be taken about the embryos lying cryogenically preserved somewhere – or nowhere – stirs up uncontainable anxieties and raises questions for which analysts also find themselves unprepared. As Apfel and Keylor testify (2002), one of them was woken in the night by her patient who had to decide by the next morning how many of the fertilised embryos should be implanted: "Very often the patients and therapists together are confronted with dilemmas and decisions which are entirely original to both and, in fact, have never been posed before the past few years of history" (p. 93). The mind of the physician, analyst, or therapist who shares this journey with the patients does not shy away from what it means to be faced with such complex questions and decisions, which also have an ethical aspect and engage the practitioner as a person and not only as a specialist. They are in fact dilemmas which profoundly affect the fantasies, conventions and convictions of every one of us. Describing her patient's analysis, Sharon Zalusky (2000) is very explicit about this point and about her personal difficulties in dealing with the patient's decision to under-take an egg donation:

> Psychologically Diana [the patient] was ready to cross that boundary [egg donation]. I was not. My feelings began to intensify. Up until now I would characterize my reactions in the analysis as usual countertransference reactions ... For me there was something profoundly different about egg donation ... This new procedure had potential meanings for me that conceivably were not related to my patient's issues. However, my way of managing my own feelings would ultimately affect my ability to help her analyze hers ... I knew that in embracing this new technique, I would have to examine my personal values privately,

at the same time that Diana was struggling with her own. Clearly the stakes were different for each of us.

(Zalusky, 2000, p. 1555)

As we also saw in the previous section, the diagnosis of infertility, especially when it is idiopathic, sounds like a "diagnosis of exclusion" (Mann, 2014), which is exclusion from the possibility of tracking down a cause or reason for the impediment, but especially an exclusion from the group of other couples and other women (mother, sisters, sisters-in-law, friends) with children. This "exclusion" is a powerful engine which sustains repeated and protracted attempts, even when this is against medical advice. In a study of a group of women who, despite the medical practitioners' contraindications, insisted on a second pregnancy with ART, after having achieved a first one by means of assisted fertilisation, Emanuela Quagliata (2016) concludes with an observation which can perhaps be extended more generally: "Difficulty in working through the mourning for an illusory belief is what seems to impel these women to persist in their desire to procreate at all costs" (p. 6). The illusory belief is in the recovery of their fertility, of their ability to imagine themselves as creative despite physical conditions and often temporal ones too. If the medical process does not make allowance for self-questioning, if it does not introduce time for waiting in which to make some background psychological profiles emerge, it reiterates the dichotomy between the urgent demand that must be granted and the denial of feelings of failure as individuals and as a couple, maintains the mind-body split, and risks disavowing the deep two-way relationship between the two terms (Vigneri, 2003; Coghi, 2005).

The relationship is two-way in another sense as well, in the rapport between physician and patient, as between therapist and patient. All the actors in the scene are involved in a project to create life. The technological repercussions affect both sides since both are simultaneously subjects and objects of the adventure in a continuous exchanging of roles. Projections invade the scene and the (male) gynaecologist is not infrequently invested by patients with the fantasy that he, having made the pregnancy possible, is the child's real father. There are other processes that can be understood as recalling the sexual act which has been missed out, such as the cytoplasmatic injection which is fantasied as an act of penetration that has not in fact happened. It is no wonder that the various individuals who take part

97

in the process of assisted fertilisation on the medical side are invested with sexual fantasies by patients and couples in the attempt to recover on the level of fantasy something that they feel disenfranchised and despoiled of on the physical level. And this may not only be a matter of fantasy. Some years ago, a patient who was undergoing level one artificial insemination[6] felt like suggesting to her gynaecologist, without her husband's knowledge, that he "mix" her husband's oligospermic seminal fluid with some healthy fluid in order to make the encounter of the gametes more efficacious. It is obvious how this would have created a secret bond between gynaecologist and patient, and made the patient the repository of something that could never be confessed, with consequences potentially lasting for the rest of her life.

The binomial Eros and Thanatos punctuates the human subject's psychic life both in alternation, in juxtaposition, and also interwoven together.[7] The link between sexuality and procreation is rooted in the idea of defying death, continuing life by means of something that is part of us and goes beyond us. Infertility, the impossibility of generating, sets in motion what we try to avoid through procreation: thoughts and feelings of death. Death represents our extreme limit, which is also, along with our origin, the limit imposed on our representative capacity. They are the blind spots of our existence because we are not there when they happen: "To give significance to the sexuality that brought one into existence, and to the death that will take one out of it, is a lifelong psychic work" (Parsons, 2014, p. 21). If the battle to defeat infertility is also the battle to defeat the sense of death connected to it, it is easy to understand what is at stake when a course of ART is undertaken, a gamble involving both doctor and patient, from different but equally engrossing perspectives.

Notes

1 "Medically assisted procreation" is the phrase generally used in Europe. The figure of the physician underpins this expression and his presence is acknowledged: hence the relational aspect of the practice is highlighted. In the Anglo-Saxon world, by contrast, the acronym ART (Assisted Reproductive Technology) is used, an expression which instead emphasises the primacy of technique.

2 Isabella Coghi, who died in 2008, worked at the Centre for Infertility at the Policlinico of Sapienza-Roma University. She witnessed the transition from the old to the new, from the traditional modes of conceiving to the new techniques, and her reflections are addressed to

the role of the physician and what this transition has meant for the medical profession, especially in terms of how they have had to adapt their ways of working to the new technological reality: "What seems absolutely necessary to me in practising reproductive medicine … is a skilled readiness to encompass the ways physicians may encounter the mind on various levels, in their specialist schools and in clinical practice. I think the key is to work with gynaecologists because all the work of dealing with the couple devolves to them, ensuring that patients are given the feeling of a unity in the various processes, including the emotional ones, and the feeling of agency in the various choices that are made" (2005, p. 80).

3 In the biblical world, but not only there, infertility is a *topos* and a recurring theme, indicating an extreme challenge to which the woman is subjected in her relationship with God. It is interesting to follow the variety of solutions in the biblical accounts that each of the protagonists (Sarah, Rebecca, Rachel, Hannah, Michal) chooses for addressing her own misfortune. On the other hand, the fact that the female reaction in emotional terms has not changed much from that of their biblical progenitors is testified not only by what we hear on the couch, but also by the statements published by women in a range of contexts, such as interviews, blogs, fiction, etc.

4 As Solano (2016) writes, "we may assert that body and mind do not possess any type of intrinsic existence distinct from the organism as a whole, but *are two categories which have to do essentially with the vertex from which the observer is positioned*" (p. 55).

5 For a review of the techniques of PMA/ART, see the relevant page of the Health Ministry's website: http://www.salute.gov.it/portale/fertility/homeFertility.jsp

6 Level one technique means simple intrauterine insemination (Homologous Intra-Uterine Insemination, HIUI) with the partner's semen. The technique entails introducing male semen into the uterine cavity simultaneously with ovulation in order to encourage the spontaneous encounter of the gametes. This can be done as part of the spontaneous cycle or by stimulating ovulation pharmacologically.

7 After 1920, with *Beyond the Pleasure Principle*, Freud introduces the great distinction between life and death drives. The concept of a death drive is one of the most controversial in Freud's work. On the one hand, it would represent the fundamental tendency of the living being to return to an inorganic state via the neutralising of tensions. When outwardly directed, the death drive manifests itself as aggressiveness and destructiveness. Freud finds it difficult to think we can find the death drive in its pure state, as he maintains in *Inhibitions, Symptoms and Anxiety* (1926). He admits the theoretical character of his hypothesis and the intrinsic

difficulties of the concept which remains in a tension with the principles of psychic functioning and the pleasure principle. Towards the end of his career, he gives a new and more convincing definition of the instinctual dualism, defining two fundamental drive: Eros and the drive to destruction. "The aim of the first of these basic instincts is to establish ever greater unities and to preserve them thus – in short, to bind together; the aim of the second is, on the contrary, to undo connections and so to destroy things. In the case of the destructive instinct we may suppose that its final aim is to lead what is living into an inorganic state. For this reason we also call it the *death instinct*" (1938, p. 148).

SEXUALITY AND BIOTECHNOLOGY

6.1 The trauma of the caesura

As we have seen in the first part of this book, by discovering psychosexuality, psychoanalytic thought has made us irreversibly aware of how human sexuality cannot be reduced to an instinctual need and how the processes which constitute subjective identity are involved in its manifestations and expressions: the pathways that form identity, the ability to establish links and to develop thought, and the institution of the temporal dimension. The recognition of psychic life's rootedness in the body and of the mutual influence between the two spheres – and in particular the way these two spheres represent specific modes of expression – has not only cast doubt on a rigid dualism but has also introduced a more complex view of the body. This is a view we have hinted at earlier, which considers body and mind as two modes of expression for the organism (De Toffoli, 2014; Matthis, 2000; Solano, 2013, 2016; Winnicott, 1988).[1] On the basis of these studies we can say that, though its language is asymbolic, the body nevertheless expresses emotions, thought and information. Indeed, the body is the place where most of the transformations that have characterised the second part of the twentieth century and characterise the present have occurred and are still occurring. Le Goff's (2003) claim that "the body is the seat of the metamorphosis of the new times" continues to have the ring of truth. It is in and on the body that this change has occurred, creating the dichotomy between sexuality and procreation, the caesura of a bond that is intrinsic to our species and could hardly be thought of until a couple of generations ago.

Sexuality, which is situated on the boundary between psychic and corporeal, constitutes a sphere that is particularly sensitive to this relationship and mutual influence. But sexuality, along with dreaming, is one of the two roots from which the tree of psychoanalysis has grown. Around it revolves a variety of different planes, intrapsychic, interpsychic, intersubjective. And that is not all. Besides reflecting the intimate history of each one of us, the events of our affective lives, our relational vicissitudes, and our experiences, the way sexuality is lived and enacted also reflects the time we live in – as Freud taught us with his hysterics – and, if we know how to read it, it functions as a reflecting surface which refers back to the temporal dimension and its transformations, and captures "the reflection that collective history projects upon the screen of individual memory" (Ernaux, 2008, p. 53). What we are witnessing in the field of choices and sexual behaviours, beyond a private dimension, also reflects one direction among the more general changes of axis that we are witnessing. The field opened up by scientific and technological research in this area confronts psychoanalysis with transformations that have a direct impact on its own object of investigation and require an adjustment in the way of thinking that is familiar to us. The caesura, *the trauma*, presented by biotechnology is represented by the inversion of terms: what used to be "fantasy" may be concretised and find realisation in reality. Today it is facts that offer "the other scene", a scene that can seem like the return of the repressed and the materialisation of unconscious fantasies.

Kaës (2009) is an author who has long reflected on the unconscious alliances which found the core of the family and by their interweaving define a psychic reality and a common identity. According to this author, the alliances made within the couple and the family, which also define the relationships between the generations, are cut across by the organisation of sexuality. When procreative practices become disconnected from sexuality, the active variables increase in number but also become more complicated, and some questions naturally arise. What outcomes and effects are created on the level of fantasy and imaginative invention in the subjects who are involved in the process of assisted procreation? Does the sexuality–procreation bond constitute an unconscious invariant?

Does its caesura indicate a structural change? These are questions which, besides involving all of us, also involve the object of psychoanalytic investigation, and as it is transformed the object tests our discipline's theoretical–clinical apparatus and our capacity for thought. We once again find ourselves faced with a double trauma. Like the "plague" which Freud was aware of carrying,[2] referring to the transformations which his investigations were producing in the image of man as "no longer master in his own house", so today the *caesura*, the trauma presented by biotechnology, engages us in a work of mourning for the symbolic points of reference and categories of thought we considered familiar until a little while ago, and compels us to face and work through the affective charge it provokes in us. Otherwise, there seems to be a risk of resorting to categories and concepts we had developed previously and of superimposing these onto the new, in order to control it and bring it back into a proper order. What is being transformed around us calls on us to problematise our knowledge so that we can once again function as "transformative objects" (Bollas, 1987) in relation to our patients' demands.

The desire and decision to have a child is a central moment in human existence. Winnicott (1965a) reminds us that every child and the act of his or her conception is located in a specific way in the fantasy of the two partners and arouses a special imaginative and emotional elaboration on both conscious and unconscious levels: "It is not possible to understand the attitude of parents to their children apart from a consideration of the meaning of each child in terms of the parents' conscious and unconscious fantasy around the act that produced the conception. Parents feel quite differently about, and act quite differently towards, each child. Much depends on the relationship between the parents at the time of conception, during the mother's pregnancy, at the time of the birth, and afterwards" (p. 61).

Winnicott's words call to mind Borges' story "The Circular Ruins" (1944) in which the author describes the dream of "the taciturn man from the South" who *imagines* his own son, "entrail by entrail, feature by feature, in a thousand and one secret nights", only to discover that he too is merely the dream of someone else who is dreaming him. We may wonder if and how far the caesura of the sexuality–procreation bond is reflected on the level of the imaginary, on that "special elaboration" in fantasy which Winnicott and Borges talk about, and on the dream which everyone has about their own child.

Indeed, choosing to have a child arouses a deep and important level of fantasy which also relates to infantile sexuality. The latter represents an unconscious but permanent dimension of the mind and performs an active function in maintaining the individual's links and fantasy life, being reactivated in the existential transitions that accompany the individual over the course of life (Marion, 2016a). The unresolved conflicts relating to infantile sexuality remain as a "residue", generating tension, restlessness, excitation, but also a creative impulse which prompts the imagining and fantasying of what remains obscure. As Widlöcher (2000) says, infantile sexuality persists in the adult mind as a source of desire and a "vector" which supports psychic work. In the second time, that of adult sexuality, the aspects of infantile sexuality that have been left mute take shape and come back into play, as they do for Francesca who, at the moment when she decides to have a baby, recovers the long-silent memory of her childhood games in which, as the mother of her doll–children, she was always alone and could not tolerate any masculine presence.

The idea of conception and of having a baby is a direct summons to sexuality and imposes a reorganisational crisis on the subject along with a profound restructuring which casts doubt on the previous solutions to the oedipal and pre-oedipal dilemmas, and affectively invests the child both on the vertical dimension of the internal world and the psychic structures and on the horizontal dimension of the relational plane. Seen in this light, the intervention of biotechnology and the possibilities it offers for overcoming the limits imposed by nature or by that specific couple may constitute a disruptive element on the plane of fantasy, altering the boundaries between reality and fantasy, since it is now the facts that offer "the other scene", giving a voice and realisation to unconscious fantasies. Luisa's decision to accept heterologous fertilisation (egg donation) in spite of her husband's doubts, thereby detaching herself from the procreative encounter through sexuality, had *also* functioned as a bulwark and defence, sheltering her from the incestuous fantasies reactivated by the idea of conception through the sexual act.

As Ansermet (2015) claims, the techniques of assisted procreation are in competition with infantile sexual theories in the sense that both aim at expelling and evacuating the sexuality from conception. The infant's encounter with sexuality, often provoked by the mother's becoming pregnant again – as we have seen with Little Hans – is at the origin of the desire to know and explore, and "the instinct for knowledge and research" (Freud, 1905, 1908a, 1908b), the "episte-mophilic instinct" (Klein, 1932, 1975), is related to sexual life. Infantile curiosity is attracted by sexual matters which are expressed in the enigma of enigmas: where do babies come from? – where do I come from? The answers which the child works out to this funda-mental question go on to constitute the "birth theories" or "infantile sexual theories" which may take on the most varied permutations in the infantile mind and fantasy: babies are born from the anus or pulled out of the tummy. How they get inside may be the result of an oral relationship or an "immaculate conception". A 4-year-old girl draws two figures quite far apart: they are smiling and brightly coloured. She tells her teacher, "They are my Mummy and Daddy waiting for me and my little brother to come out of Mummy's tummy." The teacher asks where she and her brother are in the drawing and the girl an-swers, "We're at home, but Mummy and Daddy just have to wait a bit and then we'll come." Teacher: "Where do you come from?" Girl: "From her tummy." At this point the teacher asks: "How did you get into her tummy?" and the girl replies, "Jesus sent us to Mummy and Daddy" (Marion, 2015a).

What the parents do when they are alone in their room, the primal scene, also remains a mystery for some time, one to which children try to find solutions in their own way. It may happen that their efforts give rise to anxious fantasies in which sadistic elements predominate and what goes on between the parents is imagined as an aggressive and violent scene, sometimes half way between pleasure and pain. The threat of exclusion felt by the child, cut off from the parents' intimacy and worried about the unwanted consequences which could result from the appearance of a rival, is also projected into this aggressive-ness. Or the oral element may be at the centre of the fantasy, one in which the parents feed each other or the father sucks the mother's milk, thus replicating infantile enjoyment. In the end, what infantile sexual theories expel is the sexual scene, the parents' coitus, at their origin and at the origin of other children. Infantile sexual theories (anal, oral, etc.) perform the defensive function of protecting the child from the encounter with the other's pleasure, and that of the parental couple, which is out of his or her control. The parents' sexuality tends to be taken out of the picture and denied in the infantile imagination: "In the unconscious the only couple is that of the father and mother, rather than the sexual couple of the man and the woman" (Ansermet, 2015, p. 10). The techniques of assisted fertilisation enact this fantasy of negation, expelling sexuality from the process of conception, and with it the sense of mystery linked to the origin of life. Perhaps it would be more correct to say that, when the couple's sexuality is expelled, that same sexuality goes out of the door only to come back in through the window on a fantasy level. Indeed, ART is a process which happens under the control of other figures, witnesses of the various steps and – as I was saying earlier – involved in the activity, who take the partner's place, often leading the subjects to ask themselves, "But who did I make this baby with?"

The "traumatic caesura" has a vivid representation in Gloria's ART story. In her countless foreign travels she always felt alone, and she actually was since the collecting of the seminal fluid had happened at a different time and her partner rarely accompanied her. Her prevailing perception was of a cold climate (her journeys were to destinations in Northern Europe), which mirrored the condition of her inner world. It seems to me that the extreme image provided by Gloria (fortunately it isn't always like that!) of two people who each function on their own behalf, in different times and spaces, well represents the divergence between the two terms (sexuality/procreation) through the absence of a real couple and a missing encounter at the origin of the procreative act.

6.2 Oedipus revisited

In the story entitled *The Dying of the Pythia* (1985) Friedrich Dürrenmatt revisits the story of King Oedipus in an entirely original and unexpected manner, building on the text we know, in order to construct another which interweaves the destiny of the different characters to surprising and sometimes exhilarating effect. Through the mouths of the characters themselves, especially the Pythia and Tiresias, and in a series of *coups de théâtre*, the reader learns another story where the strands of the plot are completely rearranged into a new structure which is nevertheless plausible because it is coherent in itself and therefore truthful. What makes this kind of literary fiction possible is the potency of Oedipus in his own right, his being "mythical drama in its pure state", as Starobinski emphasises (1961, p. 156). This very potency in his own right seems to enable Oedipus to contain not only many interpretations but also many varied layers of meaning. As Dürrenmatt's Tiresias says to the Pythia, "Don't worry about it … Let it be. Whatever it was, was surely different and will always be different again and again, the more we try to get to the bottom of it" (Dürrenmatt 1985, p. 300).

In fact, the task we are given today precisely matches the words that Dürrenmatt gives to Tiresias: to make our way along the trails of the diversity that is unfolding before our eyes. Picking up the question asked by Kaës (2009) that I recalled earlier, how far does the story of Oedipus which has constituted the nucleus of psychoanalytic thought, represent an unconscious invariant? Or are we being presented with structural changes that modify our very nature? How much is the nuclear family itself being redesigned by biotechnology? And how should we imagine its transformations in the light of what is taking place? And does all of this influence the journey of subjectivation?

Greek tragedy and psychoanalysis belong to the Western tradition of thought about mankind and our world of passions and emotions. For our culture and, in this respect, for psychoanalysis too, tragedy has represented a powerful anticipation and a valuable reference point in the exploration of human individuality and subjectivity[3] (Marion, 2008). The phenomenon, so distinctive and circumscribed in time, that was Attic tragedy, constitutes a stage in the psychological evolution of modern man, of interiority, and a stage in the construction of a responsible subject. The tragic, as a new affective-emotional dimension, comes onto the scene and transforms the interiority of Western man. The tragic dimension which is born when the language of myth seems to have exhausted its function and the hero has ceased to be considered a model, opens itself to the order of history and recognises the universe as one of conflict. The human and divine planes start to become distinguished and man's action becomes an object of reflection, knowledge, awareness and responsibility. The acquisition of the temporal dimension represents another central feature of tragedy because it signals the passage from a "fatal" and self-repeating (mythic) experience to the conscious (tragic) assumption of one's own destiny and the construction of one's own story. Though we have been orphaned of divinity, there remains the greatness of speech which aims at the sharing of pain and the achievement of truth, as in Antigone who opposes the law of the *polis* with the discourse of the affections, or in Oedipus who answers the question about man, and in psychoanalysis which has founded its method of knowledge and treatment on speech.[4]

Aristotle considered *Oedipus Rex* the tragedy *par excellence* in that it seems to contain within itself, in admirable form and balance, all the elements that characterise this literary genre. Freud fell under its spell and linked the foundational discovery of psychoanalysis to this tragedy. Although (as we saw in Part I) he never devoted a specific work to the oedipal theme, his theorisation of it runs through all his work and it remains the nucleus of the psychoanalytic thinking by which generations of psychoanalysts have identified themselves.[5] Freud focused his attention on the content of the oedipal experience and the significance of that part of the myth which constitutes the subject of the tragedy. As Starobinski (1975) notes, Freud almost uses the tragedy as an impersonal and collective expression to help him find an authoritative confirmation of what he was already looking for: "the mythical paradigm serves both as a corollary of the new hypothesis and as a warrant of its universality" (p. 149).

In step with the elaboration of psychoanalysis, the mythological and tragic association fades, to be replaced in the foreground by the psychological and psychopathological sense of the ideo-affective configuration structuring the human mind. The feature of the Oedipus myth and the Sophoclean tragedy that is emphasised is its significance in relation to the journey assigned to human development, which occurs by acknowledging triangulation and the difference between the generations (De Simone, 2002). After Freud, the oedipal theme will encounter an expansion of meanings which confirm the fertility of his intuition and, at the same time, the developments in psychoanalytic thought. From being a "sexual model", the Oedipus complex becomes a "model of knowledge" and attention is instead directed to the significance of the oedipal triangle in the development of the mental functions and as a method for psychoanalytic knowledge. It may be a mistake not to acknowledge that this line of thought was to some extent also captured by Freud, as is evidenced by the comparison made in the *Traumdeutung* (*The Interpretation of Dreams*) between the action of the tragedy and psychoanalytic work (1899a, pp. 261ff.), but this interpretation will only be developed by his successors, with Bion first among them. In Freud's oedipal model the emphasis was placed on the psychological and affective movements in relation to the family dynamics, and a universal value was attributed to these. By contrast, Bion aimed above all to build a model in terms of relationships and links. His reading of myths, not only of Oedipus but also of Babel and the Garden of Eden, shifts the accent from the sexual and incestuous content to the three-dimensional structure of the mind and the modes of functioning of thought. With Bion and the next generations of psychoanalysts, the myth acquires ever greater methodological value for knowledge in general, and for psychoanalytic knowledge in particular.

The paradigmatic significance of Oedipus consists in his going beyond parricide and incest, in his being a "myth of knowledge and research" (Abadi, 1978) whose latent meaning concerns the missing father-son encounter, the failure of separation from the dyadic maternal relationship and, hence, the failure of the life-project and the search for his own identity. It goes without saying that this "cognitive" dimension of the myth acquires a universal value without regard for gender – i.e. being a son or a daughter – because the necessary separating transitions and the encounter with thirdness, metaphorically represented by the paternal figure, concern all human beings indiscriminately. This is the sense in which we speak of an "oedipal function of the mind" (Di Chiara, 1985). Bollas (1992) also concentrates on this aspect and distinguishes the "oedipal dilemma" from the "oedipus complex". In the "oedipal dilemma" the child discovers and acknowledges the patriarchal line which destroys the illusion of possessing the mother. S/he resolves the Oedipus complex, renouncing rights to the mother and accepting the father who has preceded her/him, achieves "a correct identification of one's place, of one's position in time, that informs the child of the mother's prior desire" (Bollas, 1992, p. 230), and is introduced to the sphere of complexity. In fact, it is the "complex", its acknowledgement and acceptance, which signals the evolution and solution of the oedipal "dilemma".

If we shift from the sphere of tragedy to that of myth, we catch an antecedent which illuminates the story and widens its significance (Marion, 1993). When Oedipus declares, "Come what may, I want to know my birth-origins, however humble," he is speaking about an experience of negation and rejection which stands at the start of his life's journey and does not form part of the tragedy's explicit plot, but powerfully conditions its unfolding, outcome and meaning. The name Oedipus (simultaneously "swollen foot" and "he who knows") functions as the sign of his destiny and a mark of his belonging to the lame family of the Labdacids (Vernant and Vidal-Naquet, 1986). At the same time, it recalls an infirmity stamped on his body by the paternal rejection. The enigma of the name Oedipus sums up his story's tragic nature and reveals the part which precedes the tragedy, that of having been a rejected child, exposed on the mountain to await death. In a way, we could say that it reveals the importance of the pregenital period and of that period of life which concerns the idea of the child in the mind of the parents. In the myth, Oedipus is the forbidden child, and the breaking of the prohibition – Jocasta makes use of Laius's drunkenness to get around the ban and conceive a child – produces a son as a threat. Oedipus is the unwanted child, and his seeking to know/not-know is a matter of life and death. From this point of view, also following the perspective introduced by Winnicott (1988), the way is opened up for an interpretative thread which emphasises how the Oedipus "complex" represents the first interpersonal relationship, one in which bodily functioning and fantasy are involved. The dual role of the fantasies that are in play, both parental and infantile, is especially emphasised, as are the relational aspects in the field until we come to the transgenerational. The child's fantasies about the "primal scene" and the parents' fantasies about that child, before and after conception, are not detached from one another but have a reciprocal influence, each constituting for the other the nucleus which makes possible the dream of one's own life-project and sexuality.

In the light of these brief observations, it is obvious how the tragedy of Oedipus becomes multifaceted and the original theme, besides not being the only one, the exclusive reading of it, has also been the subject of constant, fruitful transformations. The way "the families of Oedipus" (De Simone, 2002) have been extended testifies to the fecundity of a story with its roots in the origins of our civilisation. Nevertheless, reminding ourselves of the words of Dürrenmatt's Tiresias confirms the idea that this story is subject to new evolutions because – in Ferro's (2002) words – this means accepting "that the development of psychoanalysis is inserted into a temporality which also proceeds by caesuras, and that its models are developed and expanded in linear fashion until a moment of rupture where there is a caesura, a quantum leap and a different model" (p. 8). So, what model can we talk about in order to address the new ways of being born, but also the new family configurations to which they are giving rise?

6.3 From the triangle to the circle

The enquiries I am proposing focus on the question of the relationship between psychoanalytic reflection and changes in progress between "what is called reality and fantasy", to use Winnicott's (1988, p. 59) expression once again. The *International Journal of*

Psychoanalysis recently asked the question in these terms: "is the nature of psychoanalytic thinking and practice (e.g. in regard to sexuality) determined by extra-analytic, social and cultural developments"? (Blass, 2016b).[6] What influence do reality and its changes have in orienting psychoanalytic thought? The significant mutations that we are detecting in the sphere of sexuality and procreation challenge the validity of the theories we have so far elaborated and their capacity for reading and understanding them. And they make us wonder about the repercussions of the innovations in progress on our theories. Is psychoanalysis in a position to welcome the ongoing *new* into its theoretical–clinical apparatus? How do we work through the discrepancy between the processes of symbolisation and the insistent rhythm which characterises what is currently going on? It is hard to establish a boundary between the *new* outside us, which we are trying to manage, and ourselves, given that we are changing as a consequence of these new facts (Marion, 2003).

The debate in the *International Journal of Psychoanalysis* brings two quite irreconcilable positions face to face: those like Paul who read the shift occurring in the Freudian idea of sexuality in terms of changes in the external arena, resulting in the replacement of old paradigms with new ones; and those like Ahumada who tend to see the new technologies, with their impact on sexuality and other areas, as the expression of forms of non-thought. For Ahumada, this would cause the affective world to come apart at the seams with a devaluing of human relations. The change in the area of sexuality is heading in the direction of promiscuity, in a search for orgiastic experiences which "just collect orgasms". According to this author, what is being called into question by the new technologies, and also represents the focus of his position, is the difficulty in establishing relationships of intimacy and dependency where the ability to love and the expressions of sexuality are in harmony. It is like the film *Her*,[7] where an operating system based on artificial intelligence using an alluring and sensual female voice calling itself Samantha replaces the physical relationship, bypassing the weight and function of corporeality in the relationship, and the machine replaces the emotional and sexual link with a real person.

Ahumada's reference to the orgiastic dimension recalls a thought expressed some years ago by Francesco Corrao who wondered if, in order to understand modern times and the anthropological transformations in progress, we might have to turn not to the myth of

Oedipus but to that of Dionysus. Dionysus also represents the origin of tragedy, the kind that precedes Oedipus and emphasises the irrational element of which the god was the bearer, the "spirit of music", ecstatic possession in search of the absolute, the dimension that is suffocated by the cloak of logocentricity and the arrival of philosophy (Arvanitakis, 1998; Fanizza, 2006). The tragic would lose its way within the domain of the *logos* and representation (Marion, 2008). This dimension of the "tragic" would indeed be more effective in capturing certain manifestations of the postmodern or even, as Riolo (2005) says, the post-human. Oedipus fills the stage with the theme of the divided subject and the transition from fate to destiny. We are at the dawn of notions like will, free choice, determinism and responsibility for one's actions, all of these being notions that will accompany the psychological history of Western man. The conflict which inhabits the internal world of Oedipus, the drama of recognising oneself in generational difference and in the separating transitions which accompany the process has no place in the world of Dionysus, which is the expression of excess and where the evacuation of the real predominates. As Riolo (2005) puts it, "*eidolopoiesis*", understood as "hypertrophy of the collective production of the imaginary" (p. 147),[8] reigns.

The new forms of procreation challenge the myth of Oedipus and "medically assisted reproduction overturns all differences, sexual as well as temporal" (Ansermet, 2015, p. 53). We can want children with people of the same sex, with unknown donors, with frozen embryos, with the uterus of another woman. Each of these situations presents us with unfamiliar scenarios: "if sperm donation can be imagined as "medically assisted adultery" (ibid., p. 55), what transformations does heterologous fertilisation produce on the level of imagination and fantasy? The fantasies about the donor get extended into the questions about one's origin: who do I belong to? … where do I come from? The answer may be even more traumatic than the question since the donors are not on the inside of a parenting project and are not recognised as biological mothers and fathers. Surrogate pregnancy complicates the panorama further, adding a new segment to all the others. In male homosexual couples, besides the donation of gametes, recourse to surrogacy is obligatory, short-circuiting the basic impediment which is also the specific characteristic of that choice of couple. What is rejected on the emotional and sexual level returns through procreation which is by definition heterosexual. In this context, I was saying before that the original therapeutic goal of the techniques of assisted fertilisation has gradually been transformed into the possibility of meeting ever more extreme demands and sometimes of short-circuiting quite different impediments which nature has imposed on reproductive possibilities, in fact throwing into crisis the anthropological continuity based on the sexuality-filiation bond.

In this new reality of multiple combinations, the oedipal triangle is subjected to demands which modify its form and structure and challenge the archetype which defines the triangular configuration, mother-father-child, an archetype that has accompanied the idea of reproduction throughout history. Diane Ehrensaft (2005) has invented a neologism to describe those who participate in the new reproduction as external players: she has replaced "birth mother" with "birth (m)other", a biological other, an individual different from the baby's parents. By the expression "birth other family", she refers to families created through the support of other figures external to the parents. While the "mind's oedipal function" (Di Chiara, 1985) – that is, the capacity, by acknowledging the third, to accept otherness and the complexity of reality – remains unaltered, the schema it is based on has been altered and complicated, confronting the subject with more complex challenges. This means not only the journey of individuation and the reframing of infantile omnipotence through the process of identifying with the parent of the same or opposite sex, according to the specific oedipal evolution of each person, the acceptance of being separate and acknowledging that a parental couple exists outside us and before us. It is also a matter of incorporating the presence of other figures who only have life on the level of fantasy and have contributed to one's generation with different roles and functions: genetic parts of unknown donors, women who have carried out gestation for others, processes often also interwoven together. Or else it is a matter of incorporating other times which preceded fertilisation, as in the case of frozen embryos waiting for the right moment to be implanted. The triangle is widened to include the totality of its protagonists and, as Ehrensaft (2014) says, it becomes a square, a pentagon, even a hexagon within an oedipal circle that is expanded ever further.

When we come to respond to such complicated processes that are also so remote from the way psychoanalysis has traditionally thought of conception, as intimately linked to the sexual act and to generation based on a heterosexual and procreative couple, we are helped out by a concept from the tradition of Winnicottian thought.[9] I am referring to the concept of "integration" (Winnicott, 1945, 1988) which constitutes one of the most sophisticated *leitmotivs* in Winnicott's theorising. Beginning with the idea that the initial state is one of non-integration, "a lack of wholeness both in space and time" (Winnicott, 1988, p. 116), the work of integration that is achieved through maternal care allows the initial fragmented experience of the new-born infant to be joined up in a single place which is the mother's mind. The environment is entrusted with the delicate task of facilitating the integrative process and of sustaining the baby in the work of appropriating the various experiences s/he is living through and of integrating them into the personality (Winnicott, 1945). This entails – an assertion which also represents a specific contribution to the development of psychoanalytic thought – the conviction that the subject's unconscious psychic space is in continual and reciprocal relation to that of the object. The mother's mind goes on an integrative journey in terms of her experiences with "that" child: how s/he was made, how s/he has come into the world, who has participated in her/his conception, what s/he represents at that specific moment in the mother's life and in the life of the couple, etc. This work is the *conditio sine qua non* which makes possible the establishment of a feeling of integration and continuity in the infantile mind. Without it, whatever happens in relation to this and is not detected or "assimilated" goes astray, ending up at the edges of the psychic universe, taking the form of a black hole, a blind spot, and sends back weak yet persistent signals, impulses that are hard to decrypt so that their existence can be noticed. It is a very familiar experience for the psychoanalyst who, using the integrative activity of his or her own mind, works to recover the mute trace, and by means of work on two temporal axes – the present time of the session and the transposition into another time that we are called upon to witness through our relationship with the patient – tries to give voice and substance to the dissociated experience and emotion.

But how does the lack of integration manifest itself in relation to the matters we are addressing? One particular example of dissociation can be traced in those cases where the parents intend to keep their child's origin a secret from them even after adolescence. Their silence on this subject, which seems to act as a defence mechanism against feelings of shame and fears about their children and their relatives, like a private nucleus which cannot be made accessible to others, reveals the failure to integrate that particular reproductive process. It is quite a common experience in consultations with parents who have children born by ART to find oneself faced with an impassable boundary. Gaia's parents bring their 6-year-old daughter for an assessment because of problems with withdrawal and inhibition that are also reflected in learning difficulties. They talk briskly about the difficulties they had encountered in conceiving Gaia and lead the therapist to understand that they had resorted to assisted fertilisation, but they do so in a confused way, sidestepping any discreet request for clarification. When the therapist comments that it certainly can't have been easy and must have demanded great commitment, the mother intervenes, saying that their daughter would react badly if she knew about it. Likewise, the parents of Marco (aged 8), referred because of his stammer, hint fleetingly and with great anxiety at the difficulties they encountered because of the father's infertility, but tenaciously avoid sharing any information with the therapist and make it clear to her that Marco is naturally in the dark about all this and must remain so. The recourse to ART, whether first or second level, seems to generate feelings of shame and guilt, as if the fantasy were inclining towards the idea of a sexual inadequacy, an unacceptable promiscuity, which might compromise them in the eyes of their children and the rest of the family. But how far is the child's symptom the effect of this lack of integration and a signal, however confused and distorted, of an alien presence within her or him and in the relationship with the parents?

Secrecy, or at least evasiveness, about the fertilisation process and, hence, about the child's origins, highlights both the parents' difficulty in "integrating" in their minds an itinerary which has required the intervention of other figures, and the child's difficult situation in having to deal not only with the two parents of the primal scene who leave him/her outside the bedroom, but also with the unconscious fantasies that may be circulating on both fronts (the child's and the parents') around the fact of being/having a parent who has made the child with someone else (Ehrensaft, 2014). Quoting Winnicott again, when the integrative process proves faulty we find ourselves faced with "disintegration", which is "an organized undoing of integration … The splitting up in disintegration occurs along lines of cleavage in the inner world set-up, or of perceived outer world cleavage" (Winnicott, 1988, p. 137). I think the feeling of being the repository of a secret around one's origin or the unveiling of a partial truth which is intended to obscure a piece of the story – the unsaid is at the origin of the journey that Oedipus makes to Delphi – represents the "cleavage" which can threaten and render fragile the subject's feeling of personal experience and their psychic and emotional growth.

Notes

1 Winnicott (1988) writes, "The psyche has a fundamental unity with the body through its relation both to the function of tissue and organs and to the brain, as well as through the way it becomes intertwined with it by new relationships developed in the individual's fantasy or mind, conscious or unconscious" (p. 52).
2 Although Freud was a man of his time and little inclined by nature to displays of transgression, this was the famous phrase he said to Jung in 1909 during their sea crossing to the United States: "They don't realise we are bringing them the plague," meaning the "revolution" introduced by psychoanalysis with regard to sexuality, dreams, and the discovery of the unconscious.
3 On the subject of tragedy, as a specific phenomenon circumscribed in time (5th century BCE) with three levels of significance – social, aesthetic, psychological – Vernant and Vidal-Naquet (1972) write that "the problem is not that of attributing one of these aspects to the other, but of understanding how they are articulated and combined in order to construct a unique human fact which appears in history under three aspects: as a social reality with the institution of the tragic competitions, as an aesthetic creation with the advent of a new literary genre, and as a psychological mutation with the arising of a tragic consciousness and a tragic man, three aspects which define the same object and belong to the same order of explanation" (p. ix). The transition to tragedy is marked by the advent of judicial thought which invests the social thinking of the *polis* and is accompanied by the concept of responsibility and guilt.
4 André Green (1975) and Jean-Luc Nancy (2006) underline how tragedy originates in religion and the sacrificial rites, and how, moving out of this sphere and away from communication with the gods through sacrifice, it preserves its ritual character in theatrical form through speech which men, "left without succour", exchange with each other (the characters among themselves and the chorus with the characters). From being an invocation to the gods, language becomes the thread which binds men together: indeed, its ethical value lies in its capacity to offer comfort and succour once divine succour has disappeared. It is

fascinating to think that a part of this legacy has transferred into the meaning and role which psychoanalysis attributes to language in treatment, language which has been modified over time, accentuating its features of sharing, acceptance, contact – "succour" – and research, at the expense of definitional and decoding interpretative functions.

5 Freud encounters Sophocles' tragedy very early on, first in his matriculation exam (Molinari, 1981) and later during his sojourn in Paris when he attends a performance of the tragedy (Jones, 1953). These two episodes seem to constitute the antecedent or "first time" of what will only be fully unveiled after 1896, the year of his father's death. The oedipal theme is picked up again in a series of letters to Fliess (21 September, 3 and 15 October 1897) which run from the crisis of the seduction theory to the moment when the analogy with the protagonists of the myth and the reference to the tragedy are made explicit. The reference to the tragedy will also be reprised in *The Interpretation of Dreams*, a work in which the accent shifts onto the action of the tragedy, which is likened to the psychoanalytic method. Oedipus is established as a guiding thread in Freud's work and the fulcrum of psychic development. Only long after his original intuition, in 1922 with *The Ego and the Id*, will he give a complete version of it, delineating its positive and negative courses.

6 This was a debate coordinated by Rachel Blass in the *International Journal of Psychoanalysis* (3, 2016b) which juxtaposed the theses of two psychoanalysts, R. A. Paul and J. L. Ahumada. The former is a training analyst at the Atlanta Psychoanalytic Society, trained in Ego Psychology, and considers himself a neo-Freudian; he is also Professor of Anthropology and Interdisciplinary Studies. Jorge Ahumada is a training analyst at the Argentine Psychoanalytic Society and describes his psychoanalytic position as being within the Freudian-Kleinian-Bionian current.

7 *Her* is a 2013 film by Spike Jonze set in Los Angeles. The protagonist, who earns his living by writing letters for other people, acquires a new operating system OS1 based on artificial intelligence and capable of adapting itself to the user's requirements. The voice he chooses for the interface is a female one performed by Scarlett Johansson. The film describes the evolution of the relationship between the protagonist and Samantha which soon develops into a romantic one. The question of the absence of physicality, the way the two protagonists experience this, and what it gives rise to in their relationship is one of the film's most interesting features.

8 According to this author, the world we are more and more concerned with is not the world of Oedipus, "an internal world inhabited by conflict", but "an external world where conflict is negated and evacuated

into the real". It is precisely this change, therefore, that would signal the transition from a postmodern culture to a post-human culture (ibid.).

9 Winnicott introduces a new view of the mother–infant relationship in his famous assertion that "the history of an individual baby cannot be written in terms of the baby alone" (1971, p. 71). In relation to our discussion, one point seems central: Winnicott changes the interpretation of the object (i.e. of the other), which, instead of being thought of in relational terms and as a bundle of projections which emanate from the subject, investing and transforming it, is recognised in its subjectivity and capacity to give more or less adequate responses. As Roussillon (2016) justly notes, the idea that the object was also a subject with its own impulses and desires, and therefore the bringer of a specific and entirely personal response to the other's gesture, was completely foreign. On the contrary, for Winnicott the quality of the object and the role of external reality as an environment and in association with internal reality are central. On Winnicott, cf. Bonaminio, 2016, 2017; Fabozzi, 2012, 2016.

---------------------------------- 7 ----------------------------------

ONE SEXUALITY OR SEVERAL?

Since the day that weddings, courts, and altars
made savage humans act compassionately
both to themselves and others ...

(Ugo Foscolo, *Dei sepolcri* (On Tombs))

7.1 Hierarchical order and difference

As we have seen in the previous chapters, the biotechnologies have
exceeded their therapeutic objective and widened the field of generative possibilities beyond the traditional couple with fertility
problems, extending them also to those situations which meet a limit
or an insurmountable impediment in the conditions given by nature,
and giving rise to the broad domain of what is called "the new
parenting". Even temporal boundaries have been overcome via the
cryogenic preservation of gametes and embryos, enabling fertilisation
past the age of fertility and the postponement of the parental project
to meet individual requirements (I am thinking, for example, of
cancer patients undergoing chemotherapy, but also the demands of a
profession or career), and now the possibility of fertilisation *post
mortem.*[1] The horizon of procreation has been extended by "combinations" that have "exploded" the Oedipus complex and its triangle. "Technological vertigo" intrudes into the question of gender
and gender identity, a question which – though not identical to the
subjects addressed so far – intersects with them in a discontent that

deeply affects a person, including their sexual self-expression. This discontent finds a concrete answer in surgery and hormonal treatments which are made ever more sophisticated by the advance of technology, thereby avoiding any lengthy pondering of the questions it raises. Interventions of this kind, sustained by the not always well-founded and often illusory hope of finding solutions to highly complex and very painful situations, provoke a consideration of the possibility of "remodelling the foundational and relational social ties" (Mazzarella, 2017) beyond the sphere of the nature-culture bond that was familiar to us until recently. My impression is that one aspect of this "remodelling" concerns the changed stance towards difference, which includes expressions of sexuality.

The tragedy of Oedipus, in all its evolutions from Freud onwards, acted as the metaphor for a central evolutionary crux which every one of us faces on the pathway of our subjectivation. The oedipal "dilemma" (Bollas, 1993, 2000) indicates the relational complexity we are immersed in, our place in time and space achieved through the acknowledgement of thirdness and otherness. The heterosexuality that is fundamental to procreation and the prohibition against incest (Lévi-Strauss, 1949) represented and still represent a universal law: "the overcoming of endogamy and the encouragement of exogamy constitutes its fundamental significance and the Oedipus myth is the one that best expresses it" (Ciaramelli, 2017, p. 465). Sexual and generational difference distils in itself the origin of all differences.

The encounter with the other's difference, the recognition that "the other is not simply the object of my desire, but exists in him/herself and has relations with a third to whom I am forbidden access" (Castoriadis, 1998, p. 59) is a foundational experience which introduces us to thought and to the process of symbolisation. However painful and disturbing it may be to have this experience, difference, the gap, is by its nature a dynamic element, an urge to the incessant revival of thought in mankind (Chervet, 2014). The author of *À la recherche*, whom we met earlier in our journey, gives us a fascinating image of this when on several pages of *Time Regained* (1927) he describes the effect produced on him by stumbling "against some unevenly placed paving stones" in the courtyard of the Guermantes' mansion. In this case the perceived difference is physical, and yet the gap between two levels which Proust encounters sets off an intense internal movement, in particular the association with sensations felt once when stepping on the uneven paving stones of the Baptistry of

St Mark's, and the recovery – like the taste of the madeleine – of the long-buried memory, still vivid and powerful, of Venice and those far off days.

Freud's *Civilisation and its Discontents* (1929) is contemporary with the publication of the final volume of Proust's search. Alongside the melancholy reflection on the price that the individual pays for being a social animal, the concept of difference, present in many parts of Freud's text, is intrinsic to the very architecture of his argument. Not so much because of that sharp and radical contrast with the formless oceanic feeling with which the paper begins. Rather, I am thinking about how the concept of "difference" supports the hierarchical structure – intrapsychic, interpsychic and relational – expressed in the structural theory. The idea of a Super-Ego, as an overseeing agency which pulls together the individual's unconscious conflict after the drives have been given up, finds its equivalent in a *Kultur-Über-Ich*, a Super-Ego of civilisation which imposes its ideal demands.[2]

In Freud's 1929 work, the sense of difference is highlighted at various points in his argument. I will just mention a couple of these. A first one concerns the Ego, which he describes as "autonomous and unitary, marked off distinctly from everything else" (Freud, 1929, p. 66). While being continued inwards towards the unconscious, it nevertheless maintains "clear and sharp lines of demarcation" (ibid.) in relation to the outside. The acceptable, indeed physiological, dissolution of boundaries in the experience of falling in love is elsewhere regarded with suspicion and considered the vector of pathological qualities. After 1920, the Freudian description of the Ego is matched by the idea of the individual conceived according to a structure capable of responding to a variety of tasks:[3] on the one hand, the demands coming from the world of the drives and of authority, on the other the mediation between the requirements of external reality and those coming from internal reality; "the ego as a defensive agent, the super-ego as a system of prohibitions, the id as the instinctual pole – which are now elevated to the rank of *agencies* of the psychical apparatus" (Laplanche and Pontalis, 1967, p. 138). The claim that "the Ego is not master in its own house" (Freud, 1916), besides being at the origin of the collapse of the illusion that man is the centre of the universe, anticipates the existence of different psychic "agencies" which are related to each other.

In Freud (1929) the very definition of civilisation – and this is the second point – depends on the concept of difference: "the word 'civilization' describes the whole sum of the achievements and the regulations which *distinguish* our lives from those of our animal ancestors and which serve two purposes – namely to protect men against nature and to adjust their mutual relations" (p. 89, my italics). The difference that Freud is thinking of and that would be at the origin of the human species seems to be in tune with the definition from Scholasticism, *definitio fit per genus proximum et differentiam specificam*, which ties the identification of a species – what makes it different from all the others – to its specific attributes.

Freud's observation and the idea of difference within a "hierarchical" spiritual and social universe is coherent with "the spirit of the age", heir of a philosophical tradition and line of thought for which the Hegelian master–slave dialectic seems to be an effective metaphor. In the second part of the short twentieth century, this type of equilibrium began to change. The image which best captures the quality of these transformations is that of a fall from verticality towards a tendency to run along the horizontal. The crisis of the grand narratives and ideologies, the meta–psychic and meta–social guarantees of Kaës and Touraine, has been accompanied by a transformation of the idea of the individual as no longer inserted, more or less harmoniously or conflictedly, into a hierarchical system of relations – the triangular structure of the traditional family or the structure of the division of labour – on which s/he depends for a role, a position, recognition. The lines of demarcation between the two parental figures and between parents and children have been made less clear and relationships have become more those of equals, just as working life has focused on problems linked to flexibility, complexity, adaptation. All of this is not without relevance for analytic practice and the idea of healing, and is also reflected in the change encountered by our position as analysts. With regard to us, the collapse of verticality has had important consequences both for the set-up of treatment and the setting, and also for the forms of training. According to Bohleber (2013), the result has been the erosion of the image of the analyst as a clinical authority, a paternalistic figure and expert on the unconscious, replacing it with the idea of greater mutuality within the analyst–analysand relationship. We are being more and more released from traditional roles and forms – both in the family and at work – and faced with links, choices and lifestyles that are highly individualised.

And yet, if we go back to Freud's text, we are somewhat surprised right at the end of the essay to find a reversal of his argument about "differences", and the topic is the very crux that is sexuality. In fact, "civilization behaves towards sexuality as a people or a stratum of its population does which has subjected another one to its exploitation" (Freud, 1929, p. 104). These are complex pages because precisely those differences which distinguish us from animal species in terms of civilising processes hide a destiny of another quality and nature, a violent oppression which leads to the wiping out of differences in relation to human sexual life, which becomes universally directed towards the heterosexual genital solution within the limits of monogamous choice. This is a choice which "disregards the dissimilarities, whether innate or acquired, in the sexual constitution of human beings; it cuts off a fair number of them from sexual enjoyment, and so becomes the source of serious injustice" (ibid.).

7.2 The crux of bisexuality

The overturning of his argument that Freud proposes in his 1929 text should no longer be so astonishing to us. The acknowledgement of the multiplicity of sexual choices which accompanies the path of human life seems coherent with the reflections that Freud had developed in his early work and especially in the *Three Essays* (1905) as we have already been able to see. In that text we find a section devoted to bisexuality, a controversial and ambiguous topic, but one that will continue to be present in Freud's thought for a long time, as is testified by certain pages of *The Ego and the Id* (1922), and this helps us understand the shadows that pass over our sexual identity and the uncertainty of our boundaries.[4] Even the revisions Freud makes to the 1905 text clearly show how his interest and attention remain clearly focused on these two elements in the individual psyche. Claiming that the co-presence of masculine and feminine characteristics, on both the physical and psychic levels, is the original element from which the later processes develop, Freud not only achieves a radical opening up of the traditional conceptions of sexuality that were dominant in his time – as we have clearly seen – but in some ways anticipates that process of deconstructing a static idea of the masculine and feminine to which gender theorists will refer many years later, a deconstruction that is a guiding thread in their own musings.

Of course, the bisexuality that Freud inherited from Fliess does not refer to social roles and the question of gender identity is not part of his sphere of observation and reflection. Some more time will need to pass before it is given theoretical-clinical status (Money et al., 1955; Stoller, 1968), establishing its early presence in the process of constructing the subject's identity and its debt to the other's gaze. Acknowledging the original co-presence of both elements in the human being, both on the biological and psychic plane, Freud's reflections took off in new directions. Many years later, in the text which attempts a definitive systematisation of the architecture of psychic functioning (Freud, 1922), he addresses the problem of the complex identificatory scenarios opened up by the resolution of the Oedipus complex and how bisexuality interferes in its destiny. In the space of half a page the term is cited several times to insist on its presence in the subject's psychic life, attributing the causes to the feminine position which the male infant adopts in relation to his father, together with ambivalence and rivalry towards the maternal object. Again in 1925, in the conclusion to his essay on *Some Psychical Consequences of the Anatomical Distinction between the Sexes*, he claims that "pure masculinity and femininity remain theoretical constructions of uncertain content" because human beings "as a result of their bisexual disposition and of cross-inheritance, combine in themselves both masculine and feminine characteristics"(Freud, 1925, p. 258).

Many years later, Winnicott (1971) will speak of the predisposition to bisexuality present in both sexes via male and female elements in men and women.[5] It is the famous interpretation he gives a patient when catching the feminine element present in him: "I am listening to a girl. I know perfectly well that you are a man but I am listening to a girl, and I am talking to a girl" (p. 73). For Winnicott, the difference is located in the contrasting ways in which one enters into a relationship with the object. While the "male" element of the person refers to the capacity for "active relating" or "passive being related to" (ibid., p. 79), the female element is concerned with the feeling of "being". Put another way, "the male element *does* while the female element (in males and females) *is*" (ibid., p. 81).[6] Winnicott's work is directed towards integration of the various parts of the self "instead of dissociated elements that exist in compartments" (ibid., p. 67) and towards the recognition and affirmation of "bisexuality as a quality of the unit or total self" (ibid., p. 76). His conception of psychic bisexuality is radical and refers to the presence of an aspect of the subject's personality which has the opposite sex. These are the terms in which he reads the tragedy of Hamlet, as the representation of an insoluble dilemma because of the dissociation produced in the main character. The hero's change towards Ophelia, his cruelty to her, is interpreted by Winnicott as the "ruthless rejection" of the female element that was in him and handed over to Ophelia; it is as if a part had been killed and the predominant male element were threatening to take over the personality completely.[7]

Psychic bisexuality, which refers to the co-presence in the same individual not only of opposed aspects of the personality but also of opposed desires, is connected to the theme of creativity (McDougall, 1989; Ferraro, 2003). The dialectic between male and female elements in the psychic structure maintains the subject's readiness to assume multiple identities, to take the other sex into oneself by means of the ability to dream its position and identify with it.[8] Heenen-Wolff writes, "the bisexual capacity – to desire, to love, to be capable of identifying with both sexes, belongs entirely to subjective psychic life and to the forces and vicissitudes which determine the singularity of every specific story" (2014, p. 148). In this respect, being able to pass through boundaries, temporarily able to assume the other's identity and to "dilute" differences, seems more productive, whereas a rigid distinction of elements which sound incompatible and risk turning out to be conflictual, indicates the fear of coming into contact with the ambiguous areas of our sexual identity and signals that splitting mechanisms are at work.

Ovid tells the myth of Hermaphroditus,[9] which is a myth of fusion, of cancelling separation to such an extent that a single body expresses both sexes. For Pontalis (1980), through the figure of Hermaphroditus, the manifest content of the myth unites the sexes of both parents in a single form, a form which, by its metamorphosis, becomes "an indeterminate being rather than a double one" (p. 52). The myth seems to give voice to a primitive desire of the human spirit, a universal fantasy, that aspiration to completeness and totality which may take us beyond our limits (old/young, living/dead, male/female) and bring us close to the divine, omnipotent, immortal order of things where all difference is obliterated, beginning with those between the sexes and the generations. And yet, doesn't such a re-conjoining which eliminates sexual difference, considered as "an existential lack that can be repaired" (ibid., 53), and eliminates it by means of a project centred and performed on itself instead of striving towards the other, perhaps turn out to be a sterile experience of impotence? Indeed, rather than attenuating sexual difference, doesn't the fantasy of unification serve to mitigate its effects, to protect from the pain of the experience of castration-separation? These are the questions Pontalis asks himself and we ask with him.

Gaddini's reflections go in the same direction, and in his paper *On Imitation* (1969) he describes two areas of the personality, the psychosensory and the psycho-oral, which coincide with the female and male elements in Winnicott. The analysis of the mechanism of imitation, its use and function in development, provides a way to approach the area of phenomena and disturbances associated with identity. Indeed, Gaddini's identification of the two areas underlines how the imitative processes of the sensory area move within the narcissistic sphere which has "more to do with the self than with the object" (Gaddini, 1969, p. 477) and represents a regressive defence against relationship and intimacy, which entails the recognition of the other-than-oneself and sets up the identificatory processes. Though not using the poetic language of Ovid, the meaning that Gaddini ascribes to this behaviour is not far from what is described in the myth. In fact, the psychic model of imitation – "imitating in order to be" – has become "that of re-establishing in a magical and omnipotent way the fusion of the self with the object" (ibid.). Eliminating or trying to eliminate differences, "the primitive imitative perception seems to lead to the hallucinatory image, to the phantasies of fusion *through modification of one's own body*, and to imitations, in the direction of the wish to be the object" (ibid., my italics). This relational mode, which Gaddini and others with him recognise as specific to narcissistic disturbances, seems to answer the need to avoid catastrophic experiences of separation and annihilation rather than generating a fluid psychic dialectic between male and female elements of the kind that Winnicott tells us about. Indeed, in cases with problems relating to gender identity – as we will see – one of the two elements, which is at odds with the physical characteristics, has taken the upper hand and we find ourselves faced with rigid and "absolute" modes of functioning.

On the other hand, the crux of bisexuality on the psychic level constitutes a crossroads in the process of development, signalling how the repression that is necessary for the transition through puberty towards the realisation of one's mature sexuality may be less definite and absolute than it seems and than we would like to believe. Adolescence represents a crucial moment for the subject from the viewpoint of identity and access to adult sexuality. It is the moment when we recognise that – with regard to our sexual characteristics – we are male or female, although this external correspondence may be coupled on the internal level with its denial, with deep conflict and uncertainty. This very theme of the problems connected to the definition of identity and gender is the focus of attention for analysts who work with adolescents. As Anna Maria Nicolò (2016) writes, "I confess that I look back with a certain nostalgia at the secure psychoanalytic set-ups for which 'working through the loss of bisexual omnipotence, the illusion of bisexuality and the illusion of the perfect body'" (Ladame and Perret-Catipovic, 1998) is a key element in psychological maturation. Today we find ourselves faced with more frequent and substantial phenomena of the kind Freud called "'polymorphous perverse functioning' typical of this age" (Nicolò, 2016, p. 187). Adolescent sexuality may well be "the litmus paper of our society and some of its discontents" (ibid., p. 182) and reflect certain changes on a societal level which influence the structuring of psychic life and have a particularly important effect during this period of life. The sexuality this author is referring to and which she considers widespread in adolescent lifestyle and behaviour is a sexuality expressed through the direct search for satisfactions that are predominantly sensual, narcissistic in kind rather than aimed at mature relational engagements of a genital kind.

Once again the image that comes to our aid is that of a loss of verticality and a loss of boundaries between clearly defined roles. This leads to a significant "identificatory dispersal" (Ruggiero, 2008, p. 279). And adolescence makes it possible to see the working and effects of "the ever-greater lability of collective reference points", "the disorganizing of the traditional models of identity, which are ever more numerous today", and "the reduction of the barrier between the generations" (ibid.). All of this seems to result in a dilution of the hierarchical structure in favour of an equalising of roles and relationships in which the sibling order predominates over that of parent and child (Mitchell, 2004). Indeed, the sibling order would the right one for expressing minimal difference as opposed to the maximal difference described by parental relations. This claim is connected to the author's hypothesis that non-reproductive sexuality, which she defines as polymorphously perverse and somewhat questionably connects to gender rather than to sexual difference, is a sexuality realised through

127

"lateral" relationships between equals, rather than vertical ones.[10] This implies a redefinition of roles which appear ever more vague, with ambiguity and difficulty, if not rejection, prevailing over the acceptance of the "limits imposed by reality, beginning with one's own body and gender identity, and the recognition of one's own differentiated subjectivity" (Ruggiero, 2017).

The difficulty in accepting these limits intersects with the expansion of technological and biotechnological developments which may feed the illusion of limitless possibilities, at least with regard to the matters that concern us, sometimes appearing "deaf" to the psychological repercussions and the consequences on the subjective level, which seem to us to be more complicated and tortuous than a linear vision adhering only to the politically correct may lead us to imagine. The direction of these changes is towards the ambiguous and the undifferentiated, and the topic of bisexuality, which used to exit through the door of the adolescent crux, comes back in through the window of custom and fashion, sustained also by the technologies and biotechnologies which allow us always to imagine, even if we can't always realise, the possibility of being simultaneously Hermaphroditus and his nymph Salmacis, and of passing through territories that would be forbidden to our manifest differences.

7.3 The question of gender

The question of gender and the new forms of sexuality seems to take in the terms of the problem with difference in a compelling and dramatic manner. The topic of psychic bisexuality and the way that psychoanalysis has addressed it run implicitly, like a *fil rouge*, through the debate about gender and about the deconstruction of the concepts of male and female as rigid and opposite categories, which is of course a fundamental idea in gender studies. Taking part in an open discussion about how the parameters for assessing sexual perversions have changed, modifying the very idea of what can and cannot be considered perversion, Ann D'Ercole (2014) in her very evocatively subtitled paper, *The Surrender of Gender*, returns to the topic of bisexuality which – in her opinion – also remains a central crux in the question of gender. The accusation levelled at Freud and psychoanalysis is that they could not or would not follow to its extreme conclusions the theme of bisexuality introduced in the *Three Essays*. Ann D'Ercole's reading seems partial. In her view, Freud's text only features "the ghost of bisexuality" and his developmental project only headed in one direction, towards the attainment of the sexuality that is considered "normal" (heterosexual, monogamous, and pro-creative) according to the *Zeitgeist*, and she certainly does not take into account his complexities and indeed contradictions on this subject in the *Essays* and in later works. Her interpretation, like others on this theme, does not seem to have absorbed the fact that for psychoanalysis, as Winnicott has clearly shown, bisexuality refers to the "play" of psychic positions (being versus doing) that are maintained within any sexual evolution. In an essay which has become a classic of the literature on gender, Judith Butler (1995)[11] uses the topic of bisexuality to maintain the thesis that heterosexuality is achieved at the cost of renunciations and prohibitions, and gender is acquired by the refusal of homosexual attachments. Thus, at the origin of "the formation of what we might call the gendered character of the ego" (p. 169) there would be a loss on the part of the self and a disavowed grief which cannot be wept for.

The theories and shifts of opinion in this sphere, which have their roots in the political and civil battles of the Eighties for women's rights and sexual equality, have often moved in a different direction from psychoanalysis, partly as the result of a certain confusion between *facts* and *rights*, as Chiland (2004) correctly notes. Starting from the presupposition that gender difference is inevitably resolved into the predominance of one over the other, where the male asserts its superiority at the expense of the female, these movements oppose this with an idea of sexual equality in which everyone exercises their own right to make a responsible choice in the construction of their own subjective world, which includes their gender. Indeed, for gender theorists the social sphere replaces the biological, and gender is the result of power relations rather than of sexual differences. In these currents of thought and their antagonism to psychoanalysis we hear the echo of Foucault's interpretation of psychoanalysis as a discipline and practice which sustains normalisation and the predominance of one gender over the other. Therefore, mistrusting and rejecting sexual difference as an acquired and static datum, these movements legitimise the demands for sex-changes in the name of the freedom of self-affirmation.

These considerations lead us to a crucial question. How can we interpret the phenomena connected to gender identity? What is the impact of the new directions in the "deconstruction of gender",[12] especially the achievement of sexual reassignment made possible by technology, on our way of thinking about sexual difference? We are confronting claims which challenge not just psychoanalytic thinking, but our thinking as a society, which tends to make sex and gender coincide and founds our identity on this coincidence. The biological difference at the base of sexual difference is a fact which precedes the construction of the idea of gender and the representations of female and male which all of us form over the course of our existence and which constitute interpretations of an undeniable difference. Studies of gender identity have focused on how the crucial step in its constitution is gender-*designation*, more or less in accordance with the assignment of sex, which is done by the other. It is not taken for granted that the attribution of sex at birth coincides with anatomical signs in the same way. It is a matter of distinguishing "between the *psychical representation of the body* – which is more a fantasmatic body than a real body, a body of drives which privileges the *felt* and the not immediately figurable – and the *body that is objective and spatialized* according to anatomy, based more on vision and the external apprehension of sexual difference" (Gibeault, 1993, p. 170).

The question of gender is relatively recent and was first used by Money in 1955 to indicate the role of the individual in society as male and female. The term "gender" does not coincide with sexuality and cannot be superimposed on it, and the "gender conundrum" (Birksted-Breen, 1993) which hides behind the male/female binomial refers as much to the journey of identity-formation as to the process of being assigned a role by the other, and to their intertwining. Later, it was Stoller (1964, 1968) who described the question of gender, connecting it to the subjective state of each individual in relation to their own sexual characters, male or female. Stoller was also the first to identify and define "core gender identity", which he differentiated from the journey through the development of gender identity which continues at least until adolescence. "Core gender identity" would be a structure that is established very early and would be unmodifiable after two or three years. In fact, over time a slightly different perspective has been introduced, one that tends instead to emphasise the variability and complexity of developmental pathways and finds a new and more appropriate definition for this type of manifestation as "atypical organization of gender identity". This is the formula advocated by Di Ceglie (2002) to describe the non-coincidence between the external reality of the body and subjective perception. The introduction of this new expression is by no means insignificant because it underlines "an element of flexibility and greater variability in the developmental pathways of children with gender identity disorders". The debate between Stoller and Di Ceglie on this point concerns the concreteness and unmodifiability of "core gender identity" maintained by Stoller as opposed to Di Ceglie's more mobile view which emphasises the multidimensional causality at the origin of these phenomena, the need to keep paying attention to the continual and complex interaction between internal and external factors without ruling out a priori the possible presence of biological factors, but without deceiving oneself into thinking that an atypical development can easily be changed. Chiland (1997, 2003, 2008), an author who has long been concerned with this subject, describes the origin of the discussion about the question of gender, connecting it to those rare but nonetheless real cases of children born with alterations in their genital organs (intersex) who receive a gender attribution at odds with their biological sex.[13] However, the real problem occurs with transsexuals, for whom problems arise on the psychological level in the firm conviction of belonging to the opposite sex rather than the one they have been assigned. For these individuals, the objective is to have a body which corresponds to their feeling of who they are, with the aim of resolving a conflict that is reduced to a purely physical event.

Outside the debate about the greater or lesser fixity of the nuclear identity, the genesis of the concept of gender identity refers to very early periods of development and is situated in that preverbal region of the mother–baby and parents–baby relationship in which physical and sensory exchanges predominate. One hypothesis would be that it could be located in the area of the subjective object, to use Winnicott's (1971) terminology, in which the "sense of being is something that antedates the idea of being-at-one-with, because there has not yet been anything else except identity" (p. 80).[14] Thinking about what, according to Parsons (2000), is decisive for a behaviour to be perverse or otherwise and about his insistence on the recognition of the *other* as a person with a separate identity, all of this also offers points for reflection about the question of gender. The atypical organisation of gender identity is a challenge to us on this specific matter of relationality. Indeed, it seems that in these situations, where the imitative mode and sensoriality predominate, the avoidance of separative processes because of catastrophic anxieties prevents *ab origine* the setting up of a relational space and the initiating of effective introjective and identificatory pathways. An author like Argentieri (2006) excludes manifestations of atypical gender identity from the classical picture of the perversions and instead interprets them as regressions towards the ambiguous and un-differentiated (in this respect, following Gaddini's line of interpreta-tion), features which characterise our era (Marion, 2015c, 2016b) and call into question the two cornerstones of the Oedipus complex, the differences between the sexes and the generations.

The treatment of children, including very young ones, who present with disturbances of gender identity offers a privileged viewpoint for catching *in fieri* the complex vicissitudes which ac-company the construction of identity (Di Ceglie, 2002; Malpas, 2011; Quagliata and Di Ceglie, 2015; Marion, 2016b; Carratelli and Massaro, 2016; Quintiliani, 2016). Carratelli and Massaro (2016) in particular write about the creation of a "baby in pink" or a "mirage object" which would represent the imitative identity supported by a defensive system based on imitation at the expense of identificatory and introjective processes. According to the authors, in these si-tuations the baby would become the object of psychic "colonisa-tion" by an unexplored maternal/parental nucleus or by unresolved problems with their roots in a transgenerational dimension.

This hypothesis is shared by Chiland (2008), according to whom

> in the case of very young children who reject their assigned gender, when we are able to observe parent-child interactions, we discover that the parents' attitude towards masculinity and femininity, together with their own sexuality, has an influence on their infant − who grasps something of the parents' inner experience beyond their manifest behaviour and interprets the conscious and unconscious messages they communicate.

According to these hypotheses, the theme of recognition is implicit in the problem of constructing gender identity since it is a process by which the subject feels seen by the other and invested with sense and meaning. If it is *seeing that gives form* (Wright, 1991) in the operation of recognition of oneself by the other, but also of oneself in the other, we can locate the dichotomies between biological sex, social sex and psychological sex (to use Chiland's terminology), between internalised identifications and anatomical sex. This line of thought calls up the presence of parental fantasies which cut across and condition biological reality: "the attribution of a sex to the infant by the parents acts as a *psychic* imprint … This imprint is constituted on the basis of the perception of the infant's body as a sexed form which is confirmed or invalidated by the parents" (Green, 1973). The early occurrence of these processes and the prevalence of primitive anti-separative defences would explain an observation made by several authors who have addressed the problem, which concerns the difficulty that these subjects have with symbolic thought, as if their problems were irreducibly "planted" in the body and left no space for any psychic working-through.

And yet, despite the hypotheses put forward about the genesis of such organisations, the fact remains that we are faced with something which still has the character of an enigma. The definition which Di Ceglie (2002) gave some years ago of those who are affected by this kind of malaise as feeling like "a stranger in my own body" still, in my opinion, effectively conveys the quality of these subjects' suffering. This is an area which touches on the mind–body relationship, or rather on the relationship between the mind and the body's sexual characteristics. The emergence of a discord between the two spheres, a discord that is not easy to access, is the source of malaise not only for the subjects it affects but also for those around them, including the professionals who have to deal with this discontent. The conviction that one's psychological sex does not correspond to one's biological sex, the perception of feeling oneself to be in the wrong body – above all, the possibility of passing from one gender to the other by modifying one's sexual characteristics and giving concrete medical and surgical answers to profound psychic discontent, challenges us to address crucial and highly delicate questions.

7.4 Difference versus indifference

The individual subjects we are talking about are bearers of a painful difference (the non-coincidence between biological sex and psychological identity) and by requesting sexual reassignment they are responding to a dysphoria that they consider intolerable. The crossing of boundaries once considered impassable is not a pain-free operation and reveals itself as a challenge to psychoanalytic thinking too since the game is being played in the theatre of the body instead of being taken on as an engine of psychic working-through.

Today progress seems to be being made by other psychoanalytic perspectives on this problem. Perhaps something similar is happening to the change in the consideration of homosexuality. Beyond the vicissitudes which have accompanied and still accompany the debate about this subject, and beyond the interpretations that can be given, there is no doubt that the therapeutic stance has changed profoundly in recent years (Bassi and Galli, 2000; Corbett, 2002; Pozzi and Thanopulos, 2006). Acknowledging the independence of sexual identity from the multiplicity of object choices, which all belong on the spectrum of expressions through which human sexual experience manifests itself, the homosexual path is one of many possible ones that the individual can follow.[15] As a consequence, and always bearing in mind the observation by Parsons, the homosexual choice cannot be considered immature, the result of a fixation and/ or regression to a pregenital stage, the criterion for judgement having shifted to the relational quality. On the other hand, several authoritative psychoanalysts such as McDougall (1989) and Loewald (1979) have admitted to changing their minds about this, especially with regard to what may be considered mature or immature from the mental viewpoint. The interpretation that sees pregenital experience accompanying the genital and fully belonging to adult sexual life (Heenen-Wolff, 2011) challenges the hierarchical idea of psychic development and intrapsychic and relational functioning where the pregenital would be located on a lower level in a hypothetical evolutionary scale: "the heterosexual genital constellation is but *one* of the forms which infantile sexuality may arrive at, the 'polymorphic perverse' elements always remaining alive and active" (p. 1218). In the end, still citing Heenen-Wolff, a person's sexual orientation tells us hardly anything about their maturity, integrity or mental health.

Returning to the question of gender, we must acknowledge another element that is not insignificant in evaluating these themes: i.e. how the way of thinking about the body and its reality has profoundly changed in recent decades. In opposition to Freud's (1924) conviction, anatomy does not seem to be destiny and the body has become part of the construction of a "subjective" world, of a "personal project" which also involves the right to modifications and constructions of reality that are different from what we are and do not want to be (Lemma, 2005). Despite our lack of "analytic models that tolerate body/psyche discontinuities" (Saketopoulou, 2014), the difference between the feeling of one's gender identity and the body which does not coincide with it is starting to be seen as no longer just a symptom of a narcissistic disorder or the expression of a perverse solution. The psychoanalytic literature, especially from the United States, uses a perspective which emphasises process rather than structure (Kulish, 2010), and complexity and fluidity are indicated as more useful concepts for approaching the topic of gender identity.

This is the direction proposed by Avgi Saketopoulou, who in 2014, in the *Journal of the American Psychoanalytic Association*, published an article about the treatment of a 5-year-old who was born male but at the time of the request for help completely and determinedly identified with the female gender. The core of the author's concept is expressed in the title of her paper, "Mourning the Body as Bedrock." Reading this study confronts us with a different perspective from those considered previously in the way we address this type of disorder. The little patient, who resolutely denies being a boy and insists on being called by a girl's name, is struggling on two fronts, an external reality at odds with what he feels inside and his sensation of gender which he compares in a doubtful and painful manner with what he encounters in his body. Like homosexuality, which cannot be considered a *single thing* but takes shape according to specific personal permutations, so, for this author, transsexual experience does not present as a unitary phenomenon but is rather the point of arrival of heterogeneous paths and compromise formations. The analyst refrains from going into aetiological factors in the origin of this situation. Indeed, from her point of view, speculations about the origin of gender dysphoria often correspond to excessively rigid clinical positions. Non-normative gender must be accepted as a vital and practicable subjective reality. In support of this idea, Saketopoulou introduces the expression "massive gender trauma" by which she means the experience of being unacknowledged by the primary object in the conflict between birth sex and the different gender identity. Gender dysphoria thus exposes the subject (generally at a very early age) to obstructive and traumatic feelings arising from the powerful desire for coherence between one's sense of belonging to a gender and one's bodily morphology.

The problems and difficulties, including the relational, which arise from this are the consequence of the situation, not its origin. The focus of the intervention should therefore be directed towards the work of mourning for the birth body and the feeling of gender ("mourning the loss of the body as bedrock"), especially addressing the distress that derives from the fantasy of having been born into the wrong body. This means helping subjects affected by gender dysphoria to mentalise the contradictory and unbearable feelings which are overwhelming them. The analyst's effort and attention are directed towards accepting the patient's feelings of being born into the wrong body and welcoming the distress which derives from this maladjustment. What becomes significant from the viewpoint of pathology are the defensive mechanisms activated in order to confront the trauma, which may acquire a life of their own, distorting and dominating the patient's psychic life from inside.

As will be understood, we find ourselves faced with an inversion of perspective because, according to this point of view, whatever solutions the patient pursues, analytic work centres on the suffering caused by the birth body and the working-through of the mourning for the painful non-coincidence/difference between the birth body and the feeling of gender. This work of mourning also becomes central because, despite surgical and hormonal interventions, which we know to be a long and painful calvary, the body will never align itself with one's experience of gender and will never produce the full matching-up that is wished for. On this last point, the various perspectives in the interpretation of gender dysphoria all agree. Indeed, shared experience reveals how confining treatment to the anatomical level never completely resolves the problem since "reconstruction" and "reassignment" will never obtain the result of making the dysphoria not have happened, with the additional awareness which the patient may acquire later on, that "the destruction is irreversible" (Argentieri, 2006, p. 79).

The panorama of gender studies seems more like a jagged set of outcrops than a unified landscape. Some currents of thought push us well beyond anatomical construction to resolve the difference. The front represented by "queer-theory", for example, affirms and exalts the concept of non–identity. What counts is ambiguity and the right to all the expressions in sexual practice, which must be celebrated through the body. It is a reality which challenges the concepts of identity, order and system, and where the meanings linked to roles, positions, and boundaries collapse (Marcus and McNamara, 2013). According to Ann D'Ercole (2014), trans desires have produced a growing clinical awareness of the subjective variety associated with gender non-conformity. The changes in this sphere, even the most extreme, are written into the ways we organise our lives and relationships differently from in the past. This is therefore to be ascribed to the sphere of difference rather than to the domain of perversion.

The very concept of perversion would be eliminated in favour of the celebration of difference. In the "age of the 'queer'" we should accept that there is no precise attribution of gender: "we should all see ourselves as transgendered … as and when we like, we ought to be able to be man, woman, or both" (Chiland, 2008, p. 28).

The theme, which is so complex and also a matter of specific geographical realities that are not marginal and the various ways in which it is elaborated and treated, can be effectively summed up in an observation which Nancy Kulish (2010) offers in her historical survey. Contemporary theories about gender certainly challenge our reference points, our psychoanalytic "magnetic north" – as Saketopoulou (2014) calls it – and prompt us to question them. And yet, if the need for coherence, for identity can hide problems, this is equally true for diversity and ambiguity, especially when "ideologically" celebrated or "idealized". One point in particular is emphasised by Kulish, and I agree with her, which concerns the risk of idealising difference, as a reaction to marginalisation. In this case what is not being taken into account is precisely the meaning of the idealisation and the objective it is meeting, that of denying the suffering caused by feelings of non-integration and depersonalisation, by the experience of being a non-conforming subject, and thereby of denying the human need of its opposite: that is, the need for coherence and certainty of identity. In the set-ups we have described and which often sound provocative, "in a transgender society, post-father and post-mother" (Chasseguet-Smirgel, 2003) we catch something paradoxical: *difference* is so affirmed and celebrated that it cancels itself out, veering towards an essential *in-difference* in which one thing is worth the same as another and all forms of expression are located on the same plane.

7.5 Who's afraid of history?

While in *Civilisation and its Discontents* (1929) and elsewhere, Freud admitted the differences in sexual constitution and the importance of acknowledging them in order not to deprive "a fair number of them from sexual enjoyment" (p. 104), discussion of this topic – as I have tried to describe – has become enormously complicated. The question posed by Kaës, whether the construction of identity models, of male-female relations, the "gender regimes" (Lett, 2014), are invariants or constructs rooted in history and modified over time, is open. We have seen that some American psychoanalysts who work on these questions of gender propose the idea, in a variety of versions, that a dynamic and non-linear theory of development may be more fruitful. As Marcus and McNamara (2013) maintain, postmodern receptivity is oriented towards a variety of narratives about gender, and the conceptualisation of psychological health cannot be constrained into evolutionary models which lead inexorably towards binary gender. These are "strong" claims which call into question the developmental guidelines that we have known, considering them prescriptive and restrictive, potentially disembodied with respect to the variety of gender paradigms.

The modifications related to the sphere of sexuality and conceptualisations of gender profoundly influence our way of thinking about it and about ourselves, even if we are not always aware of this, and "leave their mark on the anthropological landscape" (Lingiardi, 2006). The Oedipus complex, which the psychoanalytic community considered the fulcrum for understanding individual development and describing the inner world – "the sexual compass of psychoanalysis" (Chiland, 2008) – has also been violently shaken up and altered in the light of all this. And it is not only because Oedipus has been juxtaposed with Dionysus, who seems more capable of accepting certain contemporary transformations which are dominating the scene of identity and sexual practice. It is also because grand narratives are destined for grand changes and, as Ogden (2009) writes, "it is task of each new generation to make use of, destroy, and reinvent the creations of the previous generation" (p. 114). But can Dionysus really be the answer to the anxiety, the doubts which such whirling and violent changes induce in every one of us?

What we are witnessing presents us with a wider spectrum of solutions, in relation both to the binary choice of gender, and to parental links (the "new parentings" resulting from procreative choices and same-sex couples), the ties of dependency, and the demand that all of this be recognised and accepted. The plurality of subjective choices, the liberation from prescribed social forms and imposed roles, all renders difference more nuanced, and functions too become ever more interchangeable. Social and technological changes, besides being reflected in psychic life, seem also to hook onto something that is latent in it and corresponds to these changes, as the myth of Hermaphroditus teaches us. Chasseguet-Smirgel (2003), adopting a very critical stance, wonders, "Can we ask ourselves if it is biological discoveries that are arousing senseless desires or whether the desires have impelled the discoveries, or is it a reciprocal action?" (p. 14).

In this scenario, the value of personal life takes priority not only over the sense of duty, but above all over the sense of limitation, and "construction kits of biographical combination possibilities come into being ... In the transition from 'standard to elective biography', the conflictual and historically unprecedented type of the *do-it-yourself biography* separates out" (Beck, 1986, p. 135).

The right to choose and to achieve self-realisation in all spheres, alongside the decline of traditional family ties and of solid, lasting professional commitments, have contributed to the transition from an identity structure formed along an existential path marked out in ritual moments, to a mobile identity which includes the "integration" of multiple intrapsychic and interpsychic experiences (Honneth, 2002). What once drew on the willingness to accept both the authority of the role and submission to it, is today strongly shaken by the processes of levelling which penetrate individuals as much as groups and couple-relationships, by that *passion for equivalence* that Chasseguet-Smirgel speaks about (2003). The use of the Internet is a powerful detonator of these forms of parithetic relation, but it is also at the origin of a re-definition of the space we inhabit, where the "virtual" dimension widens the field and our own points of reference, offering a potential place for a new type of relational link (Corbett, 2013; Marzi, 2017).[16]

In this context of multiplying possibilities it is the sense of limitation that is under attack. The enormous potentialities offered by technology and biotechnology are becoming welded to the narcissistic root that is present in all of us and impossible to give up, and with the desire to assert ourselves omnipotently, free from any restraint. In what way do these phenomena interrogate or threaten the dogmas of psychoanalysis (Laufer, 2014)? How distant from our psychoanalytic values do we consider these new scenarios to be? What anxieties do we have to face up to "when what we have long considered to be our magnetic north becomes unmoored" (Saketopoulou, 2014, p. 799)? In order not to indulge in a "melancholy paradigm" we must acknowledge both that "psychoanalysis cannot escape the age in which it is practised" (Laufer, 2014) and that it is itself a part of that age. We are faced with the need to reflect on the significance and impact which such violent transfor-mations, capable of producing a suspension in anthropological con-tinuity (Mazzarella, 2017), have on the individual in the way we understand sexuality and the still vaster sphere of our relationships. The psychic world is the product of a complex interaction between inner world and outer environment, although we must acknowledge that it is not a straightforward matter to establish how and whether the modifications that we are recording on the external plane translate into real mutations of psychic dynamics and functioning. Indeed, tracing the links between the two domains, the social and the psychic, is a fascinating task, but not an easy one. "History is not written while the events are happening: we have to bear in mind that changes in psychoanalysis, especially in psychoanalytic theory, will be seen retrospectively" (Ungar et al., 2013, p. 482).

The expansion of limits which multiplies the possibilities of choice and solutions creates an uncertainty about boundaries. Undefined frontiers, as in Coetzee's book *Waiting for the Barbarians* (1980), undermine the stability of our Empire and risk making us feel like his protagonist, someone who has lost his way or is following a road which leads him nowhere. Perhaps, like him, we could say, "There has been something staring me in the face, and still I do not see it." The violation and alteration of boundaries opens the way to new scenarios, and certainly to a complication of intersubjectivity and intrapsychic transmission, to a "blood work"[17] that is still hard for us to think about. As Kaës (2005) puts it, paraphrasing Freud, it is about "that psychic work which is imposed on the psyche because of its fundamental link with intersubjectivity", since we are being inhabited more and more by other people inside us. We are challenged by a multiple subject and if we are to think about this we must problematise our knowledge and also revise our conceptual apparatus. "Barbarian invasions" compel us into complex operations, which Canetti (1977) described in more poetic terms as "vastness":

> The power to contain very many things within oneself no matter how contradictory they are, to know that everything that seems irreconcilable nevertheless subsists in its own environment and to feel this without losing oneself in fear, and instead knowing that one needs to call it by its own name and meditate upon it.

Notes

1 The first case of *post mortem* fertilisation in Italy dates from 1999 and involved a woman suddenly widowed at the age of 31. After a case lasting about two years, the Tribunal ruled in favour of the woman's request to use her frozen embryos.

2 It should be noted that in the Italian and English translation of *Über-Ich*, the hierarchical sense seems less evident, or fainter, than in the German formulation where *über* first of all conveys a precise reference to space, and this is its regular sense in everyday usage: "above", "up", "over". This signals a differentiated, diversified order. That this hierarchical structure also reflects an idea of man and society, "the age of Freud" (Zaretsky, 2004), in which the lights and shadows of a "solid society" converge, in contrast to Baumann's "liquid" one, is a topic which would require a separate discussion.

3 In the Freudian system of thought there are two distinct conceptions of the organisation of the psychic apparatus. A first (the so-called "topographical model") in which the main distinction is between unconscious, preconscious, and conscious, and a "structural model" after 1920, in which three different agencies are distinguished in the psychic apparatus: the *Id*, referring to the demands of the drives, the *Ego* which represents the person as such, in relation to internal and external demands, and the *Super-Ego*, the adjudicating agency, heir to the internalisation of the parental figures and of prohibitions, re-presentative of the subject's ideal requirements. There are many reasons for the impulse to imagine a different organisational system: on the one hand, greater attention paid to the role and function of unconscious defences, and on the other the discovery of the role played by identifications in the individual constitution. As Petrella (1988) writes, "in 1922, with the so-called structural model, Freud makes a considerable qualitative leap, though one that does not cancel out the previous arrangement, but in fact develops it, sharpening some of its constituent terms. To the three 'rooms' [*stanze*] of the topographical model, he adds three 'agencies' [*istanze*]" (p. 119).

4 In an unpublished paper, Giuseppe Squitieri (2007) claims that psychic bisexuality is of fundamental importance for the development of psychoanalytic theory and constitutes a decisive contribution to the understanding of the genesis of the personality. It is complex set of concepts and, for this very reason, subject to a variety of developments.

5 Winnicott addresses this topic in the chapter of *Playing and Reality* (1971) devoted to "Creativity and its Origins".

6 For Winnicott, the experience of *being* "is perhaps the simplest of all experiences ... Here one finds a true continuity of generations, being which is passed on from one generation to another, via the female element of men and women and of male and female infants" (1971, p. 80).

7 Winnicott writes, "As I see it, this difficult soliloquy is difficult be-cause Hamlet had himself not got the clue to his dilemma – since it lay

in his own changed state … If the play is looked at in this way it seems possible to use Hamlet's altered attitude to Ophelia and his cruelty to her as a picture of his ruthless rejection of his own female element, now split off and handed over to her, with his unwelcome male element threatening to take over his whole personality. The cruelty to Ophelia can be a measure of his reluctance to abandon his split-off female element" (ibid., p. 84).

8 In his *Thalassa: A Theory of Genitality* (1933), Ferenczi well captures how bisexuality integrates castration into the heterosexual union through the partners' mutual identification: "Psychoanalytic experience has established that the acts preparatory to coitus have as their function the bringing about of an identification with the sexual partner through intimate contact and embraces. Kissing, stroking, biting, embracing serve to efface the boundaries between the egos of the sexual partners … [the man] can therefore quite easily permit himself the luxury of erection, since in consequence of the identification which has taken place the carefully guarded member certainly will not get lost, seeing that it remains with a being with whom the ego has identified itself" (p. 377).

9 In *Metamorphoses*, Ovid tells how the nymph Salmacis falls in love with Hermaphroditus, son of Hermes and Aphrodite, but is rejected by him. While he is bathing in the waters of a lake belonging to the nymph, Salmacis comes up and embraces him, praying to the gods to let them never be parted. The gods grant her request by merging the two into a single body with two sexes.

10 Juliet Mitchell's (2004) thesis about the difference between the concepts of "gender" and "sexual difference" consists in linking sexual difference to reproductive sexuality, and hence bodily difference is also viewed generically as a reproductive difference. By contrast, the concept of difference is not intrinsic to "gender", which – according to Mitchell – refers instead to polymorphously perverse sexuality. This thesis has been contested by Colette Chiland (2004) for whom gender does not express any form of sexuality, reproductive or otherwise. It is an expression of being, connected to the self and the identity. I agree with this position, also considering the biological aspect that we must take into consideration when we speak of male and female sexuality, whereas gender is a psychological and social construct.

11 The essay *Melancholy Gender – Refused Identification* was presented for the first time in 1993 at the meeting of the American Psychoanalytic Association and published in 1995 in *Psychoanalytic Dialogues*, and lastly in the anthology edited by Muriel Dimen and Virginia Goldner, *Gender in Psychoanalytic Space* (2002). In its Italian version, published by Il Saggiatore in 2006, it is called *La decostruzione del genere*.

12 The subtitle to the Italian edition of Dimen and Goldner's volume well expresses the lines followed by the various contributors: *Teoria femminista, cultura postmoderna e clinica psicoanalitica*. Gender is understood as "compromise formation" and the binary solution is felt as a constraint to be overcome: "Attention to what is relative, constructed, and multiple has changed the way we think about psychic structure and its development. By affirming a 'decentred' view of the self, mental functioning is seen as a configuration of discontinuous and non-linear states of consciousness in dialectical relation to the necessary idea – the healthy illusion – of a unitary self" (Lingiardi, 2006, p. 10).

13 During the nineteenth and twentieth centuries, observation of the external genitalia was accompanied by an investigation based on the histology of the gonads, later followed by a karyotype test. The idea was to establish, on the balance of probabilities, which gender the infant might feel most at home in. To this was added the possibility of choosing whether or not intervene surgically in order to modify the imperfect genital organ. During the Nineties, in the United States, patients who were dissatisfied with the results obtained by surgical interventions on their genitals when they were babies, formed a society, not recognising themselves in their assigned gender (cf. Chiland, 2008).

14 The concept of "subjective object" is central to Winnicott's (1971) theorising. Based on the idea of a state of primary non-integration of the personality and absolute dependence on the environment, the object is experienced as a "subjective object" in which there is as yet no difference between self and other. In this phase, the mother/other guarantees the supportive function appropriate to the baby's needs in such a way that the baby feels an illusory sensation of omnipotence, different from, and not superimposable on, omnipotent defence.

15 There is a rediscovered letter from 1935 in which Freud replies to a mother who had asked him to help her gay son: "I gather from your letter, that your son is a homosexual ... Homosexuality is assuredly no advantage, but it is nothing to be ashamed of, no vice, no degradation, it cannot be classified as an illness. We consider it to be a variation of the sexual function, produced by a certain arrest of sexual development. Many highly respectable individuals of ancient and modern times have been homosexuals, several of the greatest men among them ... By asking me if I can help, you mean I suppose if I can abolish homosexuality, and make normal heterosexuality take its place. The answer is in a general way we cannot promise to achieve it ... What analysis can do for your son runs in a different line. If he is unhappy, neurotic, torn by conflicts, inhibited in his social life analysis may bring him harmony, peace of mind, full efficiency whether he remains a homosexual or gets changed ..." (Letter written in English, exhibited in London at the Wellcome Collection, 20

November 2014 – 20 September 2015). The letter is in the archive of the Kinsey Institute at Indiana University (Library of Congress ref: https://www.loc.gov/resource/mss39990.OV1317/?sp=2&r=0.256,0.418,0.477, 0.227,0) A transcript can be accessed at https://lettersofnote.com/2009/10/29/homosexuality-is-nothing-to-be-ashamed-of/.

16 Marzi (2018) writes, "We have, nevertheless, become progressively more aware of how the arrival of the digital age, by influencing the way in which one is a subject, may consequently influence the practice of psychoanalysis and the analytic relationship and setting, and thus induce a possible dynamism in the analyst's own identity. This can be brought about by the increase in his level of relational suffering faced with unfamiliar phenomena in the session, but also by reorienting and probably enriching his capacity to approach "new" patients, thereby avoiding the scotomisation of the cognitive power of psychoanalysis. Fundamentally, psychoanalysis has every right (and I would say duty) to challenge those forms of sociality and of mentalisation which put themselves forward as new. 'The feeling of being frightened exists – in the human condition – but knowing how to tie oneself to the helm of a ship tackling the storm of towering new-unknown waves also exists'" (Marzi, 2018, p. 103).

17 *Blood Work* (2002) is the title of a film directed by Clint Eastwood who, by means of a gripping detective plot, narrates the complicated circumstances of a heart transplant case and the consequences of this experience on the feeling of personal identity, on the boundaries of the self and of relations with other people.

THE LOGIC OF PLEASURE AND
THE DISCONTENT OF DESIRE

Dear love, for nothing less than thee
Would I have broke this happy dream;
     It was a theme
For reason, much too strong for fantasy,
Therefore thou wak'd'st me wisely; yet
My dream thou brok'st not, but continued'st it.
Thou art so true that thoughts of thee suffice
To make dreams truths, and fables histories;
Enter these arms, for since thou thought'st it best,
Not to dream all my dream, let's act the rest.

                    (John Donne, *The Dream*)

8.1 Pleasure at the root of psychic life

If, as Freud claims many times in his work, especially at the beginning of his first *Contribution to the Psychology of Love* (1910–17),
the task of describing the conditions of amorous life has mainly fallen
to the poets – at least up to the time in which Freud was writing –
then Donne's verse performs this task with particular grace and refined elegance. In the poem that Donne dedicates to his beloved
wife Anne, we find what Cristina Campo calls "one of those magic
circles which allow us to move into a space beyond time and beyond
the world" (1971, p. 9) and which, from our viewpoint, we would

call the capacity for describing the sexual pleasure encompassed by the carnality of the senses and the ecstasy of the imagination.

It is also the description which Freud gives in *Formulations on the Two Principles of Mental Functioning* (1911), speaking about the pleasure principle in opposition to the reality principle:

> As pleasure-principle, Freud had posited the *Lust-Prinzip*, the sexual drive; and he had placed this principle at the 'roots' of psychic life in its conflictual relationship with the *Realität-Prinzip*. He had thus developed a theory which explained the 'affects' of pleasure and unpleasure as the psychic derivatives of somatic quantities, from which in turn derived the ideational processes and cognitive functions through a long and complicated work of evolution and mediation between the demands of the body and those of the outside world.
>
> (Riolo 2017, p. 519)[1]

The activity of thought to which Freud refers, which does not function on the basis of the reality principle, is closely correlated to the sexual drive and subject to the pleasure principle. It is expressed in the imagination, in children's play, in poetry, dreaming and creative activity in the broad sense. The pleasure-Ego can only desire, but in terms of *Wunscherfüllung* (wish-fulfilment) rather than *Befriedigung*, which is directed instead to the satisfaction and gratification of a need. Indeed, the chief characteristic of desire-pleasure is mostly expressed in psychic-ludic pleasure and not in the requirements of need (Seulin, 2014). We know, of course, that the satisfaction of a need produces pleasure, and yet the pleasure we are referring to here is a different one that promotes psychic life and defines its quality. Infantile sexuality, as we have been able to see, in the multitude of forms in which it is expressed, describes this tendency to pleasure very well. On the journey that leads to adult sexuality it represents the source of the psychic apparatus's creativity and richness of functioning and maintains the "capacity for investing the world with passion" (Ambrosiano and Gaburri, 2008, p. 5). The recovery of pleasure is also a request which patients address to us, more or less explicitly and clearly. "Suffering" pain also means accepting the aspiration for life to be restored, that pleasure should flow again, that a Calvary should be followed by an Easter, as Ferro vividly puts it (2015).

Speaking about time in sexuality and the status of infantile sexuality, I have considered the hypotheses about its genesis and how the original psychic model has been joined by relational theories and the acknowledgement of the role and weight of the object's response in defining the quality of pleasure. I recalled the words of Bollas (2000) for whom, in the absence of the mother's desire for and affective investment in her baby's body, autoeroticism is configured not in terms of a search for pleasure accompanied by the production of fantasies, but instead as a substitute for a lack of sensoriality. The pleasure that infiltrates the care and nurture given by the parents is also the reflection of the pleasure that the parental couple has been able to feel in themselves and in the area of sexuality. The presence of desire, that "burlap" which Corbett (2009) speaks about, a desire that "does not evaluate" (to quote Paola Camassa's definition in a conversation with me) testifies to a link with shared pleasure, of which the sexual kind is certainly the highest and most specific form. This pleasure, which reclaims its root in the body, cannot be separated "from bodies in relation" (Riolo, 2017), and as Green claimed many years ago, reflecting on these very vicissitudes encountered by the theme of sexuality in psychoanalytic theory: "the role of a sexual relationship is not to feed and nurture but to reach ecstasy in mutual enjoyment" (1995, p. 877).[2] The same concept is expressed in another form and another way by the writer Melania Mazzucco in *La lunga attesa dell'angelo* [The long wait for the angel] through the words of the painter Jacomo Robusti *aka* Tintoretto, who at the end of his life wonders what will become of him after death: "In returning to the source of all things, how will I be able to know a perfect happiness if my body isn't given back to me in its entirety? My body, not my consciousness, has given me ecstasy and the certainty of melting into the infinite ... My body is the part of me that makes me whole" (Mazzucco, 2008, p. 106).

The metaphor of orality to which Green refers in order to contest a change of direction which had obscured the role and significance of sexuality in psychoanalytic theory – a metaphor that Freud had used himself to indicate the genesis of desire and which we have already cited – helps us to grasp a change of perspective in psychoanalytic theory with regard to the theme of pleasure and its function in promoting life. The idea originally maintained by Freud is that the early experience of pleasure leaves a mnestic trace and when, in the absence of the object, there is a renewed need to repeat that experience of satisfaction, the mnestic trace will be invested in a hallucinatory manner. In this urge to rediscover the lost object, the mnestic trace replaces the search in reality. The idea that frustration and the absence of the object, the lack of the breast, were at the origin of desire and the drive–impulse was shared by the next generations of analysts.[3] According to this line of reasoning, beginning with a gap, a deficiency, infantile sexuality remains as a residue in the activity of fantasy seeking the fulfilment of a wish (*Wunscherfüllung*). A deep nexus links absence, the lack of sensory satisfaction, the non-breast, the non-thing, to the activity of thought and the processes of learning (Bion, 1962).[4]

In my opinion, Winnicott's conceptualisation enables us to introduce a change of perspective from which to view the function of pleasure and unpleasure in the development of psychic life and the role of frustration in the birth of thought (Marion, 2014, 2016c). Winnicott proposes a distinction between two concepts, that of "early" and that of "deep", a distinction which addresses a particularly complex conceptual crux. In fact, he maintains that there exists an initial phase in the infant's life, the "early" phase, indeed, characterised by an extreme dependency on the environment. It is the phase of the subjective object (cf. supra, Chapter 3, p. 64, note 17) when the environment is an integrating part of the baby, and not differentiable as far as the baby is concerned. In this phase, the subject needs the object/other for its own survival (need), but it will be the quality of its care and nurturing – along with the satisfaction of the need and the discharge of tension – that introduces elements of pleasure, unpleasure, excitation, desire. In the phase of absolute dependency, prior to the acknowledgement of the object's existence outside the area of omnipotent control, in "the infant's journey from the purely subjective to objectivity" (1971, p. 6) the satisfaction and pleasure in its own body which the infant experiences, are perceived subjectively as not coming from outside. Only gradually is pleasure transferred onto a shared plane and into the area of play. And only gradually, does time bring "depth", which is a matter of psychic reality, imagination, fantasy life: "Deep is not synonymous with early, because an infant needs a degree of maturity before becoming gradually able to be deep" (Winnicott, 1958, p. 111).

Winnicott's thinking offers a shift in the classical psychoanalytic set-up by recognising the environment's role and function. The approach to the question is modified by the idea that the object of the drive is also a subject with its own impulses, desires and life stories (Roussillon, 2016) and that the object's characteristics, the mother's but also those of the parental couple, qualify the response. The fact that, through perception, the infant can encounter an object sufficiently like the one "created" in a hallucinatory way and which answers to his expectations, reverses the perspective. The role of external reality in association with internal reality is brought back into play and the infant's search is carried out for as long as is necessary to find a real object capable of responding to his/her demands in a more or less appropriate manner. In this way, and with the other's help, s/he will "integrate", will take ownership of the experience of satisfaction and pleasure, including the bodily, of excitation and relaxation experienced in the relationship. These are a satisfaction and pleasure which the infant, still incapable of differentiating between what is his/her own and what comes from the external environment, experiences as his/her own, perceives "subjectively" as "created" by and part of him/herself.

This experience of pleasure requires an encounter, a presence, not an absence. It is an encounter with an adult capable of investing and being invested libidinally, capable of desiring and resonating with what the infantile arouses within him or her: a presence which encounters the infant's "hallucinatory" fantasy and maintains its illusion. This final point provokes a specific reflection about the adult's relationship with pleasure, with her/his own sexuality, including the infantile kind which lives on inside her/him, is expressed on a "deep" level in psychic reality, in imagination, in fantasy life, and is reactivated by the waiting for and arrival of a baby. The experience of pleasure which the adult guarantees the baby in the "early" phase is part of the very fabric of which the subject is made, part of its ability to keep mind and body together. The adult, the parental couple, is not only there to satisfy the child's needs but also represents a source of pleasure, pleasure which becomes a foundation stone of being, of the sense of self, and of the vital project: "Autoerotic infantile sexuality therefore appears as a second phase of the sexual in the infant, whereas the first phase of sexuality unfolds in the presence of the object and via an affective sharing with it" (Seulin, 2014, pp. 56–7).

Sexuality, to which pleasure and unpleasure are so closely linked, is the continually present *skàndalon* (Riolo, 2017) in the individual's development. But it is also something that precedes it because it is in a sexual act, in a primal scene before us, behind us and unrepresentable,

149

that our roots are laid down. Our lived and enacted sexuality does not only reflect the intimate history of each of us, our affective and relational vicissitudes, but also bears the stamp of a time that precedes us, that is before us. We have considered the effects of infertility on the equilibrium of the subjects who are affected by it and the narcissistic wound that results from it, but what is the influence of the modifications introduced by the biotechnologies on the relationship with the body and sexuality? What impact do they have on pleasure? The biotechnologies "expel" sex from procreation and make generation possible by means of modalities which dispense with the sexual act and the encounter of two "bodies in relation". As we have seen, the expulsion of sexuality from procreation reminds us of the infantile sexual theories described by Freud, which tend to portray the origin of life and birth in ways that defend the child from the traumatic encounter with the "enigma" and mystery of adults' sexuality and the man–woman couple. The problem it poses is a dual one: does this expulsion modify the terms of the relationship with the pleasure-unpleasure principle and how does it influence the unconscious relationship with the child?

We often observe the consequences of these practices on sexuality. Eleonora, who had a long and challenging course of fertilisation by donor which ended positively, maintains that she now feels completely lacking in sexual desire. The determination which impelled her to make these repeated and frustrating attempts was very strong, and yet an impassable and unmoveable wall had appeared in the couple, one that seemed to reflect the missing procreative encounter. For Ginevra too (and not only for her) the fertilisation attempts, the travels abroad, in this case without positive outcomes, have resulted in a sexual block in the couple and a radical elimination of desire. Ginevra helps me to grasp how much the sexual rejection, the giving up of a shared pleasure, may also contain and express the aggression and anger felt in a physically painful and intrusive process, often with the sensation of feeling that one is alone.

Psychoanalysis has considered and continues to consider the primal scene, outside and before us, as the pivot around which the oedipal scenario unfolds and the fantasies of origin are constructed, that which allows the infant mind, step by step, to include the existence of a couple relationship and to create a representation of the nature of parental relations. Beginning with this confrontation which happens in the child's mind and which Winnicott (1988) considers

150

"the basis of individual stability" (p. 59), a relationship between reality and fantasy, between reality and dream, is set up in the infant mind. If the primal scene changes, what kind of fantasy is activated? What fantasies are provoked? In what way is all this reflected in the question about one's origin that each of us asks ourselves, and what impact does it have on the story of our life? Addressing the world of biotechnological solutions from our perspective as psychoanalysts means first of all addressing these points, remaining aware of the fact that our field of investigation always concerns single experiences and any generalisation may be risky.

The importance of the fantasy world that is set in motion and accompanies the desire to conceive a baby, the unfolding of the fantasies set in motion by that particular child, wanted in that way and at that moment, is not irrelevant to the construction of the subsequent relationship and its specific "quality". Going back to Melania Mazzucco, she describes a Tintoretto on his deathbed going back over his life, recalling its joys, griefs, loves, successes, tribulations, and defeats, and ponders the destiny he has provided for his daughters, comparing them with the feelings he nurtured for his eldest, born outside marriage: "I know what you want to say to me, Lord. I haven't given the daughters of my old age the opportunities I gave to the daughter of my pleasures" (Mazzucco, 2008, p. 260). This acute observation catches a crucial point, the significance and the role of pleasure in the very act of conception as the foundation point of origin. Care, childrearing, are subsequent, come later.

Comparative researches carried out on children born by ART and those born to same-sex parents find no differences in the stages of development and in the various areas taken into consideration (perceptual-motor, cognitive, emotional, relational, etc.) between children born in different ways or in different kinds of family.[5] Nevertheless, the enigma of origin provokes questions about the sexual relationship – the "Powerful One" (Camassa, 2014) behind us – and children born by ART, as we are beginning to understand, carry specific fantasies about their origin. Andrea is a 7-year-old boy born by homologous assisted fertilisation, and referred because of nervous tics of growing intensity and an occasional depressed mood. In a session from the third year of therapy, a session that passes rather slowly, the boy draws a tree with apples and underneath it a pencil line that suggests a snake. He associates it with the story of Adam and Eve, then quickly declares, "It's not my favourite story in religion." The boy abruptly sets aside the drawing and starts to scribble. The therapist asks what the scribble is. Andrea replies, "It's Jesus and Mary." Immediately afterwards, he draws a motorcycle helmet and a lightning bolt touching the helmet. I'm interested in the sequence, which seems to describe the way that Andrea is facing and trying to manage his conflict about sexuality and pleasure: he is trying to contact the couple Adam and Eve who perhaps represent his fantasies about the couple, including the couple he is in with the therapist, but he must quickly withdraw from them, as if wanting to protect himself against such a devastating thought. In that way, he might be able to return to an unsexed couple that reflects his perception of the parental couple and also represents his internal couple. All children are confronted with the enigma of sexuality and with defences against the idea of the parental couple's sexuality. However, I am interested in how Andrea has his own way of working out his relationship with the idea of coming into the world, whether via a couple who have eaten the fruit of sin or by means of an immaculate conception.

An unforgettable image of two different models of a couple is contained in *The Leopard* by Tomasi di Lampedusa and in the splendid, equally unforgettable, film version by Luchino Visconti. The Prince of Salina and his wife are contrasted with another couple, Tancredi and Angelica. The difference consists in how sexuality, in the sense of Eros, and hence not just procreative sexuality, is or is not part of the couple's life. The difference is an enormous one. As fulfilment of his marital duty, the Prince of Salina's sexuality lacks desire, which is satisfied elsewhere, whereas erotic desire is the glue that impels Tancredi towards Angelica and vice versa. They are a couple with vitality and we become involved in the element of passion which characterises them, just as passion involves the child and constitutes an "ingredient" of no small significance to the formation of her/his identificatory processes.

It is not unusual in analysis to have patients bring us this initial environment which seems to lack the experience of being the object of a shared pleasure, a tempered excitation like being bathed in warm light. I am thinking of certain situations where at the centre of the work is the patient's request to feel they are an object of pleasure for the analyst, like the child who enjoys being that for its mother. This is the desire to share the emotion of pleasure in being together. In other words, as analysts we are being asked to find a way of being a maternal/female figure for the patient, one who will not withdraw from the erotic valence of desire, who will not feel dominated by it, will not take fright at the sharing of pleasure, because she knows *"its nature is rigorously symbolic: 'To love each other is finally possible and a very good thing"'* (Bolognini, 2011, p. 37).[6] It was like this for Franco, who had never allowed himself to acknowledge and experience in a relationship the passionate aspect of his desire for the other as something vital and life-giving, and who was desperately seeking a relationship that might acknowledge this aspect of himself. The mother's pleasure is necessary in order for the child to experience his/her own pleasure, and the problem so acutely experienced by Franco had to do with the introjection of an object incapable of vital, libidinal investment in her child, but also perhaps in her partner. Ludovica describes this situation by means of a dream: "As I was talking, you [the analyst] were occupied with someone else. It was hard for me, because she was taking your attention away from me. I felt this situation was intolerable, I was getting into a situation I had no control over." The dream is a good description of how the distraction of the analyst reactivated the fear of not being able to gain the other's attention. Not feeling that one is the object of the other's investment arouses dramatic feelings of loss and confusion. Moreover, this seems to be the climate that marked the beginning of Ludovica's life, behind which there is a depressed and quarrelsome parental couple. Patients ask us to heal this wound by living the experience that the analyst is someone who feels genuine pleasure in encountering them. Recognising the profound and specific significance of these patient's requests, for whom a vital initial experience, a foundation stone of their being, seems to have been missed out, means differentiating the level of attachment and needs, the satisfaction of which is absolutely important but of a different nature, from that other level, of desire and pleasure on which the element of sexuality and of the body plays a fundamental part.

8.2 Altering boundaries and questioning one's origin

Besides affecting the sexual sphere and the deep nucleus of the individual's identity, the changes in fertilisation introduced by biotechnology which we have referred to so far modify the primary and foundational relational schemata. These are questions at the heart of the bioethical debate which is taking place around the themes of the "inviolability" and "unavailability of life".[7] This is not my field and I am not addressing it here, but it is interesting to cast a glance into adjacent territories for their contribution to the subject of our re-flections. The bioethical discussion also focuses on the question of what is new in this sphere, something that has never happened before, as I have repeatedly emphasised. Biotechnological practices in the field of procreation involve the alteration and manipulation of the beginning of life which until very recently had been entirely inaccessible. In this respect, the bioethicists are investigating the question of the "availability of life for use" precisely because technology has made it possible to have an impact on the original biological nucleus of the individual, making us diverge ever further from randomness and contingency in the way we come into the world. The implications of this give rise – as Chasseguet-Smirgel (2003) wrote – to "an enormous mass of problems which only lack of imagination allows us to watch with calm stupidity as it advances" (p. 14).

Seeing this multitude of problems does not mean demonising the choices, but simply being aware of them. Faure-Pragier (2008), for example, wonders if the primal scene, "procreative coitus" and the difference of the sexes connected to it, which has until today been considered the psyche's organising fantasy, is not "itself a privileged representation" (p. 47). And she also wonders if the same role and function might not be played in the process of symbolisation by "other, new representations, thus avoiding the risk of de-symbolization" (ibid.). The hypothesis that this author proposes, one we can easily share though it is an insufficient response to the problems posed earlier, is that the child's "NEW ORIGINAL FANTASY" may be built up from the certainty of being so desired and wanted that a medical intervention was accepted and made their birth possible "free from the aleatory element of a fertilising sexual act" (p. 47). And we know how true this is (the aleatory nature of a fertile sexual act) if we think of all those situations where the sexual act certainly does not have the characteristics of a shared pleasure, but is instead an imposition, sometimes a violent one, or something being done for another purpose.

In addition, the organisation of the symbolic domain – a point specifically addressed by Heenen-Wolff's (2014) reflections on same-sex parenting – may occur beyond and outside the sexual difference of the parents, in the encounter with other differences. According to this line of thought, the fact of being born to a homosexual couple does not hinder the construction of triangularity. The very necessity of resorting to a donation of sperm or ova for procreation reintroduces the third, whose function is that of

154

revealing difference. The psychic space created between parent and donor guarantees the entry of "thirdness". The unconscious message transmitted by the parental couple – same or other sex – contains the seeds of heterosexuality as much as of homosexuality, and the fantasies around individual truth dispense with historical truth.

Nevertheless, I think that the two planes – individual truth and historical truth – rather than doing without each other, interweave and influence each other, often interacting in ways that are quite complicated to decipher. From this viewpoint, I am inclined to detect more possible consequences and effects being introduced by biotechnological "manipulation" into the relationship with ourselves and with others. The times and places of procreation may be separated and dissociated. The process is broken up into many phases. In heterologous fertilisation we find ourselves faced with entirely new problems concerning genealogy and lineage, quite apart from biological continuity. The donation of genetic material, whether of sperm or ova, the anonymity of the donors, the freezing of embryos, and surrogate pregnancy are a range of conditions which stir up a variety of fantasies. They have a subversive effect on the familiar biographical scenario and on primal narrative unity as the base from which the adventure of existence begins and branches out. This primal narrative unity expresses the meaning of our identity; it is rooted in the family tree that stands behind us and in the chain of relationships from which we come and within which we exist. The biological link with our parents is a ring in this chain. The possibility of intervening, modifying and manipulating the original biological nucleus which involves other lives beyond our own, and the possible forms of fertilisation and generation to which it gives rise confront us with a scenario for which we are often unprepared.

The practices of assisted procreation present a variety of steps: homologous, heterologous, surrogate pregnancy, and possible combinations of the three, the possibility for same-sex couples to have children, and delayed or even *post mortem* fertilisation. Each of these possibilities offers solutions to problems that previously seemed insoluble, but impose not just ethical challenges, but ever more psychically challenging demands which include their emotional and psychologically profound resonances. Even homologous fertilisation which may appear apparently innocuous gives rise to far from trivial problems for the participating individuals (sperm-collection, the monitoring of ovulation, insemination, and adherence to precise protocols even with regard to sexual intercourse) and imposes the presence of extraneous figures who may have substantial effects on the couple's life. The question becomes still more complex when we are talking about heterology, with regard to both heterosexual and homosexual couples. In male couples there is the additional element of surrogate pregnancy. The specific and characteristic element of these situations is the multiplicity of places and figures who inhabit the physical and temporal space of conception and hence the moment of origin. A *fil rouge* seems to link all these experiences, from the slightest to the most extreme, and that is the shifting of the personal centre of gravity to an *elsewhere*. The *elsewhere* is the wrenching effect on the foundation of the child's origin, which may remain an open question as much in the child as in the parents and become a "family secret". In the end, it is this very search for his own origins that sends Oedipus off to Delphi.

The urgent need felt by children born via heterologous techniques to come together in associations[8] reveals an anxiety about an unknown part of their origins, which makes the subject concerned feel deeply unsure about their kinship links and comes close to what Racamier (1995) calls the "incestual". He uses this term to define "a register of psychic and relational life" which "instils suspicion, silence, and secrecy" (1995, p. 21). Unfortunately, this is what happens when it is so difficult to reveal to the child the truth about his or her coming into the world and – as I was saying earlier – to acknowledge that the answer may be even worse than the question. Federico has had a son via heterologous fertilisation (sperm donation). He brings the following dream to his analyst:

> I dreamt I was in a cave, maybe an undersea cave. The inside of the cave was like a dark swimming pool surrounded by stones which marked out its boundary. Luca [his son] was diving, as if he had to retrieve something and he was disappearing into the water.

He describes it as a distressing dream from which he woke deeply disturbed. He associates the dream and the feelings of anxiety with the growth of his son, now a teenager, who is withdrawing from him and whom he is afraid of losing. He carries on along this line of thought, recounting episodes from his son's life. The session proceeds and at a certain point the patient starts to talk about something to do with Luca's origin. The analyst intervenes and tells him that perhaps this is also the subject of the dream where he is talking about Luca's origin, that part of his origin which neither he nor Luca know anything about. As if the dream represented a search he might get lost in and disappear. The patient lights up, saying that it is a question he has recently been pondering intensely and it is greatly distressing him because there is something he and his son will never know, something that will forever be alien. The analyst comments, "The black hole." The patient, "Yes, and I feel the weight of a secret that is being built up between the two of us." Using the second time, his son's adolescence, and the dream image, Federico seems able to give representation to a much more radical and original separation.

We have already said that keeping a secret about a son or daughter's origin highlights not only the parental difficulty in mentally "integrating" a process which has required intervention by other figures but also the difficult situation for the child who must deal with something unspoken that concerns them. It is this "cleavage", that I referred to earlier, which threatens the sense of self and psychic and emotional growth. As Faure-Pragier (2008) rightly notes, "the child perceives – we find this all the time – not the truth, but the secret: they blame themselves for it and display inhibition or unconscious guilt" (p. 35). The secret corresponds to the ignorance caused by anonymity, but also by the parents' denial about the fertilisation techniques employed. Psychoanalysts likewise agree that the "secret" is "one of the most, so to speak, 'pregnant' features of ART couples, and this is fully apparent in clinical work with these people" (Vigneri, 2011, p. 133). As Federico's dream shows, the prolonging of the secret also increases the anxiety about how and when to lift the silence around an event which indissolubly links the parent to the child.

The changing of the identity-schema, which includes the concepts of kinship and lineage, and *origin in an elsewhere* represent transformations of the "natural" bond or limit that has been a guiding thread throughout mankind's anthropological history. In order to comprehend "the new ways of being born", it seems necessary to accept the birth of new ways of thinking about the relationship with ourselves and with others. If until a short time ago biography tended to be understood in linear terms of development according to a precise division of roles anchored to sexual gender, today this paradigm is being modified. A stable biological identity with concomitant, pre-established relational schemata is being replaced with a more fluid identity characterised by the ability to "integrate", including parts of other people, as the experience of transplants has shown and as the broad spectrum of fertilisation techniques leads us to think. The experience of altered personal boundaries is well known to those who have studied the psychological consequences of transplants. Indeed, the integration of the new organ entails delicate problems connected to the redefinition of the Self, to the fear of uncontrollable physiological changes and loss of the integrity of one's own person. The intrapsychic integration of the new organ is accompanied by a process of taking on the characteristics of the donor, a process which remains for the most part unconscious and is influenced by the nature of the relationship between donor and recipient. The implanted organ – and we can think of a donor's genetic material in the same way – is not a mechanical object but a "piece" of the other person, laden with history, fantasies, speculations, which become part of us and which we integrate into our personally lived experience (Basch, 1973; Castelnuovo-Tedesco, 1978; Freedman, 1983; Assou, 2016).

In a paper confronting the psychoanalytic paradigm with the problems posed by postmodern identity, Axel Honneth (2002) emphasises how the image of the individual which is being asserted is that of a subject characterised by an internal multiplication of identities. In essence, Honneth's thesis is that "at least in highly developed societies, there is an increased tendency for subjects to allow and imagine greater possibilities of inner identity than those permitted by the conventional attribution of a rigid role and the expectations of behaviour" (Honneth, p. 14). The postmodern personality is therefore characterised by an intrapsychic complexity which redefines the subject's relationship with her/himself. The orientation that privileges a rigid identity-schema based on the selective, synthetic, and normative capacity of the Ego, proves inadequate to explain a more elaborate and extended subject resulting from an extreme "fluidification" (*Verflüssigung*) of psychic life capable of living intrapsychic and relational experiences that are diversified in time and space, and doing so with a sense of coherence. The subject's maturity would therefore be measured by the individual capacity for accepting the many layers of her/his personality and the many times of his/her history, and for constructing an intrapsychic space where all these aspects live together and are in dialogue with each other: "the goal of inner vitality, of intrapsychic richness, has taken the place that was occupied in early psycho-analysis by the concept of Ego strength" (ibid., p. 26).

In this revisiting of the construction of identity, Winnicott's (1945, 1965b) concept of integration once again comes to our aid. The integrative journey of the sensory and motor elements ac-companied by their imaginative elaboration is guaranteed by the maternal presence, which is tasked with carrying out this role and thereby guaranteeing the sense of continuity of existence: "I am, I exist, I gather experiences and enrich myself and have an introjective and projective interaction with the NOT-ME, the actual world of shared reality" (1965b, p. 61). Patients – adults or children – who have been through experiences like those we have described so far, whether actively chosen or unintentionally undergone, ask us for specific help in this direction. How to accept, integrate and perso-nalise events which appear so extreme in relation to the unity of the Self? It is the challenge addressed to psychoanalysis and to the help it can give to individual patients bearing an "enigma" which has been transformed from the sexuality of the oedipal scene to the "enigma" of their own origin.[9] Federico's dream is a good representation of the anxiety about the "black hole" in which one can be lost, but the most significant aspect is that, through his son's anxiety in diving into the well of the secret, Federico dreams his own anxiety because a piece of Luca's origin remains a secret for him too. The emotional echo of the events they have gone through must find a listening and a recognition which enables it to be shared and imaginatively worked through, and helps events with an alien character to be made personal. This is "that psychic work which is imposed on the psyche by the fact of its fundamental link with intersubjectivity", says Kaës (2005) paraphrasing Freud, by the fact that we are more and more inhabited by others inside us. The challenge, which psychoanalysis also faces, is posed by a multiple subject who in order to be thought about requires a problematising of our knowledge and also a revision of our conceptual apparatus in the complex terms of that "vastness" that we recalled earlier in words of Canetti.

8.3 Desire and its discontents

The theme of desire intersects with the question of whether and how the expulsion of sexuality from procreation modifies the re-lationship with pleasure in the couple and also modifies a unitary view of the individual who is being reflected in the child's fantasies. Ansermet (2015) wonders if, when desires become rights, to the point where they take no account of the limits imposed by reality and breach them, we can still rank them within the domain of desire. It is a question which opens up a range of substantial questions both on the bioethical and psychoanalytic fronts. Mary Warnock, who chaired the Committee of Inquiry into Human Fertilisation and Embryology in the United Kingdom (1982–84), addresses the problem with customary Anglo-Saxon pragmatism and wonders if "there is a right to have children"? In a brief but very clear and lucid text (Warnock, 2002), several questions are raised and discussed, such as the difference between wanting something and needing something, between needs and rights, the distinction between clinical and non-clinical criteria for defining "suitability for treatment", the consideration of the child's well-being and the terms in which it should be expressed. However, the central point of the argument in favour of the "right to treatment" is that in the case of infertility we find ourselves faced with something that can cause great suffering. This is a suffering which cannot always be alleviated by adoption and, from the medical viewpoint, justifies access to clinical interventions and a cure for the malaise. "Trying" to have a child is an individual right and must be attended to.

Mary Warnock's reasoning raises a more general problem which closely concerns us, and relates to the nature and specific quality of the desire to have a child. It is a desire which goes beyond the problem of infertility and may "possess" the individuals involved to the point where it becomes hard to deal with. In globalised societies like ours it is easy to cross the boundaries that may have been put in place by local legislation and thus to satisfy one's wishes elsewhere. Heterologous fertilisation and surrogate pregnancy are the most obvious examples. So the question shifts onto the quality of this desire and what its repercussions may for the children. From a thoroughly psychoanalytic perspective, Ansermet wonders what is hidden "beyond" the desire for a child at any cost. Going "beyond" the limit would shift the game "beyond" desire and pleasure towards an entitlement to gratification (*jouissance*) at all costs: "The satisfaction of having a child is claimed as a right. Sometimes it is no longer clear if it is still the child that is wanted or if it is only the satisfaction that is wanted at any cost" (Ansermet, 2005, p. 14). In these cases it is a "demiurgic scheme" that grips the protagonists.

The difference that separates the plan for a child from a "demiurgic scheme" is not so clear and easy to establish. The theme of parental narcissism replicated by means of the child, in "His Majesty the Baby", was well known long before medically assisted reproduction came along: "At the most touchy point in the narcissistic system, the immortality of the ego, which is so hard pressed by reality, security is achieved by taking refuge in the child. Parental love, which is so moving and at bottom so childish, is nothing but the parents' narcissism born again, which, transformed into object-love, unmistakably reveals its former nature" (Freud, 1914c, p. 91). Desire arises from a lack and the plan to have a child is also the response to the need for somebody besides ourselves, someone to survive us and continue us after our death. The child represents "the tenacious shadow" that is projected beyond our limit in time, in the generations to come, the attempt to fill the sense of emptiness that accompanies the idea of the end, our defiance of time and death. Viviana, whose multiple and repeated attempts using various techniques have not achieved success and in the end have also led to separation from her husband, has not stopped hoping that something may yet happen. The end of her fertile years represents a harsh awakening which she will dream as holding a dead baby, whose features she cannot see, in her arms.

The desire for a child brings into play the body and "bodies in relation". The subjects are deeply involved, as much on the psychic level as the physical, in a desire and a pleasure which needs the other in order to be fully expressed, and produces the most profound transformation of the couple. In poetic terms this pleasure is described by the figure of the embrace. In it is realised the sensation of the "infantile embrace" – as an incestuous return to the maternal embrace – and the force of the genital which is asserted and cuts off that "indistinct sensuality". According to Barthes (1977), the act of the amorous embrace serves to represent the realisation of the dream of total union:

1. Besides intercourse ... there is that other embrace, which is a motionless cradling: we are enchanted, bewitched ... we are within the voluptuous infantilism of *sleepiness* ... this is the return of the mother ("In the loving calm of your arms," says a poem set to music by Duparc) ...

161

2. Yet, within this infantile embrace, the genital unfailingly appears; it cuts off the diffuse sensuality of the incestuous embrace; the logic of desire begins to function, the will-to-possess returns, the adult is superimposed upon the child: I am then two subjects at once: I want maternity *and* genitality.

(Barthes, 1977, pp. 104–105)

Conception mobilises all the fantasies of origin. The body is engaged to give expression to the fantasy, but also to oppose it. Biotechnology, which introduces an alien and artificial dimension, rearranges the reality of conception and tries to get around the body's discourse, giving life to other fantasies. The way out of "technological vertigo" requires us to deal with the traumatic aspects stirred up by the use of biotechnology. Using the dream of Laura, who has had a child with ART, we can reconstruct the fantasy which has accompanied and supported her journey: protecting herself from the idea that sexual intercourse may entail an incestuous act and affirming within herself the conviction that she has made this child by herself. In these cases the desire for a child is no longer a desire that moves towards the other and meets with the other's desire so as to recognise the third to which it has given life. The trans-formative force of the desire is in fact revealed in the "engagement/disengagement of the subject's bodily structure" achieved through co-penetration with the other and in the gratification that this produces (Thanopulos, 2016). By contrast, in the situations I alluded to earlier, the desire is asserted in a determined but sometimes also violent way and betrays its obscure origin. The child too can become the object of a peremptory need for possession and control, rather than the consequence of a shared pleasure.

Lacan is a writer who has given much reflection to the theme of desire. For this author, desire is not so much connected to redis-covering and recreating the lost object of the original satisfaction, that "finding of an object" which "is in fact a refinding of it" as Freud said in the *Three Essays*. Rather, it is rooted in an essential lack (the lack of being) which every child experiences at birth in the moment of separation from the mother's body. The child desires to be the Other's desire, the desire of the mother's desire, thereby at-tempting to complete this lack at his origin. The striving to stop up this wound that cannot be staunched will then rely on replacements and be expressed in demands which, because they refer to repressed

162

desires, will never be satisfied.[10] Contrasting gratification (*jouissance*) with desire introduces a new level which dodges the encounter with the Other, the intersubjective logic, and asserts itself as an absolute. Antigone, *the extreme image of desire*, may be taken as an epitome of this absolutising move which imposes its conviction to the death, neither asking for nor claiming recognition by the Other, but only fidelity to itself.[11]

At times, the desire for a child and the decision to undergo ART also seems to hide a radical absoluteness and a shift towards *Beyond the Pleasure Principle* (Freud, 1920b).[12] It is a *beyond* which questions the significance of those situations in which the link with suffering seems to represent a source of pleasure for the patient. In order that the destructive drives which operate in the individual do not gain the upper hand, it is necessary for the vital drives to be able to "bind" and bridle them.[13] Whereas Eros is a force that links, that transforms in the service of pleasure, the opposite, the work of the negative, consists in an untying of subject from object maintained by a fantasy of self-sufficiency which gives rise to a sort of negative narcissism (Green, 1993, 2002).

The desire for a baby is a complex desire, ambivalent in nature, and not infrequently located more in the idea of pregnancy than in what comes afterwards. Infertility is a wound which overwhelms desire and alters its mobile nature addressed to and through the other with the aim of shared gratification and pleasure. We are witnessing a transformation of desire into need, often an obsessive, relentless need directed towards the achieving of a goal in order to overcome such a disappointing image of oneself and one's couple. The shadow of the wound has fallen onto the desire. I do not want to be mis-understood: I think that in the determination of many women and many couples, perhaps most, there really is a sincere desire for and striving towards motherhood: so strong that it urges them to ob-literate or not see this risk of transforming desire into necessity and an obligation to themselves.

The discontent of desire is expressed by means of this sometimes violent distortion to which it is subjected. As I said at the start (Part I, Chapter 1) the discontent of the desire for the object "always sought and never found" is a desire that has to do with the unsaturated, with a void; by contrast, in these journeys that involve the protagonists in such a degree of physical, psychological and emotion engagement, the desire presents itself as a *too much* that may compulsively saturate

163

heart and mind. Pleasure is replaced by difficulties and suffering – *in primis*, physical suffering: i.e. the contrary of sexual pleasure. Above all, the mobility that is so natural to desire, both in its being addressed to an object outside the self and in the ways in which it is sublimated, stiffens into a repetitive compulsion. The reality of the solutions responds to the fantasies in play which accompany every biotechnological choice, including those of making a child on one's own. And these are perhaps the cases in which, further down the line, we see a frozen sexuality, whether as desire for the other or as desire to feel like a living body and to experience pleasure.

Having a child is a creative act, involving the individual on deep levels and stimulating a special pleasure, that of feeling alive. "It is creative apperception more than anything else that makes the individual feel that life is worth living", writes Winnicott (1971, p. 65). The decision to have a child brings our inventiveness into play and opens new horizons. Bollas (2000) claims that "thinking futuristically ... is an erotic drive" (p. 36). In search of the sexual object located outside us, which marks the transition from childhood to adolescence, the individual accepts external reality and the need to negotiate with the outside world: "Eros is reality oriented in spite of its nature; Thanatos hates the world of reality and uses fantasy to replace the real" (ibid.).

These observations bring us back to where we started, to that fine boundary between "what is called reality and fantasy" which is brought back to our attention by the decision to give birth to someone and by the new ways of being born. Abandoning the seduction theory, Freud had revolutionised the approach to the human subject, recognising the role of psychic reality, fantasy, and the unconscious in determining the individual's destiny: *Wo Es war, soll Ich werden*. Winnicott breaks the traditional conception of psychic space and carries out a new "silent yet radical future revolution" (Fabozzi, 2012). In fact, Winnicott looks at the vicissitudes of that intermediate area between subject and object, between internal and external, at the transitional space that is created between the two poles and where creativity is situated. The recognition of the environment's role, of the other's reality in interaction and deep exchange with the subject are central for understanding this dialectic. Indeed, according to Winnicott, "creativity ... belongs to the approach of the individual to external reality" (Winnicott, 1971, pp. 68) and in the absence of this acceptance (of external reality), creativity itself becomes "lethal", in the definition which Ogden (2012) gives it, reading Winnicott.

"The point", writes Winnicott,

> is that in fantasy things work by magic: there are no brakes on fantasy, and love and hate cause alarming effects. External reality has brakes on it, and can be studied and known, and, in fact, fantasy is only tolerable at full blast when objective reality is appreciated well. The subjective has tremendous value but is so alarming and magical that it cannot be enjoyed except as a parallel to the objective.
>
> (1975, p. 153)

Objectivity and external reality constitute the clog, the barrier, the brake against an explosion of unbounded fantasy, the yearning for limitless possibilities. In the sphere we have been considering up to now, the body constitutes the fine boundary between what is real and what is fantasy. The body, the mind's birthplace but also its limit, is presented as a reality which puts on the brakes and may rebel against the demands made of it if it considers them excessive and if these demands become too strongly a source of discontent and reveal a destructive valence.

The theme of the limit recurs at the moment when technological progress offers ever more advanced solutions and something that a moment before may have seemed a terminus can be surpassed. There are certainly limits to human action and not every demand can be satisfied, just as there are limits to clinical efficacy. Nevertheless, the limit of sense seems to be most challenged because it is not always easy to recognise what is acceptable for each of us and find a feeling of goodness and good sense in what we are doing. Maria tells how at yet another attempt at heterologous ART, which forced the couple to make exhausting journeys abroad, something inside her rebelled. Even though they were about to make a new "pilgrimage" and everything had been organised, she decided to stop, to direct her desire elsewhere because what she was doing seemed excessive and made no sense. Maria, and other women and men like her, seems to have reached the crossroads "between creative living and living itself, and the reasons ... why it is that creative living can be lost and why the individual's feeling that life is real or meaningful can disappear" (Winnicott, 1971, p. 69).

At the end of this journey I wonder if, instead of being about the concept of limit, it is in fact a question of responsibility.[14] The bounds of freedom have increased and expanded enormously; ever greater progress in medicine, advances in technology and science, and the legal rulings which have become more and more progressive and respectful of individual choices and the dignity of the person are being confronted with much more complex psychological consequences. From our point of view, the responsibility that these situations face us with is that of transforming into thoughts, into emotional events, the experiences, choices and vicissitudes that otherwise risk being deposited as mental "pieces" that are not and cannot be elaborated, as we have seen may happen with the secret of origins, bringing consequences for the self and the other. It is to be hoped that the expansion and multiplication of the possibilities of choice may be matched by an equal awareness of the effects on us and others of what we are doing, and an equally great and deep recognition of the limits of being human and how far each of us can push against them. We have a responsibility to our inner world, towards the other, and the obligation to know how to think about ourselves as beings in time.

Notes

1 In his brief but illuminating paper on *Pleasure*, Riolo (2017) shows how the description given by Freud, though approximate, achieves "a scientific revolution". Indeed, Freud introduced "the explanation of psychic phenomena as processes of nature, removing them, as he would later claim many times, both from the domain of metaphysics and the domain of spirit and consciousness. A naturalistic but not necessarily mechanistic conception, since it was not resolved into the contradistinction between discharge and inhibition, but posited that contradistinction as the engine and organizer of the entire development of the psychic apparatus, since this development essentially consists in the transition from the primary process to the secondary: in other words, in the work required of the psyche in order to achieve, in an indirect way – by means of thought – the satisfaction it is forbidden by means of action. In this way, Freud posited a continuity between the somatic-quantitative pleasure-principle and the psychic-qualitative transformations made necessary by unpleasure" (p. 520). The author goes on to assert that this conception does not place pleasure/unpleasure, *Lust/Unlust*, in opposition because the two processes are concomitant: "The consequence of

this dual suppression is not, therefore, 'pain' but *apathy*." And the result is the loss of meaning.

2 As we saw earlier in Part I, Green (1995) refers explicitly to the change of viewpoint introduced by Kleinian theory, which replaces the pairing of pleasure/unpleasure with good/bad object and in which the model of the breast (good breast/ bad breast) acquires a dominant position.

3 After Freud, Klein (1975) will use similar terms to describe how "the main processes which come into play in idealization are also operative in hallucinatory gratification" (p. 7). The lost or absent breast is regained through fantasy activity and the creation of an ideal breast. In particular, Klein highlights how the denial of frustration operates in hallucination by recourse to the splitting of the ideal breast and the absent, persecutory breast.

4 Bion's theory of thinking, which moves in this direction, actually describes an antecedent level involving the formation of a conception that depends crucially on the encounter between the pre-conception and its realisation. In *Elements of Psychoanalysis* (1963), Bion describes pre-conception as "a state of mind adapted to receive a restricted range of phenomena. An early occurrence might be an infant's expectation of the breast. The mating of pre-conception and realization brings into being the conception" (p. 23). In this respect, if it is to be realised and transformed into a conception, the pre-conception requires an encounter. According to Alvarez (2012), Bion would in fact dedicate less attention to this phase, concentrating instead on the later transition which, with absence and the tolerance of frustration as its starting point, brings to life the apparatus for thinking thoughts and makes thinking possible.

5 A not very recent paper (Ceccotti, 2004) reviews the various researches conducted on children born by ART and their parental couples. These researches into the impact of ART from the psychological viewpoint seem to rule out differences from the control group. However, the author notes how in this type of research the number of children considered is often low and opportunities for follow-up are not taken. One body of research merits a separate discussion, that led by Susan Golombok, Director of the Family and Child Psychology Research Centre, City University of London. Research published in *Human Reproduction* in 1996 entitled *The European Study of Assisted Reproduction Families: Family Functioning and Child Development* considers 400 families and children between four and eight years old from various European countries. The sample was followed longitudinally. The results do not seem to reveal significant differences from the viewpoint of psychological wellbeing and social-emotional development. In relation to same-sex parenting, the studies that have been

conducted seem to rule out differences between children brought up by heterosexual or homosexual couples (Golombok and Tasker, 1996; MacCallum and Golombok, 2004; Vecho and Schneider, 2005).

6 Bolognini (2008) writes that it is very important for the analyst to attend to his capacity for working in an un-eroticised way at those moments when the intimate mental pairing with the patient could be perceived by the latter as eroticised. The central point that arises is the importance of the analyst's role in performing a containing and transformative function for the patient's excitatory tension. The *"paroxysmal excitatory state"* in which the patient is imprisoned tasks the analyst with translating it into an experience, which the patient lacks, of sharing with the object.

7 Habermas (2001) distinguishes between life's "inviolability" and "unavailability for use". In the first case, human life across its whole course from conception to death cannot be interfered with, ruling out abortion, the ending of life, etc. By contrast, the question of "un-availability for use" touches on the topic of manipulating the vital processes and so, in this case, we are concerned "with the claim to have life at our disposal, whether via the decision to bring something into being that would not otherwise have existed or via the decision to make it in a certain way, different from what it would naturally have been. This step entails a series of problems which have never arisen before." The ethical question relating to the topic of re-production concerns the status of an *other* who is involved in the process (Moneti Codignola, 2008).

8 Wendy Kramer and her son Ryan have founded the Donor Sibling Registry, a non-profit organisation which helps those born from do-nated gametes to find people "with whom they have genetic links". There are a great many online forums where children born via het-erologous techniques in many countries, especially the USA, are con-stantly looking for their "donor" and their biological siblings. Many of them admit to the fantasy and fear of having a relationship with bio-logical brothers/sisters of whose existence they know nothing.

9 Clearly, the secret about one's origin is not confined to situations involving ART. Many others may give rise to such a secret: extra-marital relationships, adultery, not acknowledging the child at birth and abandoning it, and adoption. What differentiates these cases is the fact that they are deliberately chosen by the parental couple and pursued with enormous effort and sacrifices. It is this which induces many people to see the force of this determination as an element favourable to the child's journey towards an identity: you were really wanted.

168

10 Lacan especially addressed this topic in the *Écrits*. The word "desire" is steadily abolished and the primacy of desire gives way to that of gratification (*jouissance*). The difference between the two terms goes back to the fact that the first refers to the desire for the Other (*l'Autre* is always upper case in Lacanian language) – that is, the desire to be the desire of the Other – whereas the second makes absolute the solipsistic primacy of gratification: "While desire can only find its satisfaction through the Other – or, more precisely, while desire cannot do without its exposure to the Other – gratification cuts the Other out … Compared to the open field of desire, the figure of gratification tends to take shape as an absolute figure of the One" (Recalcati, 2012, pp. 241–2). It should also be added that in Lacan desire draws its origin from a fundamental lack, that lack of being (*manque d'être*) which Sartre also speaks about, and which not only indicates the distinguishing feature of mankind but also something irremediably lost and unrecoverable.

11 Lacan's reading of the figure of Antigone is opposed to Hegel's. Whereas, for Hegel, Antigone in Sophocles' tragedy represents the conflict between the universal law of the *polis* and the private law of the affections, of the family, for Lacan Antigone expresses the absolute relationship with desire: the subject is possessed, "subjugated" by desire, and not the other way round. On this point, see Recalcati, 2012.

12 In the second part of his theoretical elaboration, Freud finds himself forced to rethink the opposition between pleasure and unpleasure. Led by his reflections on his clinical practice, which seemed to contradict this principle, beginning with the compulsion to repeat, masochism and sadism, he enquires into the link with suffering when it represents a source of pleasure for the patient. As we saw earlier, with the change of direction in 1920, Freud modifies his thesis and advances a new hypothesis about the psychic functioning of the individual, proposing a more radical conflict than that of pleasure and unpleasure: that is to say, the conflict between life and death drives.

13 In a note to the penultimate paragraph of the text, Freud gives a particularly clear and pleasing description of the interplay between these two forces: "What are commonly called the sexual instincts are looked upon by us as the part of Eros which is directed towards objects. Our speculations have suggested that Eros operates from the beginning of life and appears as a 'life instinct' in opposition to the 'death instinct' which was brought into being by the coming to life of inorganic substance." Then he continues in a note added the following year: "The opposition between the ego instincts and the sexual instincts was transformed into one between the ego instincts and the

object instincts, both of a libidinal nature. But in its place a fresh opposition appeared between the libidinal (ego and object) instincts and others, which must be presumed to be present in the ego and which may perhaps actually be observed in the destructive instincts. Our speculations have transformed this opposition into one between the life instincts (Eros) and the death instincts" (Freud, 1920b, p. 60).

14 I am not referring here to the use of the term in the legal lexicon, but to its moral meaning, indicating the consequences which a choice may incur and which may or may not be foreseen. We owe to Max Weber the distinction between ethic of intention and ethic of responsibility. Other authors who have dealt with the ethic of responsibility are Emmanuel Lévinas (1972) and Hans Jonas (1979).

BIBLIOGRAPHY

Abadi, M. 1978, Meditazione su (l') Edipo, in *Rivista di Psicoanalisi*, XXIV, pp. 391–424.

Allison, G. H. 1997, Motherhood, Motherliness, and Psychogenic Infertility, in *Psychoanalytic Quarterly*, 66, pp. 1–17.

Alvarez, A. 2012, *The Thinking Heart: Three Levels of Psychoanalytic Therapy with Disturbed Children*, Routledge, Hove.

Ambrosiano, L. and Gaburri, E. 2008, La spinta a esistere. Note cliniche sulla sessualità oggi, Borla, Rome.

André, J. 2009, Evento e temporalità. L'après-coup nella cura, in M. Balsamo (ed.), *Forme dell'après- coup*, Franco Angeli, Milan.

André, J. 2011, Laura: Or the Sexual Borders of Need, in *International Journal of Psychoanalysis*, 92, pp. 761–771.

André, J. 2014, Perché, dopo tutto, l'eterosessualità?, lavoro presentato alla giornata su *I disagi della contemporaneità. Nuove patologie e variazioni nella cura. Stati-limite della sessualità*, Rome Centre for Psychoanalysis, Rome, 10 May.

Ansermet, F. 2015, *La fabrication des enfants. Un vertige technologique*, Odile Jacob, Paris (Eng. trans., *The Art of Making Children: The New World of Assisted Reproductive Technology*, Routledge, Abingdon, 2018).

Ansermet, F. and Magistretti, P. 2010, *Les Enigmes du plaisir*, Odile Jacob, Paris.

Apfel, R. J. and Keylor, R. G. 2002, Psychoanalysis and Infertility: Myths and Realities, in *The International Journal of Psychoanalysis*, 83, pp. 85–104.

Argentieri, S. 2006, Travestitismo, transessualismo, transgender: Identificazione e imitazione, in *Psicoanalisi*, X, 2, pp. 55–92.

Arvanitakis, K. I. 1998, Some Thoughts on the Essence of the Tragic, in *International Journal of Psychoanalysis*, 79, pp. 955–964.

Assous, A. 2017, La psychanalyse et l'expérience-limite médicale, relazione presentata al Colloquio internazionale La psychanalise interpréte du temps present, Rome, 17–19 February.

Baranes, J.-J. 1991, *La Question psychotique à l'adolescence*, Dunod, Paris.

Barthes, R. 1977, *Fragments d'un discours amoureux*, Éditions du Seuil, Paris (Eng. trans., *A Lover's Discourse: Fragments*, Vintage, London, 2002).

Basch, S. H. 1973, The Intrapsychic Integration of a New Organ: A Clinical Study of Kidney Transplantation, in *Psychoanalytic Quarterly*, 42, pp. 364–384.

Bassi, F. and Galli P. F. (eds.) 1999, *L'omosessualità nella psicoanalisi*, Einaudi, Turin.

Bauman, Z. 2000, *Liquid Modernity*, Polity Press, Cambridge.

Beck, U. 1986, *Risk Society: Towards a New Modernity*, Sage, London, 1992.

Benedeck, T. 1952, Infertility as a Psychosomatic Defense, in *Fertility and Sterility*, 3, pp. 527–541.

Bion, W. R. 1962, *Learning from Experience*, Heinemann, London.

Bion, W. R. 1963, *Elements of Psychoanalysis*, Heinemann, London.

Birksted-Breen, D. (ed.) 1993, *The Gender Conundrum: Contemporary Psychoanalytic Perspectives on Femininity and Masculinity*, Institute of Psychoanalysis, London.

Blass, R. 2016a, Understanding Freud's Conflicted View of the Object-Relatedness of Sexuality and its Implications for Contemporary Psychoanalysis: A Re-Examination of Three Essays on Theory of Sexuality, in *International Journal of Psychoanalysis*, 97, pp. 591–613.

Blass, R. 2016b, Introduction to "Is the Nature of Psychoanalytic Thinking and Practice (e.g., in Regard to Sexuality) Determined by Extra-Analytic, Social and Cultural Developments?, in *International Journal of Psychoanalysis*, 97, pp. 811–821.

Blass, R. and Simon, B. 1994, The Value of the Historical Perspective to Contemporary Psychoanalysis: Freud's Seduction Hypothesis, in *International Journal of Psychoanalysis*, 75, pp. 677–693.

Blum, H. 2007, Little Hans: A Centennial Review and Reconsideration, in *Journal of the American Psychoanalytic Association*, 65(3), pp. 749–765.

Bohleber, W. 2013, Gesellschaftige Demokratisierung und der Aufstieg des intersubjektiven Paradigmas in der Psychanalyse. Eine kritische Bestandsaufnahme, paper presented at the Anniversary Conference of the Deutsche Gesellschaft für Psychoanalyse, Psychotherapie, Psychosomatik und Tiefenpsychologie (DGPT), Berlin, 27–29 September.

Bollas, C. 1987, *The Shadow of the Object: Psychoanalysis of the Unthought Known*, Free Association Books, London.

Bollas, C. 1992, *Being a Character: Psychoanalysis and Self Experience*, Routledge, Hove.

Bollas, C. 2000, *Hysteria*, Routledge, London.

Bolognini, S. 2008, *Passaggi segreti. Teoria e tecnica della relazione interpsichica*, Bollati Boringhieri, Turin.

Bolognini, S. 2011, The Analyst's Awkward Gift: Balancing Recognition of Sexuality with Parental Protectiveness, in *Psychoanalytic Quarterly*, 80, pp. 33–54.

Bonaminio, V. 2016, Clinical Winnicott: il suo quieto ma determinato percorso lungo una strada rivoluzionaria, paper presented at the conference *Donald Winnicott e la psicoanalisi del futuro*, organized by the Rome Centre for Psychoanalysis, Rome, 30–31 January.

Bonaminio, V. 2017, Clinical Winnicott: Travelling a Revolutionary Road, in *The Psychoanalytic Quarterly*, 3, pp. 609–626.

Borges, J. L. 1956, The Circular Ruins, in *Ficciones*, Grove Press, New York, 1962.

Borgogno, F. 1999, *Psychoanalysis as a Journey*, Open Gate Press, London, 2007.

Britton, R. 1989, The Missing Link: Parental Sexuality in the Oedipus Complex, in R. Britton, M. Feldman and E. O'Shaughnessy (eds.), *The Oedipus Complex Today: Clinical Implications*, Karnac, London.

Butler, J. 1995, Melancholy Gender: Refused Identification in *Psychoanalytic Dialogues*, 5(2), pp. 165–180 (and in M. Dimen and V. Goldner (eds.), *Gender in Psychoanalytic Space: Between Clinic and Culture*, Other Press, New York, 2002).

Cahn, R. 1998, *L'Aadolescent dans la psychanalyse. L'aventure de la subjectivation*, PUF, Paris.

Caldwell, L. 2005, *Sex and Sexuality: Winnicottian Perspectives*, Routledge, London.

Caldwell, L. 2015, panel discussion, One Sexuality, Many Sexualities: What Challenge for Psychoanalysis? XLIX IPA Congress, Boston, 22–25 July.

Camassa, P. 2014, *La Potente*, Nottetempo, Rome.

Campo, C. 1971, Introduction to *J. Donne, Poesie amorose e poesie teologiche*, ed. C. Campo, Einaudi, Turin.

Canetti, E. 1983 [1977], *The Tongue Set Free*, Farrar Straus and Giroux, New York.

Carratelli, T. and Massaro, V. 2016, Il bambino rosa: alla ricerca della leggerezza dell'essere. Note teorico-cliniche, in *Richard e Piggle*, 4, pp. 356–372.

Castelnuovo-Tedesco, P. 1978, Ego Vicissitudes in Response to Replacement or Loss to Body Parts: Certain Analogies to Events during Psychoanalytic Treatment, in *Psychoanalytic Quarterly*, 47.

Castoriadis, C. (ed.) 1998, *L'enigma del soggetto. L'immaginario e le istituzioni* (Epilogue by F. Ciaramelli), Dedalo, Bari.

Ceccotti, M. 2004, *Procreazione medicalmente assistita*, Armando, Rome.

Chasseguet-Smirgel, J. 2003, *Le Corps comme miroir du monde*, PUF, Paris (Eng. trans., *The Body as Mirror of the World*, Free Association, London, 2005).

Chervet, B. 2014, Il presente, una qualità psichica. Elementi per una metapsicologia della coscienza, in *Psiche*, 1, pp. 99–116.

Chianese, D. and Fontana, A. 2010, *Immaginando. Il visivo e l'inconscio*, Franco Angeli, Milan.

Chiland, C. 1997, *Transsexualism: Illusion and Reality*, Wesleyan University Press, Middletown 2003.

Chiland, C. 2003, *Exploring Transsexualism*, Karnac, London.

Chiland, C. 2004, Gender and Sexual Difference, in Matthis 2004, pp. 79–91.

Chiland, C. 2008, *Sex Makes the World Go Round*, Karnac, London.

Chused, J. 2007, Little Hans "Analyzed" in the Twenty-First Century, in *Journal of the American Psychoanalytic Association*, 55, 3, pp. 767–778.

Ciaramelli, F. 2017, La proibizione dell'incesto come prima forma di socializzazione del desiderio, in *Rivista di Psicoanalisi*, 2, pp. 465–471.

Coates, E. and Person, E. S. 1985, Extreme Boyhood Femininity: Isolated Behavior or Pervasive Disorder?, in *Journal of the American Academy of Child and Adolescent Psychiatry*, 24, pp. 702–709.

Coates, E., Freidman, R., and Wolfe, S. 1991, Aetiology of Boyhood Gender Disorder: Model for Integrating Temperament, Development, and Psychodynamics, in *Psychoanalytic Dialogue*, 1, pp. 481–523.

Coetzee, J. M. 1980, *Waiting for the Barbarians*, Vintage, London, 2004.

Cogeval, G. and Pludermacher, I. 2013, 'Venere di Urbino e Olympia': due donne scandalose, in Fondazione Musei Civici Venezia, *Manet. Ritorno a Venezia*, Skira, Milan.

Coghi, I. M. 2005, Le problematiche psicologiche del ginecologo di fronte alla Procreazione Medicalmente Assistita, in *Richard e Piggle*, 1, pp. 73–81.

Conrad, R. et al. 2001, Alexithymia in Male Infertility, in *Human Reproduction*, 16, pp. 578–592.

Conrotto, F. 2002, Introduction to the Italian edition of Widlöcher, D., *Sexualité infantile et attachement*, PUF, Paris, 2002 (Ital. trans. by F. Conrotto, *Sessualità infantile e attaccamento*, Franco Angeli, Milan).

Corbett, K. 2002, The Mystery of Homosexuality, in M. Dimen and V. Goldner (eds.), *Gender in Psychoanalytic Space: Between Clinic and Culture*, Other Press, New York (Italian trans. *La decostruzione del genere*, Il Saggiatore, Milan, 2006).

Corbett, K. 2009, *Boyhoods: Rethinking Masculinities*, Yale University Press, New Haven.

Corbett, K. 2013, Shifting Sexual Cultures, the Potential Space of Online Relations, and the Promise of Psychoanalytic Listening, in *Journal of the American Psychoanalytic Association*, 61, pp. 25–44.

D'Amelia, M. (ed.) 1997, *Storia della maternità*, Laterza, Rome-Bari.

Denber, H. C. 1978, Psychiatric Aspects of Infertility, in *Journal of Reproductive Medicine*, 20, pp. 23–29.

D'Ercole, A. 2014, Be Careful What You Wish For! The Surrender of Gender, in *Psychoanalytic Quarterly*, 2, pp. 250–279.

De Seta, C. 2013, Manet e i 'Voyages d'Italie', in Fondazione Musei Civici Venezia, *Manet. Ritorno a Venezia*, Skira, Milan.

De Simone, G. (ed.) 2002, *Le famiglie di Edipo*, Borla, Rome.

De Toffoli, C. 2014, *Transiti corpo-mente* (ed. B. Bonfiglio), Franco Angeli, Milan.

Deutsch, H. 1945, *Psychology of Women: Motherhood*, Green & Stratton, New York.

Di Ceglie, D. 2002, *Straniero nel mio corpo. Sviluppo atipico nell'identità di genere e salute*, Franco Angeli, Milan (Eng. trans., A Stranger in my Own Body: Atypical Gender Identity Development and Mental Health, Karnac, London, 1998).

Di Chiara, G. et al. 1985, Preconcezione edipica e funzione psicoanalitica della mente, in *Rivista di psicoanalisi*, 3, pp. 327–341.

Dimen, M. and Goldner, V. 2002, *Gender in Psychoanalytic Space: Between Clinic and Culture*, Other Press, New York. (Italian trans. *La decostruzione del genere*, Il Saggiatore, Milan, 2006).

Dürrenmatt, F. 1985, *Das Sterben der Pythia*, Diogenes Verlag, Zürich (Eng. trans. The Dying of the Pythia, in *Friedrich Dürrenmatt: Selected Writings, Volume 2*, University of Chicago, Chicago, 2006).

Egidi Morpurgo, V. 2013, Da Prometeo al Big Brother, in A. Marzi (ed.), *Psicoanalisi, Identità e Internet. Esplorazioni nel cyberspace*, Franco Angeli, Milan.

Ehrensaft, D. 2014, Family Complexes and Oedipal Circles: Mothers, Fathers, Babies, Donors, and Surrogates, in Mann 2014, pp. 19–43.

Ehrensaft, D. 2005, *Mommies, Daddies, Donors, Surrogates*, Guilford, New York.

Eisner, B. G. 1963, Some Psychological Differences between Fertile and Infertile Women, in *Journal of Clinical Psychology*, 19, pp. 391–395.

Ernaux, A. 2008, *Les Années*, Gallimard, Paris. (Eng. trans., *The Years*, Seven Stories Press, New York, 2017.)

Fabozzi, P. 2012, A Silent yet Radical Revolution: Winnicott's Innovative Perspective, in *The Psychoanalytic Quarterly*, 3, pp. 601–626.

Fabozzi, P. 2016, The Use of the Analyst and the Sense of Being Real: The Clinical Meanings of Winnicott's The Use of an Object, in *The Psychoanalytic Quarterly*, 1, pp. 1–34.

Facchinetti, F. et al. 1992, Psychosomatic Disorders Related to Gynecology, in *Psychotherapy & Psychosomatics*, 58, pp. 137–154.

Faimberg, H. 2005 Après-coup, in *International Journal of Psychoanalysis*, 86, pp. 1–6.

Faimberg, H. 2006, *The Telescoping of Generations: Listening to the Narcissistic Links between Generations*, The New library of Psychoanalysis, London.

Faimberg, H. 2007, A Plea for a Broader Concept of Nachträglichkeit, in *Psychoanalytic Quarterly*, 76, pp. 1221–1227.

Fanizza, F. 2006, Il Tragico e l'Occidente, in A. Giannakoulas and S. Thanopulos (eds.), *L'eredità della tragedia*, Borla, Rome.

Faure-Pragier, S. 2008, Famiglie o parentalità caotiche?, in *Psiche*, 2, pp. 31–48.

Ferenczi, S. 1932, Confusion of the Tongues between the Adults and the Child: The Language of Tenderness and of Passion, in *International Journal of Psychoanalysis*, 30, pp. 225–230 (1949).

Ferenczi, S. 1933, *Thalassa: A Theory of Genitality*, in *Psychoanalytic Quarterly*, 2, 361–403 and 3, 1–3, 200–222.

Ferraro, F. 2003, Psychic Bisexuality and Creativity, in *International Journal of Psychoanalysis*, 84, pp. 1451–1467.

Ferraro, F. and Garella, A. 2001, Nachträglichkeit, in *Rivista di psicoanalisi*, 47, pp. 79–106.

Ferro, A. 1996, *In the Analyst's Consulting Room*, Routledge, Hove, 2013.

Ferro, A. 1999, *Psychoanalysis as Therapy and Storytelling*, Routledge, Hove, 2006.

Ferro, A. 2002, Introduction, in De Simone 2002, pp. 5–9.

Ferro, A. 2007, *Avoiding Emotions, Living Emotions*, Routledge, London, 2011.

Ferro, A. 2013, Preface, in *Psicoanalisi, Identità e Internet. Esplorazioni nel cyberspace* (ed. A. Marzi), Franco Angeli, Milan.

Ferro, A. 2015, Prefazione, in M. A. Lupinacci et al. (eds.), *Il dolore dell'analista. Dolore psichico e metodo psicoanalitico*, Astrolabio-Ubaldini, Rome.

Ferruta, A. 2012, A Reconsideration of Freud's Essays on Sexuality and Their Clinical Implications, in *Psychoanalytic Quarterly*, 81, 2, pp. 259–278.

Flamigni, C. 2002, *La procreazione assistita*, Il Mulino, Bologna.

Fonagy, P. 2006, Psychosexuality and Psychoanalysis: An Overview, in P. Fonagy, R. Krause and M. Leuzinger-Bohleber (eds.), *Identity, Gender, and Sexuality:150 Years after Freud*, The International Psychoanalytical Association, London.

Fonagy, P. 2008, A Genuinely Developmental Theory of Sexual Enjoyment, in *Journal of the American Psychoanalytic Association*, 56(1), pp. 11–36.

Freedman, A. 1983, Psychoanalysis of a Patient who Received a Kidney Transplantation, in *Journal of American Psychoanalytic Association*, 31.

Freud, S. 1892–95, Studies on Hysteria, in *The Standard Edition of the Complete Psychological Works of Sigmund Freud (S.E.)*, II.

Freud, S. 1892–97, Draft K, in S.E., I.

Freud, S. 1895, *Project for a Scientific Psychology*, in S.E., I.

Freud, S. 1896a, *Heredity and the Aetiology of the Neuroses*, in S.E., III.

Freud, S. 1896b, *Further Remarks on the Neuro-Psychoses of Defence*, in S.E., III.

Freud, S. 1896c, *The Aetiology of Hysteria*, in S.E., III.

Freud, S. 1899a, *The Interpretation of Dreams*, in S.E., IV–V.

Freud, S. 1899b, *Screen Memories*, in S.E., III.

Freud, S. 1901, *Fragment of an Analysis of a Case of Hysteria* (Case history of Dora), in S.E., VII.

Freud, S. 1905, *Three Essays on the Theory of Sexuality*, in S.E., VII.

Freud, S. 1906, *My Views on the Part Played by Sexuality in the Aetiology of the Neuroses,* in S.E., VII.

Freud, S. 1908a, *Analysis of a Phobia in a Five-Year-Old Boy* ("Little Hans"), in S.E., X.

Freud, S. 1908b, *On the Sexual Theories of Children*, in S.E., IX.

Freud, S. 1910–17, *Contributions to the Psychology of Love*, in S.E., XI.

Freud, S. 1911, *Formulations on the Two Principles of Mental Functioning*, in S.E., XII.

Freud, S. 1914a, *On the History of the Psycho-Analytic Movement*, in S.E., XIV.

Freud, S. 1914b, *From the History of an Infantile Neurosis* ('The Wolf Man'), in S.E., XVII.

Freud, S. 1914c, *On Narcissism: An Introduction*, in S.E., XIV.

Freud, S. 1915, *Repression*, in S.E., XIV.

Freud, S. 1916, *A Difficulty in the Path of Psychoanalysis*, in S.E., XVII.

Freud, S. 1919, *"A Child is Being Beaten": A Contribution to the Study of the Origin of Sexual Perversions*, in S.E., XVII.

Freud, S. 1920a, *Psychogenesis of a Case of Homosexuality in a Woman*, in S.E., XVIII.

Freud, S. 1920b, *Beyond the Pleasure Principle*, in S.E., XVIII.

Freud, S. 1922a, *The Ego and the Id*, in S.E., XIX.

Freud, S. 1922b, Two Encyclopaedia Articles: "Psycho-Analysis" and "The Libido Theory," in S.E., XVIII.

Freud, S. 1923, *The Infantile Genital Organization*, in S.E., XIX.

Freud, S. 1924, *An Autobiographical Study*, in S.E., XX.

Freud, S. 1925, *Some Psychical Consequences of the Anatomical Distinction between the Sexes*, in S.E., XIX,

Freud, S. 1929, *Civilisation and its Discontents*, in S.E., XXI.

Freud, S. 1938, *An Outline of Psycho-Analysis* in S.E., XXIII.

Freud, S. (1985) (Masson, J. ed.) *The Complete Letters of Sigmund Freud to Wilhelm Fliess, 1887–1904.*

Gaddini, E. 1969, On Imitation, in *International Journal of Psychoanalysis*, 50, 475–484.

Gibeault, A. 1993, Riflessioni a partire dal libro di Jacquelin Cosnier *Destins de la fémininité*, in Birksted-Breen, 1993, pp. 213–231.

Golombok, S. and Tasker, F. 1996, Do Parents Influence the Sexual Orientation of their Children? Findings from a Longitudinal Study of Lesbian Families, in *Developmental Psychology*, 32, pp. 3–11.

Graf, M. 1952, interview with K. Eissler, Box 112, Sigmund Freud Papers, Sigmund Freud Collection, Manuscript division, Library of Congress, Washington, DC.

Graf, H. 1972, Memoirs of an Invisible Man: A Dialogue with Francis Rizzo, in *Opera News*, 5 February, pp. 5–28; ibid. 12 February, pp. 26–9; ibid. 19 February, pp. 26–9; ibid. 26 February, pp. 26–9.

Green, A. 1973, Le Genre neutre, in *Narcissisme de vie, Narcissisme de mort*, Les Éditions de Minuit, Paris (Eng. trans., *Life Narcissism Death Narcissism*, Karnac, London, 2001).

Green, A. 1975, Orestes and Oedipus, in *International Review of Psychoanalysis*, 2, pp. 355–364.

Green, A. 1993, *Le Travail du négatif*, Les Éditions de Minuit, Paris (Eng. trans., *The Work of the Negative*, Karnac, London, 1999).

Green, A. 1995, Has Sexuality Anything to Do with Psychoanalysis? in *International Journal of Psychoanalysis*, 76, pp. 871–883.

Green, A. 2000, *Le temps eclaté*, Les Éditions de Minuits, Paris.

Green, A. 2002, *Idées directrices pour une psychanalyse contemporaine. Méconnaisance et reconnaissance de l'inconscient*, PUF, Paris (Eng. trans., Key Ideas for a Contemporary Psychoanalysis, Routledge, Hove, 2005).

Green, A. 2008, Freud's Concept of Temporality: Differences with Current Ideas, in *International Journal of Psychoanalysis*, 89, 5, pp. 1029–1039.

Greil, A. l. 1997, Infertility and Psychological Distress: A Critical Review of the Literature, in *Social Science & Medicine*, 45, pp. 1679–1704.

Grotstein, J. 2009, *"... But at the Same Time and on Another Level...": Clinical Applications in the Kleinian/Bionian Mode*, Karnac, London.

Guignard, F. 2010, Lo psicoanalista e il bambino nella società occidentale di oggi, in *Rivista di Psicoanalisi*, 56, pp. 901–920.

Gutton, P. 2000, *Psychothérapie et adolescence*, PUF, Paris.

Habermas, J. 2001, *Die Zukunft der menschlichen Natur. Auf dem Weg zu einer liberalen Eugenik?*, Suhrkamp, Frankfurt am Main (Eng. trans., The Future of Human Nature, Polity, Cambridge, 2003).

Haynal, A. 2006, Sexuality: A Conceptual and Historical Essay, in P. Fonagy, R. Krause and M. Leuzinger-Bohleber (eds.), *Identity, Gender, and Sexuality:150 Years after Freud*, The International Psychoanalytical Association, London.

Heenen-Wolff, S. 2011, Infantile Bisexuality and the "Complete Oedipal Complex": Freudian Views on Heterosexuality and Homosexuality, in *International Journal of Psychoanalysis*, 92, pp. 1209–1220.

Heenen-Wolff, S. 2014, Same Sex Parenthood, in *Rivista di Psicoanalisi*, 1, pp. 147–158.

Honneth, A. 2002, Teoria delle relazioni oggettuali e identità post-moderna. Sulla presunta obsolescenza della psicoanalisi, in *Psiche*, 1, pp. 13–29.

Hynes, G. J. et al. 1992, The Psychological Well-Being of Infertile Women after a Failed IVF Attempt: The Effects of Coping, in *British Journal of Medical Psychology*, 65, pp. 269–277.

Isaacs, S. 1948, The Nature and Function of Phantasy, in *International Journal of Psychoanalysis*, 29, pp. 73–97.

Jacobson, E. 1946, A Case of Sterility, in *Psychoanalytic Quarterly*, 15, pp. 330–350.

Janik, A. and Toulmin, S. 1973, *Wittgenstein's Vienna*, Touchstone, New York.

Jonas, H. 1979, *Das Prinzip Verantwortung: Versuch einer Ethik für die technologische Zivilisation*, Insel Verlag, Frankfurt am Main (Eng trans. The Imperative of Responsibility: In Search of an Ethics for the Technological Age, University of Chicago, Chicago and London, 1984).

Jones, E. 1953, *Sigmund Freud: Life and Work, Volume 2: Years of Maturity, 1901–1919*, Hogarth Press, London.

Kaës, R. 2005, Il disagio del mondo moderno e la sofferenza del nostro tempo. Saggio sui garanti metapsichici, in *Psiche*, 13, pp. 57–65.

Kaës, R. 2009, *Les Alliances inconscientes*, Dunod, Paris.

Kahn, M. 1979, *Alienation in Perversions*, Hogarth Press, London.

Kandel, E. R. 2012, *The Age of Insight: The Quest to Understand the Unconscious in Art, Mind, and Brain. From Vienna 1900 to the Present*, Random House, New York.

Kernberg, O. 1992, *Aggression in Personality Disorders and Perversions*, Yale University Press, New Haven.

Keylor, R. and Apfel, R. 2010, Male Infertility: Integrating an Old Psychoanalytic Story with the Research Literature, in *Studies in Gender and Sexuality*, 11, pp. 60–77.

Klein, M. 1932, *The Psychoanalysis of Children*, Hogarth Press, London.

Klein, M. 1975, *Envy and Gratitude and Other Works 1946–1963*, edited by M. Masud and R. Khan (The International Psycho-Analytical Library, 104), The Hogarth Press and the Institute of Psycho-Analysis, London, pp. 1–346.

Knight, R. P. 1943, Functional Disturbances in the Sexual Life of Women: Frigidity and Related Disorders, in *Bulletin of the Menninger Clinic*, 7, pp. 25–35.

Kohon, G. 2018, Reflections on Dora: The Case of Hysteria, in G. Kohon (ed.), *British Psychoanalysis: New Perspectives in the Independent Tradition*, Routledge, Abingdon,

Krafft-Ebing, R. von 1886, *Psychopathia Sexualis mit besonderer Berücksichtigung der conträren Sexualempfindung. Eine klinische.forensische Studie, Enke, Stuttgart (Eng. trans. Psychopathia Sexualis: With Especial Reference to the Antipathic Sexual Instinct. A Medico-Forensic Study*, Arcade, New York, 1965).

Kulish, N. 2010, Clinical Implications of Contemporary Gender Theory, in *Journal of the American Psychoanalytic Association*, 58, pp. 231–258.

Lacan, J. 1966, *Écrits*, Les Éditions du Seuil, Paris.

Ladame, F. and Perret-Catipovic, M. 1998, Jeu, fantasme et realités. Le Psychodrame psychanalytique à l'adolescence. Masson, Paris.

Langer, M. 1958, Sterility and Envy, in *International Journal of Psychoanalysis*, 39, pp. 139–143.

Laplanche, J. 1970, *Vie et mort en psychanalyse*, Flammarion, Paris (Eng. trans., *Life and Death in Psychoanalysis*, Johns Hopkins University, Baltimore).

Laplanche, J. 1997, The Theory of Seduction and the Problem of the Other, in *International Journal of Psychoanalysis*, 78, pp. 653–666.

Laplanche, J. 1999, Isteria oggi, in F. Scalzone and G. Zontini (eds.), *Perché l'isteria*, Liguori, Naples.

Laplanche, J. 2007, *Sexuel. La Sexualité élargie au sens freudien 2000–2006*, PUF, Paris (Eng. trans., J. House and N. Ray, *Freud and the Sexual: Essays 2000–2006*, International Psychoanalytic Books, New York, 2011).

Laplanche, J. and Pontalis, J.-B. 1967, *Vocabulaire de la psychanalyse*, PUF, Paris (Eng. trans., *The Language of Psycho-Analysis*, Hogarth Press, London, 1973).

Laufer, L. 2014, La soggettività di un'epoca. Che cosa porta l'omoparentalità alla psicoanalisi, in *Rivista Italiana di Psicoanalisi*, 60, pp. 131–146.

Laufer, M. and Laufer, E. 1984, *Adolescence and Developmental Breakdown*, Yale University Press, New Haven.

Le Goff, J. 2003, *Une histoire du corps au Moyen Age*, Liana Levi, Paris.

Lemma, A. 2005, *Under the Skin: A Psychoanalytic Study of Body Modification*, Routledge, London.

Lemma, A. and Lynch, P. (eds.) 2015, *Sexualities: Contemporary Psychoanalytic Perspectives*, Routledge, London.

Leon, I. G. 2010, Understanding and Treating Infertility: Psychoanalytic Considerations, in *Journal of the American Academy of Psychoanalysis and Dynamic Psychiatry*, 38, pp. 47–75.

Lett, D. 2014, *Uomini e donne nel Medioevo. Storia del genere (secoli XII–XV)* (It. trans., R. Ferrara), Il Mulino, Bologna.

Lévinas, E. 1972, *Humanisme de l'autre homme*, Éditions Fata Morgana, Saint-Clément-de-Rivière (Eng. trans. *Humanism of the Other*, University of Illinois, Urbana, 2003).

Lévi-Strauss, C. 1947, *Les Structures élémentaires de la parenté*, Masson, Paris (Eng trans., The Elementary Structures of Kinship, Beacon, Boston, 1969).

Lingiardi, V. 2006, La generazione del soggetto, in M. Dimen and V. Goldner (eds.), *La decostruzione del genere*, Il Saggiatore, Milan.

Loewald, H. W. 1979, The Waning of the Oedipus Complex, in *Journal of the American Psychoanalytic Association*, 27, pp. 751–775.

Lucchetti, A. 2010, Il segreto della sessualità, introduzione a S. Freud, *Tre saggi sulla teoria sessuale*, BUR, Milan.

Lupinacci, M. A. 1994, Riflettendo sull'Edipo precoce: la coppia genitoriale nel lavoro dell'analista, in *Rivista di Psicoanalisi*, 40(1), pp. 5–23.

MacCallum, F. and Golombok, S. 2004, Children Raised in Fatherless Families from Infancy: A Follow up of Children of Lesbian and Single Heterosexual Mother at Early Adolescence, in *Journal of Child Psychology and Psychiatry*, 45, pp. 1407–1419.

Malpas, J. 2011, Between Pink and Blue: A Multi-dimensional Family Approach to Gender Nonconforming Children and their Families, in *Family Process*, 1 (4).

Mann, M. (ed.) 2014, *Psychoanalytic Aspects of Assisted Reproductive Technology*, Karnac, London.

Mann, T. 1927–42, *Joseph and his Brothers* (Eng. trans., H. C. Lowe-Porter, Secker and Warburg, London, 1959).

Marcus, B. F. and McNamara, S. 2013, "Strange and Otherwise Unaccountable Actions": Category, Conundrum, and Trans Identities, in *Journal of the American Psychoanalytic Association*, 61, pp. 45–66.

Marion, P. 1991, L'Edipo Re tra mito e tragedia, in C. Bollas et al., *Perchè Edipo? Intorno mito e alla tragedia*, Rome, Borla, pp. 47–61.

Marion, P. 2003, Nascere nell'era delle biotecnologie. Introduzione, in *Richard e Piggle*, 11, pp. 241–249.

Marion, P. 2005, 'Invasioni barbariche' o 'Debito di sangue'? Note intorno ai nuovi con- fini della soggettività, in *Psiche*, 2, pp. 131–153.

Marion, P. 2008, Alcune note intorno alla tragedia greca e alla sua eredità per la psicoanalisi, in *Parricidio e figlicidio: crocevia d'Edipo. Fondamenti della teoria e della clinica psicoanalitiche*, Borla, series Rivista di psicoanalisi, Monografie, Rome.

Marion, P. 2009, Brèves considérations sur la Nachträglichkeit dans la cure, in *Revue Française de Psychanalyse*, 73, pp. 1723–1730.

Marion, P. 2010, Il tempo della Nachträglichkeit, in *Rivista di Psicoanalisi*, 2, pp. 297–318.

181

Marion, P. 2011, Some Notes on Sexuality in Psychoanalysis and Freud's Heritage, paper presented at the XLVII IPA Congress, Mexico City, 3–6 August.

Marion, P. 2012, Some Reflections on the Unique Time of Nachträglichkeit in Theory and Clinical Practice, in *International Journal of Psychoanalysis*, 93, pp. 317–340.

Marion, P. 2013, I Tre saggi e la sessualità infantile in psicoanalisi, in *Rivista di Psicoanalisi*, 2, pp. 359–382.

Marion, P. 2014, La sessualità infantile è 'precoce' o 'profonda'? Alcune considerazioni sulla sessualità infantile nel processo di soggettivazione, paper presented at the XVII Congress of the Italian Psychoanalytic Society, Milan, 22–25 May.

Marion, P. 2015a, Introduzione al tema della sessualità infantile, in Quagliata and Di Ceglie 2015.

Marion, P. 2015b, Sexuality in the Time of Biotechnologies, paper presented at the XLIX IPA Congress, Boston, 21–25 July.

Marion, P. 2015c, Alcune note sul concetto di differenza vs indifferenza nella sessualità oggi, in *Psiche*, ii, 1, pp. 107–126.

Marion, P. 2016a, Infantile Sexuality and Freud's Legacy, in *International Journal of Psychoanalysis*, 97, pp. 641–664.

Marion, P. 2016b, Prospettive attuali nella variabilità e complessità nell'identità di genere, in *Richard e Piggle*, 4, pp. 344–355.

Marion, P. 2016c, La logica del piacere all'origine dello psichico, in *Rivista di Psicoanalisi*, 62, pp. 845–860.

Marion, P. and Bonaminio, V. 1986, Esiste una specifica tecnica di analisi infantile nel periodo di latenza? Rie- same della letteratura psicoanalitica, in *Psichiatria dell'infanzia e dell'adolescenza*, 53(4), pp. 473–487.

Marzi, A. 2018, The Analyst's Identity and the Digital World: A New Frontier in Psychoanalysis, in *The Italian Psychoanalytic Annual*, 12, pp. 99–113.

Matthis, I. (ed.) 2004, *Dialogues on Sexuality, Gender and Psychoanalysis*, Karnac, London.

Mazzarella, E. 2017, *L'uomo che deve rimanere. La 'smoralizzazione' del mondo*, Quodlibet Studio, Naples.

Mazzucco, M. 2008, *La lunga attesa dell'angelo*, Rizzoli, Milan.

McDougall, J. 1982, *Théâtres du Je*, Gallimard, Paris (Eng. trans., *Theatres of the Mind: Illusion and Truth on the Psychoanalytic Stage*, Routledge, Abingdon, 1992).

McDougall, J. 1989, *Theatres of the Body*, Free Association Books, London.

McDougall, J. 1995, *The Many Faces of Eros*, W. W. Norton & Company, New York.

Meltzer, D. 1973, *Sexual States of Mind*, Clunie Press, Perthshire.

Mitchell, J. 2004, The Difference between Gender and Sexual Difference, in Matthis 2004, pp. 67–78.

Mitchell, S. 1988, *Relational Concepts in Psychoanalysis: An Integration*, Harvard University Press, Cambridge, MA.

Modell, A. 1990, *Other Times, Other Realities: Toward a Theory of Psychoanalytic Treatment*, Harvard University Press, Cambridge, MA.

Molinari, S. 1981, Freud di fronte al mito di Edipo, in *Rivista di Psicoanalisi*, 2, pp. 274–293.

Moneti Codignola, M. 2008, *L'enigma della maternità. Etica e ontologia della riproduzione*, Carocci, Rome.

Money, J. et al. 1955, An Examination of Some Basic Sexual Concepts: The Evidence of Human Hermaphroditism, in *Bulletin of Johns Hopkins Hospital*, 97, pp. 301–309.

Nancy, J.-L. 2000, *L'Intrus*, Galilée, Paris (Eng. trans., in *Corpus*, Fordham University Press, New York, 2008).

Nancy, J.-L. 2006, Dopo la tragedia, in *L'eredità della tragedia* (ed. A. Giannakoulas and S. Thanopulos), Borla, Rome, pp. 31–42.

Nicolò, A. M. 2016, Le nuove sessualità in adolescenza e non solo, in M. Nicolò and I. Ruggiero (eds.), *La mente adolescente e il corpo ripudiato*, Franco Angeli, Milan, pp. 181–193.

Norsa, D. 2006, Rappresentazione e Scena Primaria, paper read to the Associazione Italiana di Psicoanalisi, 11 June.

Ogden, T. H. 2009, *Rediscovering Psychoanalysis: Thinking and Dreaming, Learning and Forgetting*, Routledge, Hove.

Ogden, T. H. 2012, *Creative Readings: Essays on Seminal Analytic Works*, Routledge, Hove.

Ovid 1953, *Metamorphoses* (ed. A. G. Lee), Bristol Classical Press, Bristol, 1984.

Parsons, M. 2014, *Living Psychoanalysis: From Theory to Experience*, Routledge, London.

Perelberg, R. 2006, The Controversial Discussion and après-coup, in *International Journal of Psychoanalysis*, 87, pp. 1199–1220.

Perelberg, R. 2009, Après-coup dynamique: Implications pour une théorie de la clinique, in *Revue Française de Psychanalyse*, 73, pp. 1583–1589.

Petrella, F. 1988, Il modello freudiano, in *Trattato di psicoanalisi*, vol. 1 (ed. A. A. Semi), Raffaello Cortina, Milan.

Pines, D. 1990, Emotional Aspects of Infertility and its Remedies, in *International Journal of Psychoanalysis*, 71, pp. 561–568.

Pontalis, J. 1973, L'inafferrabile via di mezzo, in *Fliess, Groddeck, Pontalis, Winnicott: Bisessualità e differenza dei sessi*, Savelli, Rome, 1980.

Pozzi, O. and Thanopulos, T. (eds.) 2006, *Ipotesi Gay. Materiali per un confronto*, Borla, Rome.

Proust, M. (1913), *À la recherche du temps perdu: Du côté de chez Swann* (Eng. trans., C. K. Scott Moncrieff and T. Kilmartin, *Remembrance of Things Past*, vol. 1: *Swann's Way*, Penguin Books, Harmondsworth, 1996).

Proust, M. (1921), *À la recherche du temps perdu: Sodome et Gomorrhe* (Eng. trans., C. K. Scott Moncrieff and T. Kilmartin, *Remembrance of Things Past*, vol. 4: *Sodom and Gomorrah*, Penguin Books, Harmondsworth, 1996).

Proust, M. (1927), *À la recherche du temps perdu: Le Temps retrouvé* (Eng. trans., C. K. Scott Moncrieff and T. Kilmartin, *Remembrance of Things Past*, vol. 7: *Time Regained*, Vintage, London, 2000).

Quagliata, E. 2016, Credenza, illusione e lutto: riflessioni sull'esperienza del limite e della perdita nella procreazione medicalmente assistita [Belief, illusion, and mourning: Reflections on the experience of limit and loss in medically assisted procreation], paper presented to the Società italiana di psicoterapia psicoanalitica dell'infanzia, dell'adolescenza e della coppia (Sipsia) [The Italian Society of Child, Adolescent, and Couple Psychotherapy], 23 January.

Quagliata, E. and Di Ceglie, D. (eds.) 2015, *Lo sviluppo dell'identità sessuale e l'identità di genere*, Astrolabio, Rome.

Quintiliani, R. 2016, Annullare le differenze di genere. Il bambino che non voleva essere maschio, in *Richard e Piggle*, 4, pp. 373–382.

Racamier, P.-C. 1995, *L'Inceste et l'incestuel*, Les Éditions du Collège, Paris.

Recalcati, M. 2012, *Jacques Lacan. Desiderio, godimento e soggettivazione*, Raffaello Cortina, Milan.

Rifkin, J. 1998, *The Biotech Century: Harnessing the Gene and Remaking the World*, Gollancz, London.

Riolo, F. 2005, Eidolopoiesi, in *Psiche*, 2, pp. 147–150.

Riolo, F. 2017, Del principio del piacere, paper presented at the XVIII Congress of the Italian Psychoanalytic Society, Rome, 26–29 May, and published in *Rivista Italiana di Psicoanalisi*, 3, pp. 519–25.

Rose, J. 2007, Distortions of Time in the Transference: Some Clinical and Theoretical Implications, in R. Perelberg (ed.), *Time and Memory* Karnac, London.

Rosen, A. and Rosen, J. 2005, *Frozen Dreams: Psychodynamic Dimensions of Infertility and Assisted Reproduction*, Routledge, London.

Roudinesco, E. 2014, *Sigmund Freud en son temps et dans le nôtre*, Seuil, Paris (Eng. trans. C. Porter, *Freud in His Time and Ours*, Harvard University Press, Cambridge, MA, 2016).

Roussillon, R. 2010, *La Psychanalyse de l'adolescent existe-t-elle?*, PUF, Paris.

Roussillon R. 2016, Le Trouvé et le crée, paper presented at the conference Donald Winnicott e la psicoanalisi del futuro, Rome, 30–31 January.

Ruggiero, I. 2008, Bisogni fusionali e pulsioni sessuali: una difficile integrazione nella vita sessuale delle adolescenti, in *Rivista di Psicoanalisi*, 2, pp. 277–291.

Ruggiero, I. 2017, C'è ancora qualcuno che vuole diventare adulto? La progressiva adolescentizzazione della società adulta, in *Rivista di Psicoanalisi*, 3, pp. 673–684.

Saketopoulou, A. 2014, Mourning the Body as Bedrock: Developmental Considerations in Treating Transsexual Patients Analytically, in *Journal of the American Psychoanalytic Association*, 62, pp. 773–806.

Saraceno, C. 1997, Verso il 2000: la pluralizzazione delle esperienze delle figure materne, in D'Amelia 1997, pp. 318–351.

Say, R. E. and Thomson, R. 2003, The Importance of Patient Preferences in Treatment Decisions: Challenges for Doctors, in *British Medical Journal*, 327, pp. 542–545.

Scalzone, F. and Zontini, G. (eds.) 1999, *Perché l'isteria*, Liguori, Naples.

Seulin, C. 2014, Émergence et transformations de la sexualité infantile dans la cure. 75° Congrès des psychanalystes de langue française: le sexuel infantile et ses destins, Lyon, 14–17 May 2015, in *Bulletin de la Société psychanalytique de Paris*.

Seward, G. H. et al. 1965, The Question of Psychophysiologic Infertility: Some Negative Answers, in *Psychosomatic Medicine*, 27, pp. 533–545.

Solano, L. 2013, *Tra mente e corpo. Come si costruisce la salute*, Raffaello Cortina, Milan.

Solano, L. 2016, Al di là di Cartesio. Riflessioni sul CorpoMente, in *Rivista di Psicoanalisi*, 62, pp. 49–72.

Squitieri, G. 2007, Bisessualità e scena primaria. Osservazioni a proposito di un paziente maschio omosessuale, unpublished.

Starobinski, J. 1961, *L'Oeil vivant*, Gallimard, Paris (Eng. trans. *The Living Eye*, Harvard University Press, Cambridge, MA, 1989).

Stein, R. 1998a, The Enigmatic Dimension of Sexual Experience: The "Otherness" of Sexuality and Primal Seduction, in *Psychoanalytic Quarterly*, 4, pp. 594–625.

Stein, R. 1998b, The Poignant, the Excessive and the Enigmatic in Sexuality, in *International Journal of Psychoanalysis*, 79, pp. 253–268.

Stein, R. 2008, The Otherness of Sexuality: Excess, in *International Journal of Psychoanalysis*, 56, 1, pp. 37–71.

Stoller, R. 1964, A Contribution to the Study of Gender Identity, in *International Journal of Psychoanalysis*, 45, pp. 220–226.

Stoller, R. 1968, *Sex and Gender*, Science House, New York.

Stuart, J. 2007, Little Hans and Freud's Self-Analysis: A Biographical View of Clinical Theory in the Making, in *International Journal of Psychoanalysis*, 55(3), pp. 799–819.

Sulloway, F. J. 1979, *Freud, Biologist of the Mind: Beyond the Psychoanalytic Legend*, Basic Books, New York.

Thanopulos, S. 2016, *Il desiderio che ama il lutto*, Quodlibet, Macerata.

Thomä, H. and Cheshire, N. 1991, Freud's Nachträglichkeit and Strachey's "Deferred Action": Trauma, Constructions and the Direction of Causality, in *International Review of Psychoanalysis*, 18, pp. 407–427.

Ungar, V. et al. 2013, La relazione con i genitori nell'analisi dei bambini, in *Rivista Italiana di Psicoanalisi*, 59, pp. 473–490.

Van Haute, P. and Westerink, H. 2016, Sexuality and its Object in Freud's 1905 edition of *Three Essays on Theory of Sexuality*, in *International Journal of Psychoanalysis*, 97, pp. 563–589.

Vecho, O. and Schneider, B. 2005, Homoparentalité et développement de l'enfant: bilan de trente ans de publications, in *La Psychiatrie de l'enfant*, 48, pp. 271–328.

Vernant, J.-P. and Vidal-Naquet, P. 1972, *Mythe et tragédie en Grèce ancienne*, F. Maspero, Paris (Eng. trans. *Tragedy and Myth in Ancient Greece*, Harvester Press, Brighton, 1981).

Vernant, J.-P. and Vidal-Naquet, P. 1986, *Mythe et tragédie deux*, La Découverte, Paris.

Vigneri, M. 2003, Mater dolorosa (sulle donne e la procreazione assistita), in *Richard e Piggle*, 11, pp. 285–300.

Vigneri, M. 2011, I bambini che vengono dal freddo. Sulla donna infertile e le nuove frontiere procreative, in *Rivista Italiana di Psicoanalisi*, 1, pp. 117–145.

Warnock, M. 2002, *Making Babies: Is There a Right to Have Children?*, Oxford University Press, Oxford.

Widlöcher, D. et al. 2000, *Sexualité infantile et attachement*, PUF, Paris (Eng. trans. *Infantile Sexuality and Attachment*, Abingdon, Routledge, 2018.).

Winnicott, D. W. 1963, Fear of Breakdown, in *International Journal of Psychoanalysis*, 1, pp. 103–107.

Winnicott, D. W. 1965a, *The Family and Individual Development*, Tavistock Publications, London.

Winnicott, D. W. 1965b, *The Maturational Processes and the Facilitating Environment: Studies in the Theory of Emotional Development*, Hogarth Press, London.

Winnicott, D. W. 1971, *Playing and Reality*, Tavistock Publications, London.

Winnicott, D. W. 1975, *Collected Papers: Through Paediatrics to Psycho-Analysis*, Tavistock Publications, London.

Winnicott, D. W. 1986, *Home is Where We Start From*, Penguin Books, London.

Winnicott, D. W. 1988, *Human Nature*, The Winnicott Trust, London.

Wright, K. 1991, *Vision and Separation: Between Mother and Baby*, Free Association Press, London.

Zalusky, S. 2000, Infertility in the Age of Technology, in *Journal of the American Psychoanalytic Association*, 48, pp. 1541–1562.

Zaretsky, E. 2004, *Secrets of the Soul: A Social and Cultural History of Psychoanalysis*, A. Knopf, New York.

Zweig, S. 1944, *Die Welt von gestern. Erinnerungen eines Europäers*, Bermann-Fischer Verlag, Stockholm (Eng. trans., *The World of Yesterday*, Pushkin, London, 2011).

Zweig, S. 1932, *Die Heilung durch den Geist. Mesmer, Mary Baker-Eddy, Freud*, (Eng. trans., Mental Healers: Franz Mesmer, Mary Baker Eddy, Sigmund Freud, Plunkett Lake, Lexington, 2012).

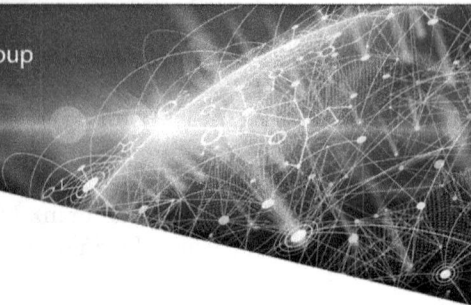

For Product Safety Concerns and Information please contact our EU
representative GPSR@taylorandfrancis.com
Taylor & Francis Verlag GmbH, Kaufingerstraße 24, 80331 München, Germany

www.ingramcontent.com/pod-product-compliance
Lightning Source LLC
Chambersburg PA
CBHW070331270326
41926CB00017B/3838

9 781032 003689